Desperately Seeking Mary

A Feminist Appropriation of a Traditional Religious Symbol

Promotores :   prof. dr. L.A. Hoedemaker
                 prof. dr. P. Vandermeersch
                 prof. dr. M. Grey

The investigations were supported in part by the Foundation for Research in the field of Theology and the science of Religions in the Netherlands which is subsidized by the Netherlands Organisation for the Advancement of Research (N.W.O.).

Els Maeckelberghe

Desperately Seeking Mary

A Feminist Appropriation of a Traditional Religious Symbol

In memory of my grandmothers

Anna Catrysse (1900-1991)

Elvira Mombert (1893-1977)

CIP-GEGEVENS KONINKLIJKE BIBLIOTHEEK, DEN HAAG

Maeckelberghe, Els Lisette Maria

Desperately seeking Mary : a feminist appropriation of a traditional religious symbol /
Els Lisette Maria
Maeckelberghe. - Kampen : Kok. - Ill.
Proefschrift Groningen. - Met bibliogr. - Met samenvatting in het Nederlands.
ISBN 90-242-3077-2
NUGI 631
Trefw.: mariologie / feministische theologie.

© 1991, Kok Pharos Publishing House,
Kampen, The Netherlands
Cover by Inge Steenhuis
ISBN 90-242-3077-2
NUGI 631

Acknowledgements

I am grateful to many people who have supported me while I was writing this book. The conversations with friends during meals and drinks have encouraged me to continue. I only mention here Door-Elske, Nelie, and Saskia who helped me in being a *seeking* but not a *despairing* person.

I thank my promotors for giving me the freedom to persue my own goals. Bert Hoedemaker taught me the necessity of definitions, but he never stopped trying to follow my associative mind. Patrick Vandermeersch has been supportive of this project from the start. His sometimes teasing but always stimulating questions have been highly influential. I enjoyed the discussions with Mary Grey. They enabled me in formulating my own point of view more clearly.

Drs. Posthumus has mended my clumsy English, explained me about dangling participles, and put sentences in order. Needless to say that the limitations and the errors of this book are mine. Stefaan Baeten and Patrick Vandermeersch have taken care of the outlook of this book, amazing me with the wide variety of layout. I finally want to thank the Department of Theology of the University of Groningen. It has provided me with 'a room of myself' and an atmosphere of comradeship that has made it easier writing this book.

Contents

Chapter 3   Mary : A Nineteenth Century Heritage

Chapter 4   Desperately Seeking Mary

Introduction

The novelist Connie Palmen writes in her book *De wetten*:

> "One day the soul was no longer a thing, sin no longer an erasable word, and God no longer a man. Without any longer having an image for them, I have remained attached to the words as such. They are persisting metaphors from the very first stories that reached my ears. They constitute the topography of my primal story, in which the great questions of life and death happened to have acquired this form and no other. I do not avoid them. I see no sense in replacing them by other words that would come down to the same thing" (C. Palmen, 1991, 114-115)[1].

The fundamental questions of life and death have been formulated in a specific way in different traditions. Perpetual repetition seems to have eroded the formulas of these traditions. They are worn out by too much use. These formulas, however, also provide a feeling of comfort. They fit like an indispensable, old sweater with faded colours and pads on the elbows. Even though the sweater is outmoded, you continue wearing it when reason tells you to throw it away. It has become an intimate part of yourself. As a twentieth-century European woman with a Christian upbringing, I am confronted with the question whether Christianity and the words and the concepts used in the Christian tradition, are still meaningful. Is Christianity an outmoded but familiar sweater that any reasonable person would jettison? Or is it still capable of vivifying faith? Do we continue using certain words and images because they are familiar without necessarily being significant? Or do we use them because they are indeed still meaningful?

It is confusing to live in a society that claims to be secularised, but that is at the same time imbued with Christian elements. Are these el-

---

1. "Op een dag was de ziel geen ding, de zonde geen uitwisbaar woord en God geen man meer. Zonder er nog een voorstelling bij te hebben ben ik blijven hechten aan de woorden zelf. Het zijn hardnekkige metaforen uit de allereerste verhalen die mij ter ore kwamen. Ze vormen de topografie van mijn oerverhaal, waarin de grote vragen over het leven en de dood toevallig deze vorm hadden gekregen en geen andere. Ik schuw ze niet. Ik zie er de zin niet van in ze te vervangen door andere woorden die toch op hetzelfde neerkomen."

ements ornamental, or do they still enable us to speak about the fundamental questions of life and death? The observation of one of the characters in André Brink's novel *The Ambassador*, reflecting on a Christmas service, is acute, but killing:

> "It is very silent now. Every word and gesture is in code, pure symbol. And I have lost the key. Is this the only way in which we can survive --through an endless series of symbols? For things are unique; the smallest event can never be repeated; even last night's emotion is absent today with the repetition of the same ceremony. And because it is impossible for two experiences ever to be similar the only solution is this search for common denominators, symbols to render life intelligible. We cannot go without them. Yet this very habit keeps us away from essentials, from truth, from the things themselves!" (Brink, 1985, 221).

Are we indeed condemned to an endless repetition of symbols that prevent us from finding truth? Or are symbols leading us to truth?

This book is written out of an ambiguous attitude towards the Christian tradition: on the one hand I feel very ambivalent toward the limiting doctrines that Christianity has produced and that have caused much pain, especially for women. On the other hand, I am attracted by its seemingly inherent life promoting power. The volume *Immaculate and Powerful* (Atkinson, 1985), with its emphasis on the idea that traditional religions not only oppress women, but also provide them with tools for developing critical perspectives, stimulated me to explore the ambiguity of traditional religious symbols: both liberating and oppressive. How is it possible that religious symbols contain this double capacity?

This study has been written with a very practical and vital aim in mind. My commitment as a feminist has confronted me with many stories of women. Too often I have heard stories of pain and anger. Stories that can only be answered with silence. I did not want this silence to continue. I have been searching for a way to verbalise or to symbolise the extraordinary resilient power that was often contained in these stories so that others could be empowered as well. The words and the symbols that traditionally have expressed these experiences are burdened with a heritage of patriarchal abuse. New words or symbols are not created ex nihilo. They are always connected with the past. Is this an insurmountable impasse?

I acknowledge the search of women for images and symbols that are not oppressive as a major evolution in the twentieth century religious spectrum. It has produced questions ranging from *The Christian Past: Does it Hold a Future for Women?* (McLaughlin, 1979), *What Became of God the Mother?* (Pagels, 1979), *Why Women Need the Goddess* (Christ,

1979), to the affirmation that *God is Inside You and Inside Everybody Else* (Walker, 1989).

All these questions and observations come together in the figure of Mary. She is an ambiguous religious symbol. She has evoked strong emotions in the faithful throughout centuries of Christianity. She has been a model for women and men, but the ambiguity has been especially devastating for women. On the one hand, womanhood was elevated in Mary; on the other hand it was impossible for women to be like Mary. The ideal of simultaneous virginity and motherhood was an impossible one. It nevertheless did not refrain women from praying to Mary, going on pilgrimages to Marian shrines, seeking comfort in chapels devoted to Mary. It seems that Mary is more than an oppressive image.

Feminists have tried to clear away the oppressive images of Mary and they have made proposals for the liberation of Marian interpretations. In the first chapter I will present these attempts, in doing I so clarify the query of this book. The central question is whether there are limitations to interpretations of Mary. In order to answer this question, I will concentrate on the process of interpretation. I will compile tools for a model of feminist interpretation of symbols in chapter 2. Two authors form the core of this model: Paul Ricoeur and Rosi Braidotti. I do not offer an exegesis of their work but I indicate how their thoughts are helpful in developing a feminist model of interpretation. Chapters 3 and 4 are an exercise in applying this feminist model of interpretation and asking the question whether the symbol 'Mary' is capable of a liberating interpretation for women.

Chapter 1

Feminist Interpretations of Mary

Introduction

This chapter sets out to present a number of different positions that can be taken by twentieth century authors who write about Mary from a women's studies perspective. Mary can indeed be seen from different angles as part of a dogmatic exposition, as a subject that deserves historical analysis, as a psychological category, as part of a particular cultural setting, as belonging to our religious heritage, as an object of devotion. It will become clear that I look upon Mary as belonging to a specific cultural and religious heritage. In Mary a way of speaking has been transmitted about what is called divine. In Western Europe Mary also belongs to the cultural patrimony. The intersection of those two areas determines my interest in Mary.

In this first chapter I will take a look at different, contrasting, interpretations of Mary. W. Beinert (Beinert, 1988, 22-26), in discussing feminist approaches to Mary, distinguishes five categories: 1. authors who consider Mary to be the symbol of the eternal feminine; 2. those who see Mary as a symbol of anti-feminism in the Church; 3. Mary interpreted as the Christian symbol of the original myth of the feminine; 4. Mary as a symbol of self-esteem of women; 5. Mary as sign of the *heilsgeschichtliche* meaning of women. This categorisation can be meaningful, but I do not intend to make use of such classifications, as most authors transgress the boundaries of any particular arrangement. Furthermore, I will also present authors who do not belong to the category of 'feminist Mariology'. The authors I have studied approach Mary from very different angles. We could distinguish between a philosophical/theological interest and an historical interest. It is also possible to categorise the authors according to their religious adherence, e.g. Roman Catholic, goddess-movement, etc. Another classification could be made starting from the question whether the authors recognise what they call the Goddess in Mary or not. Yet another listing could organise the authors as seeing Mary as a cultural given or as a religious factor. More schemes are possible. All classifications are limiting and tend to highlight one aspect while covering up the rest. Furthermore, authors very often could be assigned more than one label. The difficulty of classifying feminist authors has been shown well in H. Meyer-Wilmes' book *Rebellion auf der Grenze* (Meyer-Wilmes, 1990, 76-144).[1] As my aim is not to categorise the different approaches but to

---

1. The schedule on page 111 shows that heterogeneity is the characteristic that applies most of all to feminist theological authors. The schedule differs according to the angle of incidence that has been chosen.

see *how* Mary is broached, I opt for a presentation of authors without forcing them into an ill-fitting frame. This leads to a presentation of authors accompanied with some critical remarks, but without the pressure of trying to make unnecessary comparisons. All authors selected for treatment, however, identify themselves as working within a frame of women's studies. I limit this presentation to these authors, as they more or less explicitly recognise and theorize about the differences between, or the differences attributed to, the sexes.

In commenting on their approach, I step beyond the limits of a mere presentation of the authors. It will soon be clear that my remarks are inspired by a hermeneutical and historical interest. The question "How can women conceive of Mary in a liberating way?" has canalised the selection of authors. While studying these authors I will show that a hermeneutical-historical approach can be constructive. I will point out in what way the authors presented here contribute to this approach, or give indications for such an approach.

At the beginning of this chapter, it is useful to give a brief sketch of the development of Mariology, i.e. the way in which thought about Mary has 'traditionally' been given voice.

Preface: Mariology?

While working on this dissertation, I have heard many people respond to my topic as "How nice, are you writing a new Mariology?". My rather vague but brisk response was: "No, not a Mariology, I am doing something with Mary, but it definitely is not a Mariology". This conversation needs to be clarified: what is a Mariology? We will notice that the term 'Mariology' is also used in feminist interpretations. This is another reason to start with some background information about this concept. I will not only refer to the term as such, but also sketch some of the developments in the approach of Mary. The reasons why I reject a new Mariology will become clearer as this study progresses.

Several definitions can be given. In the *Kleines theologisches Wörterbuch* we read that Mariology is the theological doctrine about Mary. The authors continue: Mariology is entitled to be a separate theological doctrine, but it must be seen as part of a larger whole. Mariology must be in accordance with christology and soteriology; it is the inner moment and first chapter of a dogmatic ecclesiology. The authors do not give us a description of what Mariology could stand for, but immediately propose their own interpretation. Most authors agree that historically Mariology is a fairly young discipline. As a systematic approach of enunciations about Mary, Mariology only appears from the seventeenth century onwards. In the first five centuries of Christianity 'Mariology' is part of the economy of salvation which in turn belonged to christology. Mary is especially important for the humanity of Christ. Later on Mary more and more becomes a figure who contributes to salvation. The history of salvation becomes personalized in Mary. In the seventeenth century Mariology becomes that part of theology that systematically reflects on Mary. Recently (first half of the twentieth century) it has become a separate chapter (Delius, 1963, 288-290). Delius, a Protestant, describes Mariology as dealing with the relation between Mary and God, a relation that is characteristic for Mary as she is the mother of God and as such mother of the divine Redeemer. According to Delius Mariology contains a speculative and a practical side. A speculative Mariology is the "notwendige Ergänzung der Lehre von der Menschwerdung Christi und der Erlösung durch Ihn" (Delius, 1963, 290). Mary presents a new and special world, Mariology is part and consequence of the revealed reality. A practical Mariology concerns the cult and devotion of Mary. Söll makes a stricter distinction: "für den lehrhaften Teil (wird) von Marienlehre (Mariologie) und mariologisch gesprochen, für den Bereich der Frömmigkeit von Marienverehrung bzw. von marianisch" (Söll, 1984, 94)[2].

We must take a look at two important evolutions that form the background to the feminist discourse about Mary: the Second Vatican Council and the ecumenical dialogue about Mary. The Second Vatican Council has been interpreted as a major breakthrough for Catholic thought in the twentieth century. This Council announced a period of openness and experimentation, of renewal and dialogue. It promised to focus on the "People of God" as centre of interest. Mary Daly, one of the authors I will present in this chapter, wrote her first feminist book in those days of hope. The Second Vatican Council has opened doors and windows in the Roman Catholic Church that have stimulated discussions. It is in this climate that Catholic feminists were able to start formulating their own questions. In a similar way, the ecumenical dialogue opened up possibilities for exchanging ideas. The most important outcome of both the Second Vatican Council and the ecumenical dialogue in regard to Mary is, to me, that questions about Mary could be asked outside the strict ecclesial framework. Several groups could enter the debate now. I will give a brief sketch of the evolution in the Vatican documents from the Second Vatican Council on and I will point at some important discussions in the ecumenical dialogue.

In the Roman Catholic Church we see that the Second Vatican Council by its refusal to write a separate document about Mary returned

---

2. The book's title is 'Handbuch der Marienkunde' and not 'Handbuch der Mariologie'.

Mariology to its former status of belonging under ecclesiology (Logister, 1990, 63-64). Several Roman Catholic documents have been produced about Mary in the Vatican these last decades. Even though it is not our aim to analyse these documents, it is necessary to highlight the tenor of some of the documents. We will take a brief look at four documents that have been influential: the eighth chapter of *Lumen Gentium* (1964), *Marialis Cultis* (1974), *Redemptoris Mater* (1987), and *Mulieris Dignitatem* (1988). *Lumen Gentium*[3] is the result of the deliberations concerning the Church by the assembly of bishops during the Second Vatican Council. The assembly decided that no separate document would be written about Mary. Mary's place is with the Church. The document emphasises that Mary is the model of the Church. The parallel of Mary and the Church as Mother and Virgin is extensively elaborated (nr. 64). A remarkable element is the consolidation of Mary's voluntary act of faith and obedience[4] (nr. 56).

On November 21st 1964 Pope Paul VI declared Mary to be 'Mother of the Church'. On February 2nd 1974 Paul VI wrote a letter to the bishops concerning the devotion to Mary: the apostolic adhortation *Marialis Cultis*. This letter is written to stress the necessity of a Marian devotion, but this must be a Marian devotion that is christologically embedded (nr. 4). All Marian devotion must measure up to the christological and trinitarian orientation of Mary (nr. 25). Mary is a teacher of devotion as listening Virgin, praying Virgin, child-bearing Virgin, and as sacrificing Virgin (nrs. 16-21). The Pope shows understanding for the difficulties concerning the imitation of Mary, especially for women in contemporary culture. However, Mary should not be taken as an example because of the kind of life she lived nor because of the socio-cultural conditions of her life, but because she accepted God's will in her life (nr.35). Paul VI blames the devotional, popular images of Mary that swerve from the evangelic image of Mary as being unchristian. (I contend that this attitude shows a complete undervaluation, even denial of the 'voice of the masses'. This does not imply that one has to accept everything that arises from 'the masses', but that one must at least take seriously the message they convey.) The document continues by offering examples of how Marian devotion can be practised.

3. A more elaborate and critical analysis of this text is to be found in Söll, 1984, 223-227 and Laurentin, 1965.

4. This emphasis seems remarkable if one reads feminist authors who bring to the fore this aspect of Mary's attitude as something that has not been acknowledged before. Considering the Roman Catholic doctrine of grace, this interpretation of Mary's obedient, faithful but voluntary fiat is not really surprising at all.

John Paul II has written two documents. The encyclical *Redemptoris Mater* re-emphasises the christological and ecclesiological character of all Mariology. Apart from Jesus, Mary is the most perfect image of the freedom and liberation of humanity and the cosmos (nr. 37). Christian life should be Marian. Women especially should feel invited by Mary to live a Christian life: femininity, according to John Paul II, has a special connection with Mary. Every woman should find in herself total sacrifice in love, the power that resists greatest grief, unlimited loyalty and never-ending care, the capacity to unite penetrating intuition with words of comfort and help. For these after all are the characteristics of Mary (nr. 46). This document was the opening chord for a Marian year and an apostolic letter about the dignity and vocation of woman: *Mulieris Dignitatem*. The document reiterates that one can only say and know something about women by looking at Mary. Human beings are characterised as relational beings, but both sexes realise this relationality according to their specific nature. Women are called to be mother or virgin. Womanhood is openness which can be found in motherhood as this is genuine self-donation, or in virginity as this is spiritual motherhood, an openness for all people. These papal documents stress a Mariology that is christological and ecclesiological, and they emphasise that there is a special connection between Mary and women.

Apart from the Vatican documents which can be criticised because of their theology, the eclectic use of sources, and the image of women that they display, many other voices can be heard in the Roman Catholic Church. One of the more striking interpretations is found in liberation theology. Mary is Mother of the poor. Marian devotion is a popular and persevering characteristic of Latin American Catholicism. Mary has chosen the side of the despised, she has given hope to the exploited, and she has empowered movements working for liberation. This understanding of Mary does not belong in the context of Western theologies and practices, but must be situated in the context of Latin America. Clues here are colonisation and Indian religion (Elizondo, 1983, 76-82). The Mary of the liberation theologies is a challenge to the Western theologies.

The emphasis on christology and ecclesiology displayed by the Second Vatican Council and the later documents seems to have removed barriers to ecumenical discussion (Courth, 1989, 9). The position of Mary has been a controversial point in the dialogue between the Churches. The problems relate to the dogmatic reflection on Mary and the spiritual meaning of Mary. A short survey will give an indication of the differing positions. The Protestant Churches can be characterised as very reluctant towards Mariology and Marian devotion. The primacy of Scripture is central. All reflection about Mary must be situated within this context. Dogmas about Mary are only acceptable when they are based in Scripture.

Mary as Mother of God, and Virgin have references in Scripture. They are not mariological dogmas, but dogmatic pronouncements about Mary that are added to the christological dogma (Feiner, 1973, 610-614). This leads to 'Marian minimalism' (Petri, 1984, 330). Adriaan Soeting, for instance, describes the attention given by Dutch Protestants to Mary as separated from a living reality. Mary is safely packed away in the books on the shelves. Dogmatic discussions about e.g. Mary's virginity, nevertheless, make passions rise (Soeting, 1980, 52-53).

There are historical reasons for the reluctant attitude towards Mary: the Catholic reformation has used Mary as its hallmark. Mary became associated with anti-protestantism, or seen from the opposite perspective, Mary became typically Roman Catholic. The theological background is that for Protestants the centrality of Jesus as reference to the New Testament is crucial. Jesus is at the heart of Protestant religious life. The proximity of God is shown in Jesus. It is not necessary to make a detour via Mary or the saints. Prayer should not be directed at Mary. According to Luther praise of Mary can only be praise of the abundant grace of God (Courth, 1989, 12). Mary can be the human being who is the recipient of the miracle of revelation (K. Barth in Petri, 1984, 335). She is the witness of Jesus. From the Roman Catholic side attempts to bridge the differences between the churches have often been made by writing articles that centre around New Testament texts about Mary (see Mussner, 1964; Mussner, 1967; Langemeyer, 1967; Scheele, 1975; Schmidt, 1975; Kertelge, 1986). In contemporary ecumenical dialogue thoughts about prayer to Mary are set in the context of solidarity in salvation (*Heilssolidarität*) of the faithful. The Roman Catholic identification of Mary and the Church is problematic. "Die ganze Härte der evangelischen Kritik an der römisch-katholischen Mariologie (ist) Kritik an der römisch-katholischen Ekklesiologie" (Döring in Courth, 1989, 28). The idea that the Church is in Mary is unacceptable; Mary as a person who belongs to the Church is a perspective that is less problematic. The question what kind of Church Mary belongs to, remains a point of discussion. Another problematic field is the idea of Mary's mediatorship. Mary as mediator seems to suggest that human beings somehow can cooperate in establishing salvation. This is contrary to the idea of God's redeeming activity as belonging to God only. The controversy around this topic seems to have come to an end in the distinction that "Gottes *All*wirksamkeit nicht seine *Allein*wirksamkeit besage" (Courth, 1989, 20-21)[5]. Feminist theologians have been acutely

---

5. More literature: Schimmelpfenning, 1952; Tappolet, 1962; Oberman, 1964; Brandenburg, 1965; Thurian, 1962; Düffel, 1968; Voss, 1981; Ott, 1984; Lackmann, 1985; Schütte, 1985; Ritschl, 1986, 40-59; Courth, 1986.

aware of the difficult position of Mary in ecumenical dialogue. As we will now turn to authors who have written about Mary from a women's studies perspective, I will start in presenting someone who has rooted her reflections about Mary in the ecumenical question: Catherine Halkes.

1. C. Halkes: Mary as an antidote for patriarchal religion

In her oeuvre, Tine Halkes regularly reflects on the figure of Mary. She herself sketches an evolution in her life with Mary: from a childhood saturated with Mary and saints in which Mary functioned as the ultimate example for women, via a banishing of all 'superstitious' belief at the emergence of the *nouvelle théologie*, to a discovery of the Mary of the gospels, i.e. Mary as the first person to accept faith (Halkes, 1980, 87-88).

Whereas in 1962 she writes that Mariology is Christology -- Mary has to be seen in relation with Christ who represents redeemed humanity (Halkes, 1962, 40-41) -- more recent articles reject this notion. Halkes states that this interpretation is a reduction: it does not ask the question who Mary actually is, what person she was, and what images were made of her (Halkes, 1977, 87; Halkes, 1984, 85-87). Halkes is convinced that talking about Mary is necessary. She gives five reasons: Mary needs to be liberated; women need to be liberated from restrictive images of Mary; feminist theologians have to participate in the discourse about Mary in order to introduce the female experience in theology; the ecumenical basis of feminist theology can bridge the gap between the different denominations when Mary is discussed; and the figure of Mary reveals the ambivalent attitude of Church and theology towards sexuality and women (Halkes, 1983, 83-84).

Halkes expresses the hope[6] of finding a picture of Mary by applying various disciplines: comparative religion, history of religion, psychology of religion, depth psychology, theology, etc. (Halkes, 1983, 85; Halkes, 1980, 111; Halkes, 1984, 96). A different Mary appears when popular piety rather than theological treatises is studied. Mary is the life-giving, feeding, and preserving one (Halkes, 1983, 85). She is a reminder of the Magna Mater (Halkes, 1980, 102). Mary confronts people with their female side (Halkes, 1980, 102). She is the revelation of the female dimension of an androgynous God (Halkes, 1980, 112; Halkes, 1980, 126). She can be the triumph over patriarchal one-sidedness as she forces the

---

6. This hope, expressed in several articles, has not been realized up till now. It would be most interesting to see the outcome of this research.

Church to acknowledge the aspects of the "Great Mother" she embodies (Halkes, 1983, 90, Halkes, 1984, 92-94)[7].

It is a pity that Halkes, up till now, has not yet written a systematic article on Mary. The overviews she has produced present us with a rather diffuse and scattered vision. On the one hand she wants to discover the historical Mary, the person she really was, how she lived. On the other hand she wants to see Mary as a reminder of the Magna Mater. She views her therefore both as human being and as Goddess. Does this mean that Mary is the incarnation of the Goddess? Does not this statement conflict with her Christian belief that Jesus is the incarnation of God? Or do we need two incarnations: one of God and one of the Goddess? Or does she talk about two different Marys: a strictly human one and a strictly divine one? Halkes distinguishes between the historical Mary and the images of Mary. Do humanity and divinity of Mary also follow this distinction? These questions cannot be answered, as Halkes has not yet offered clues in the articles she has written.

I want to mention one more problem: Halkes wants to picture the person Mary actually was. This seems to me an impossible task, as there are no data available about the historical Mary. The only accounts we have are the New Testament writings and the apocrypha. These writings, however, do not offer a historical account. They are a reflection upon the experience that Jesus is Christ. This faith is communicated by way of stories, and Mary is part of these. The stories function so as to proclaim this faith in Christ and all elements have to underpin this, also Mary. As a consequence these writings offer only an image of Mary. This becomes obvious if one for instance compares the Matthean and the Lukan Mary. Every attempt to tell something about Mary how she really was thus has to run aground.

2. R. Radford Ruether: Mary, vision of a new Church

Rosemary Radford Ruether is one of the few feminist theologians who has reflected systematically on Mary and who has tried to develop a theology that integrates the figure of Mary. In *Disputed Questions* she relates her childhood memories and recalls that "Even the divine appeared to be

---

7. Marianne Katoppo interprets Mary in a similar way. For her Mary is the figure who is sensitive to injustice and who tries to promote social changes. She also is the image of full humanity. She is "the new human being (man-woman) who is open to God who invites him/her to be imago Dei" (Katoppo, 1979, 34). Sölle describes Mary as a "sympathizer". She chooses the side of the poor and the despised of this earth and incites resistance (Sölle, 1979, 48-52).

immediately represented by a female, Mary. God and Christ were somewhere in the distance, like the priests, but Mary was the one you talked to
if you wanted to pray" (Ruether, 1989, 111-112). This early experience has
set the tone for a life that can be characterised as "a cosy, female run
world where I felt myself a favored daughter" (Ruether, 1989, 112) and
where men were "distant and unavailable figures" (Ibid.). Far from psy-
chologizing Ruether's preoccupation with Mary, this experience has been
the foundation for the serious and truly searching way in which Ruether
has written about Mary. On a theoretical level she claims that "Human
experience is both the starting point and the ending point of the circle of
interpretation" (Ruether, 1985, 111).

Regarding Mary, it seems that her own positive experience with Mary
early on in life has effected a constructive approach, without closing her
eyes to the destructive and debasing interpretations of Mary. Ruether
finds it worthwhile to ask over and over again: is Mary a symbol of liberation, or is she an instrument of male power? (Ruether, 1977, 12) She
claims that Mariology has much to account for. It has a history of canalis-
ing people's fears of sexuality (Ruether, 1972, 111-112). There is a possible relationship between increasing misogyny (as manifested in the late
medieval witch craze) and a blooming Mariology (Ruether, 1976, 16-17).
Mariology has emphasised the passive receptivity of women (Ruether,
1983, 139). The nineteenth century ideology of the cult of true womanhood appears to be Mariology in secular clothes (Ruether, 1976, 45-49[8]).
For these reasons, a new and fresh look at Mariology is demanded. Once
more the question arises: whose side is Mary on? (Ruether, 1975, 36-37)

In trying to expose the roots of Mariology, Ruether first of all
focuses on biblical and pre-biblical sources. She uncovers the links between the Goddesses of non-Israelite cultures and biblical imagery
(Ruether, 1975, 37-41; Ruether, 1977, 13-18). The Mediterranean religions see the Goddess in multifarious images and symbols. Several of these
appear in the Old Testament (Ruether, 1977, 19-30). Very little of this
survives in the New Testament. Mary plays a minor role in all these writings (Ruether, 1977, 31-42). The female symbols applied to God in the
Old Testament did not disappear in early Christianity. This inheritance
was handed down and appropriated in the description of the "New Israel"
(Ruether, 1977, 43-48). It was only when an attempt was made to develop
a Mariology, that female symbols became connected with the mother of
Jesus. The second century (C.E.) fathers represented Mary as the new

---

8. See also Ruether, 1985, 110-111 where the author links medieval Mariology with
nineteenth century post-revolutionary France where she discovers a secular restatement of
woman worship.

Eve, the new Church. Mary is the daughter of the old covenant and member of the new covenant in Christ (Ruether, 1977, 53-57). Ruether also points out that there is a link between Isis and the Christian cult of Mary in third century (C.E.) Egypt (Ruether, 1985a, 6). From the end of the fourth century on Mariology becomes a real topic. Mariology tries to centre a theology of female experience around the person of Mary. Mary is "a symbol of the self and the community in relation to God, or a maternal mediator between the patriarchal Lord of Heaven and the faithful of the Church" (Ruether, 1975, 46; Ruether, 1977, 48). Ruether indicates that Latin theology situated Mary's importance around her function of representative of humanity in its original goodness: Mary is the "persona ecclesiae" (Ruether, 1975, 55).

Ruether wants to integrate Mariology in contemporary theology. She asks:

> "Is there any basis for an alternative Mariology, one that is not the expression of the male feminine which scapegoats female sexuality for sin and death? Is there a Mariology -- a doctrine of the Church as symbolically female -- that would allow us to name sexism itself as sin and point toward the liberation of women and men from the dualisms of carnal femaleness and spiritual femininity?" (Ruether, 1983, 152).

In her earlier work Ruether pleads for a liberation Mariology, i.e. a Mariology that gives rise to a new vision of Gods power, and that enhances a new humanity. Ruether rejects the idea that the introduction of the Goddess will liberate women from an oppressive and sexist religion. She fears that this will limit women to the cliché: "woman is the symbol of nature" (Ruether, 1977, 76-77). She tries to develop a non-sexist way of thinking about God. Of ultimate importance is the question: 'How can God's transcendence be conceived?'. Is it possible to imagine the relation between God and the world in terms other than 'above' and 'below', 'Lord' and 'servant' ... ? Ruether believes that a change in this relationship can incite a change in the relations between people. According to Ruether, the solution is a model of mutual relationship in which the dichotomy dominance-receptivity is transcended. The new model of reciprocity is characterised by support of autonomy and actualization of others (Ruether,1977, 77-78; Ruether, 1975, 58). This destroys the idea of male activity and female passivity.

In Mary this new way of relating becomes visible. Mary embodies the co-creatorship between God and humanity (see Luke's Magnificat). She shows a receptivity that has nothing to do with a sexist interpretation that equals receptivity with powerless passivity and self-abnegation. Mary's 'yes' to God is a free act of faith. Mary can be a liberating symbol if she is seen from this angle. She is the new humanity freed from hierarchical power. She represents the original wholeness of humanity. The sin that destroyed this original wholeness is sexism (Ruether, 1975, 58). The Church becomes a community of people redeemed from sexism (Ruether, 1983, 151-156; Ruether, 1977, 82-88). Christ's message urges rulers and mighty persons to serve in order to promote authenticity, dignity, and goodness. Ruether proposes to interpret tradition as having revealed this new community in a woman. Mary or the Church represents liberated humanity (Ruether, 1977, 86). Or in other terms: "Mary as Church represents God's 'preferential option for the poor', to use the language of Latin-American liberation theology" (Ruether, 1983, 157). Mary can take this special place as representative of the Church not because she is mother of Jesus -- Ruether interprets Luk.11:27-28 as Jesus' refusal to honour his mother only because of her motherhood -- but because she heard God's word and responded to it (Ruether, 1977, 85-87).

> "If we take seriously the female personification of the Church within this perspective, then we must take the analysis of oppression and liberation a step further. If women of the oppressed classes and social groups represent the poorest of the poor, the most despised of society, then such women can become the models of faith and their liberation becomes the special locus of the believing and liberated community. We need to move beyond the typology of Christ and the Church as dominant male and submissive female. Rather, what we see here is an ongoing process of *kenosis* and transformation. God's power no longer remains in Heaven where it can be used as a model of the 'thrones of the mighty'. In the iconoclastic and messianic prophet, it has been emptied out into the human situation of suffering and hope" (Ruether, 1983, 157).

(Ruether's indebtedness to Latin American liberation theologies is obvious here: the centrality of the Lucan Mary and the privileged position of the poor.)

Ruether is very clear: even though she recognises links between the Goddesses of non-Israelite cultures and the Old Testament, she does not want to introduce Goddesses into contemporary Christianity. She fears it will pin women down to the 'woman = nature' caricature they have been reduced to for ages. It seems that Ruether's rejection of the insertion of Goddesses, and as a consequence the restriction on imaging Mary as Goddess, is strongly connected with her adherence to the Christian tradition. She wants to stay in line with this tradition. The question why Mary in popular devotion was venerated as a Goddess remains unanswered. This question has too many implications to be left aside. A possible answer could be deduced from Ruether's design for a new God-image that is rooted in another interpretation of God's power. This would mean that, in popular piety, Mary took on some functions people missed in God. This thesis, however, is still speculative and needs further research. It is her opinion that the escape from a patriarchal image of God is a new vision of God's power. Mary can be helpful in establishing this. In this approach Mary becomes the human being in whom God shows how s/he can be conceived[9].

In Ruether's design, which is clearly Christian, and also circumscribed by her Roman Catholic background, Mary becomes a theological concept. Ruether makes a move similar to that made by the Second Vatican Council: back to the biblical roots. It seems that what lies between the biblical period and the present must be forgotten, or maybe it must be seen as folklore. It is questionable whether this entire history can be neglected.

3. E. Schüssler Fiorenza: Mary, a myth

Elisabeth Schüssler Fiorenza in an article in Theological Studies, *Feminist Theology as a Critical Theology of Liberation* (Schüssler Fiorenza, 1975), shows what the Mary myth meant for women and what we have to do with it. The article offers an insight into what feminist theology is. It first sketches the point which feminism, and feminist theology along with it, makes when it criticises contemporary culture and its inherent dangers. The awareness that "not only Christian institutions but also Christian theology operates in a sexist framework and language" (Schüssler Fiorenza, 1975, 611), enhances the attempts of Christian feminists to reconceptualize and to transform Christian theology from a feminist perspective. Secondly the article describes what feminist theology as critical theology means: it demands a radical change of ecclesial institutions and structures, of theology and history in order to overcome sexism. This, however, can only happen if language, imagery and myth participate in this radical change. The third part of the article tackles the question of new symbols, images, and myths. This is where Mary appears on the scene.

---

9. The suspicion arises that the stress on the need for a Mariology is still the result of a problematic christology. Is it not in Jesus, who was recognized as Christ that the co-creatorship between God and humanity took shape? Is it not also in Jesus that a new way of relating to each other takes shape? The outstanding position of Mary has the tendency to denigrate Jesus. It leads to the supposition that Jesus' gender was after all important, so we need a female counterpart. It also has to be noticed that Ruether's interpretation stays very much in line with contemporary official Catholic teachings about Mary: Mary is the church-person. Her interpretation differs, however, when it comes to the place of Mary as object of devotion and as example for women.

Images and myths, according to Schüssler Fiorenza, "provide a world view and give meaning to our lives" (Schüssler Fiorenza, 1975, 620). Contrary to the abstract and rational input of theological reflection, images and myths not only inform people about the world but also invite imitation.

> " They encourage particular forms of behavior and implicitly embody goals and value judgments. Insofar as a myth is a story which provides a common vision, feminists have to find new myths and stories in order to embody their goals and value judgments. (...) Yet feminist theologians are aware that myths also have a stabilizing, retarding function insofar as they sanction the existing social order and justify its power structure by providing communal identity and a rationale for societal and ecclesial institutions. Therefore, exactly because feminist theologians value myths and images, they have first to analyze and to 'demythologize' the myths of the sexist society and patriarchal religion in order to liberate them." (Schüssler Fiorenza, 1975, 620).

The 'myth' of Mary has been, and still is, one of those life-guiding myths. It is therefore not only possible but also necessary to dissect this myth and uncover its psychological and ecclesial functions. The guiding question is whether the Mary myth ever provided women with a new vision of equality and wholeness. Elements can be traced that point in the direction of a divinization of Mary that was difficult to combat. As such Mary is reminiscent of the ancient Goddess mythologies. The powerful radiation of this divine Mary, however, never affected the hierarchical organisation of the Church, nor did it integrate women into it.

When we look at the New Testament stories, it is plain that the roots of the Mary myth are not found there. On the contrary, Schüssler Fiorenza radically points out that male, clerical, ascetic culture and theology is the producer of the Mary myth. The main theme that pervades this myth is the image of Mary as the Virginal Mother. Mary is seen as the pure woman, without sin, obedient, subservient. This myth in the first place undergirds the body-soul dualism that has affected all of Christianity. It pins women down to their 'natural' capacities, i.e. bearing children. Dualistic thinking subordinates everything that is connected with nature, or body. The mind, or spirit, is to be cultivated and is 'men's' goal. Men are linked with mind-spirit, women with body-nature. Spirit dominates nature, man dominates woman. The male-invented Mary myth also connected human capacities like love, nurture, emotionality, and care exclusively with mothering, which in its turn was reserved for women. Schüssler Fiorenza claims that "this stereotyping of these human qualities led not only to their elimination from public life but also to a privatization of Christian values, which are, according to the New Testament, concentrated and climaxed in the command of love" (Schüssler Fiorenza, 1975, 623).

The Mary myth secondly separates women in the Catholic community from one another. Catholic women have to be either mother or nun. Virginal existence is valued as being the better choice: one truly embodies the ideal of the humble handmaiden through a rejection of earthly desires and dependencies. It is necessary to overcome this dichotomy and establish a true sisterhood.

Schüssler Fiorenza's conclusion is clear: if a myth of a woman, as in traditional Mariology, is preached to women by men, the outcome can be that women are prevented from being fully independent and whole human beings. This observation must lead to a particularly careful use in feminist theology of contemporary attempts to emphasise feminine imagery and myths. These new images do not stand apart from sexist society. They therefore must undergo the same critical analyses that traditional imagery has to endure[10].

A second article in which Mary is mentioned appeared in 1978 and was reprinted in *Womanspirit Rising* (Schüssler Fiorenza, 1979, 136-148). Schüssler Fiorenza describes the Goddess of radical feminist spirituality and does not find her so very different from the God of Jesus. She states that "the traditions about the Goddess and those of the New Testament are conflated in the Catholic community's cult of Mary" (Ibid., 138). The patriarchalisation of God and Jesus effected the turn to Mary.

> "Even though any Catholic school child can explain on an *intellectual-theological* level the difference between the worship of God and Christ and the veneration of Mary, on an *emotional, imaginative, experiential* level the Catholic child experiences the love of God in the figure of a woman" (Ibid., 138).

The Catholic cult of Mary not only provided experience of the divine in a female figure, it also provided female language and imagery to speak of the divine. We have to use this language, according to Schüssler Fiorenza, in order to talk about God in a nonsexist way but we should not absolutise it.

---

10. Schüssler Fiorenza continues the article with a suggestion for new imagery that can be empowering for Christian women. She gives the example of Mary Magdalen.

4. E.A. Johnson: The symbolic Character of Theological Statements about Mary

Elizabeth A. Johnson has written several articles about Mary in a very short period. The first, which appeared in 1984, contained an analysis of the christologies of Rahner and Schillebeeckx in their connection with Mary (Johnson, 1984, 155-182). Johnson shows how the place of Mary in both authors' works changes in correlation with the development of new christologies. Remarkable for Rahner as well as for Schillebeeckx is the intensification of the christological focus. This results in a displacement of characteristics formerly attributed to Mary towards Jesus. This diagnosis induced Johnson to propose ten theses for the reconstruction of a theology of Mary: 1. a theology of Mary must be constructed in dialogue with the primary doctrines of God, Christ, Church, and the reality of humanity, sinful and redeemed; 2. there must be Trinitarian reference; 3. a theology of Mary differs from Christology as it "reflects on the intelligibility of the symbol of this woman as responsive to the Christ event" (Johnson, 1984, 181); 4. Mary is the first of the believing Christian disciples; 5. affirmations about Mary are affirmations about the nature of human salvation; 6. a theology of Mary is connected with pneumatology, a connection that has not yet been explored[11]; 7. the Marian image has revealed 'the feminine dimension of the divine'; 8. the interpretation of the Marian doctrine is to be ecclesiological; 9. the communion of saints is the principle that relates present-day believers to Mary; 10. Mary, member of the Church, is the embodiment of discipleship.

In an article in the *Journal of Ecumenical Studies*, 1985 Johnson argues that

> "Theological statements about Mary have a symbolic structure, so that while they refer immediately and in an obvious way to this one woman, they reach their intended and theological referent when interpreted finally as statements about the Church, the community of faithful disciples, of which she is a member and in which she participates" (Johnson, 1985a, 313).

This elaboration throws new light on the ten theses of the previous article. Johnson distinguishes between two opposite interpretative traditions concerning statements about Mary. One pole is formed by the Roman Catholic tradition and is supposed to be historical. Point of departure is the historical events in Mary's life. A search for this historical Mary provides few clues: she was the mother of Jesus, she was a Jewish woman,

---

11. Johnson overlooks the Orthodox Mariology. Other example is Boff, 1989.

she did not understand the intentions of her own son, and later on she became a faithful disciple. The points differentiating her from Jesus and the consequent christology are that no specific events characterise Mary's demeanour nor does her personality offer any reason for her special status. It is

> "the graced reality of the ekklesia (that) grounds her symbol; the community of disciples in which she participated creates the symbol, sees itself reflected in it, and, in the measure in which the symbol evokes through the grace of God a similar response of faith-filled discipleship, benefits from it" (Johnson, 1985a, 317).

The other side of the interpretative spectrum is formed by a more Protestant, meditative approach. The statements about Mary are read as stories, poetic meditations that clarify and enhance the central themes of the gospels. As a consequence -- so mourns Johnson -- the historical Mary is lost. (Johnson stages an opposition between Catholicism and Protestantism that sounds familiar: S. McFague, 1982, 13-14 also refers to this distinction. I do not agree with this simplified and simplifying division, nor do I agree with an oppositional approach to metaphors and symbols -- an approach that can also be found in Morton, 1985, 153ff. Over against this, Soskice, for example, clearly distinguishes between symbols and metaphors: metaphors are figures of speech, symbols are a category that includes the non-linguistic, Soskice, 1985).

A symbolic interpretation, according to Johnson, avoids the pitfalls of naïve historicism and of losing the real Mary. She understands symbols in terms of P. Tillich and P. Ricoeur's theories. Tillich sees religious symbols as pointing to what is transcending the world, what is beyond the human and the finite, what can never be objectified. A symbol is 1. a sign that refers to something outside itself; 2. in contrast with a sign, a symbol participates in what it refers to; 3. a symbol gives access to dimensions in the human mind that otherwise would remain hidden; 4. it unlocks dimensions of the human spirit that correspond to this reality; 5. symbols cannot be created or replaced at random; 6. a symbol is dynamic, it is born, it develops, and it dies in relation to a group. Johnson brings in Ricoeur because he describes religious language and "the way in which its structure carries the human subject into the meaning which it gives" (Johnson, 1985a, 312).

In summary, Johnson defines a symbol as follows:

> "A symbol is a species of sign which carries a fullness of meaning going beyond what can be explicitly and exhaustively stated. It characteristically introduces us into realms of awareness not usually

accessible to discursive thought, giving participatory rather than simply speculative knowledge" (Johnson, 1985a, 322).

Concerning Mary, Johnson contends that we can give Marian statements a symbolic interpretation because she "personifies or 'symbolizes' the characteristics of the new humankind of faith" (Johnson, 1985a, 323). Any interpretation of the Marian symbol will be structured by its nature. According to Johnson, Marian statements are best interpreted as "statements about aspects of the church's relationship to God in Christ, that ekklesia of which she is a member and in which she participates" (Johnson, 1985a, 327).

A third article written by Johnson explicitly addresses the relation between the Marian tradition and women (Johnson, 1985b). The crucial questions are how the Marian tradition has kept women inferior because of their gender, and how this tradition can possibly be reinterpreted in such a way that it becomes liberating and enhances mutuality between women and men. Johnson analyses three major criticisms: 1. "The Marian tradition has been intrinsically associated with the denigration of the nature of women as a group" (Johnson, 1985b, 121) ; 2. "The Marian tradition has dichotomized the being and roles of women and men in the community of disciples following Christ" (Johnson, 1985b, 124); 3. "The Marian tradition has truncated the ideal of feminine fulfilment and wholeness" (Johnson, 1985b, 126). Johnson has three proposals for directions that could lead to new interpretations: 1. the imaginatively historical approach that by identifying Mary as a real person in history makes her more accessible. Even though the imagery sprouting from this approach is not necessarily historically based, it shows a realism that brings Mary within imaginable reach; 2. a more theological approach that interprets Mary as a type of the Church, a type of the community of believing disciples; 3. an approach that explores and discovers new symbolic aspects of Mary as the proclaimer of liberation and reinterpreting the meaning of the traditional qualities of virginity and motherhood. Johnson concludes that she believes a resymbolisation of Mary is possible, but she also warns against premature complacency.

These three articles by Johnson are fundamental for any reinterpretation of Mary. The consistent interpretation of Mary as symbol is promising. Johnson limits this to theological statements, but it would be interesting to broaden this to all utterances about Mary.

5. I. Gebara and M. Bingemer: Mary: Mother of God, Mother of the Poor

Gebara and Bingemer have conceived of "a Marian theology whose start-ing point is women and Latin America" (Gebara, 1989, xi). The authors try to reread Mary with the questions of this age in mind, an age that is characterised by the awakening of women's historical consciousness (Gebara, 1989, 16). Any Marian theology must first of all clarify its an-thropological assumptions. They understand anthropology to be "the fun-damental lines governing our understanding of what human beings are and what their task in history is" (Gebara, 1989, 2). Most of the anthro-pology in existing Mariologies is, according to Gebara and Bingemer, male-centred, dualistic, idealist and one-dimensional. The development of a human-centred, unifying, realist, and pluri-dimensional anthropology can do justice to the complexity of human reality. Their insistent emphasis on anthropology is fundamental for the kind of theology these authors have in mind: "when we speak of anthropology we are speaking of theology" (Gebara, 1989, 2). The divine is manifested in the human, breaks through in human history. This is how 'human word' about Mary becomes 'divine word' for human beings. "Mary is the divine creation of the human and in the human" (Gebara, 1989, 17).

In offering some hermeneutical remarks, the authors set out the direction the readers must follow. They emphasise the centrality of the faith relationship between "believers within history and those 'who live in God'" (Gebara, 1989, 20). The yearning for the unlimited, the belief that human life continues in God, structures the lives of those who live in history.

> "For a Marian theology it is not enough to analyze the texts of previous tradition. It is crucial to recognise what kind of human experience devotion to Mary, or relationships with her, is. In other words, we must ask to what kind of 'yearnings,' manifest or latent, our relationship with Mary, who 'lives in God' and lives in us, belongs" (Gebara, 1989, 260).

The hermeneutics of the authors is dialogical: they converse with the texts, bringing their own life experience to the text. Their lives are marked by the rejection of capitalist oppression of Latin American people. Their reading of texts is "a committed reading, on the side of the poor and op-pressed" (Gebara, 1989, 30).

Scripture, read in order to develop a Marian theology, provides the central idea of the Kingdom of God. This concept unites God's saving activities on behalf of women and men. It emphasises the concrete actions that characterise God's saving activity. Mary's actions can be seen "as actions that bring signs of the reign of God to the fore, concrete actions that make the presence of salvation in human history manifest" (Gebara, 1989, 33). Gebara and Bingemer read the New Testament as a text that says "that God's gesture of love is repeated again in Mary and Jesus, or in other words, is repeated in humankind as a new creation" (Gebara, 1989, 45).

Tradition, here limited to the Marian dogmas, is reread from the perspective of the poor. Interesting is the question of "the people's dogmatics as related to the dogmatics established by the church institution" (Gebara, 1989, 125). Saving life is the core of the existence of the people, saving power is what institutional dogmatics seem to be about. The relation to Mary is experienced as immediate and vital for those whose children are hungry. "(...) the formulation of institutional dogmatics is 'not much of a problem' for the poor, since it is not very well understood, and ultimately the poor transform it to serve their own situation in history" (Gebara, 1989, 127).

The experience of faith in Mary by the poor, is illustrated with several examples: the colonial background of Marian devotion, Marian apparitions, cures and miracles, and the place of Mary in the base communities. The new Marian theology developed by these authors brings a new word about the world: this world is the meeting place of those who 'live in history' and those who 'live in God'. It also brings a new word about the human being: "Mary, collective figure, symbol of the faithful people from whose womb emerges the New Creation, unfolds before human beings all their infinite horizons with their indescribable possibilities" (Gebara, 1989, 174). It also brings a new word about God: Mary, who is a human being totally open to the divine, shows something of God in her participatory activity in the Kingdom of God.

The strength of this book lies in its radical contextualised approach. The authors unravel the myth of an unproblematic universal discourse about Mary. Without denying the possibility of universal communicative discourse, they elaborate an approach that starts with a contextual analysis. Gebara and Bingemer are a warning to feminist theologians who try to bring a feminist Mariology, or a feminist Marian theology. It is necessary to specify what kind of feminist Mariology this is: a North American white Mariology, or a European feminist Marian theology? Gebara and Bingemer point out that the actors in the hermeneutical field must be specified.

6. Mary Daly: Arch-Image

Mary Daly, the controversial professor of Boston College, has, as a former Catholic, experienced what impact Mary can have in a person's life.

Daly's preoccupation with Mary in all of her books, especially in *Pure Lust*, consequently is not fortuitous. A remarkable evolution is noticeable, an evolution that characterises her entire oeuvre: Daly moves from being a feminist Catholic theologian (*The Church and the Second Sex*) to being a radical feminist philosopher (*Beyond God the Father, Gyn/Ecology, Pure Lust*). The second, present-day Daly is estranged from the first Daly. She no longer recognises herself in the author of *The Church and the Second Sex* (cf. the Post-christian Introduction to this book in the 1975 edition). From a historical point of view it is interesting to read what the first Daly has written about Mary. *The Church and the Second Sex* was an eye-opener, as it pointed out the distortions of patriarchal religion regarding women. Daly has proved to be a seer who has set out tracks that have provided a full agenda for authors after her. We have to keep in mind, however, that the present-day Daly has disconnected herself from this author.

The Church and the Second Sex can be regarded as the first major critical feminist theological work. The title already suggests that the author is acquainted with Simone de Beauvoir. Indeed, Daly draws heavily upon the ideas found in *'Le deuxième sexe'*. Daly agrees with de Beauvoir's analysis of the figure of Mary, mother of God: the power of motherhood is threatening to men. In order to control this power, motherhood needs to be enslaved and transformed. Mary is the ideal mother: she kneels before her son and she freely accepts her subordinate role. This makes her the outstanding role model for women. This image of Mary has "devastating effects" (Daly, 1975, 61). Identically devastating effects can be found in the ambivalent attitude towards sexuality: Mary is supposed to counterbalance Eve. The message that is supposed to be conveyed by the Eve-Mary polarity is that women are guilty of the Fall but that they also take part in the redemptive activity through Mary. This balancing effect has not gained much popularity. A more confused image appeared: in Mary women are good, but Mary is unique, she does not really connect with real women (Daly, 1975, 68). As a consequence Mary appears to be an impossible model for women. Furthermore, says Daly, we should remember that the Mary symbol is the product of the brains of a celibate clergy who hope to capture the essence of womanhood through this man-made symbol. Daly calls this phenomenon "the Catholic symbol syndrome" (Daly, 1975, 157). It is obvious that this static, hierarchical, polar image is not exactly the most adequate role model for women, and that it will prevent men from acquiring a realistic view of women (Daly, 1975, 160-164).

The later Daly looks at Mary from a very different angle. She has stopped her dialogue with the institution of the "Church". This applies to the Roman Catholic Church and all other institutional forms of religion.

Daly now uses her energy to develop a new way of being, of loving and living that is proper to women. Her critique of Christian and other symbols, ideas, words, etc. focuses on the distortions, the sublimation, the obscuring of original meanings.

In *Beyond God the Father* Daly consolidates the impossibility of using Mary as a model for women of flesh and blood (Daly, 1974, 62, 81). This is a reiteration of her previous book. Instead of finishing the discussion here, she moves on and discovers a prophetic dimension in Mary. This prophetic message does not lie in the all too often quoted Magnificat (Lk.1,46-55) but in Mary herself: Daly sees Mary as a remnant of the ancient Mother Goddess (Daly, 1974, 82-84). She not only is some distant reflection of an almost completely forgotten and denied past (Daly, 1974, 90-94), she also is the precursor of a new age in which women are becoming God (Daly, 1974, 84). The big silence that covered up the universally matriarchal world is about to be broken: we are on the verge of a new coming of female presence (Daly, 1974, 93-96).

Gyn/Ecology and *Pure Lust* elaborate and travel beyond the ideas of *Beyond God the Father*. More clearly than in her previous books Daly states that "despite all the theological minimizing of Mary's 'role', the mythic presence of the Goddess was perceivable in this faded and reversed mirror image" (Daly, 1978, 85; also Daly, 1984, 73). Mary has been turned into a vessel of male progeniture, a human being who is not entitled to live a life of her own. Her life and being is secondary to that of the male species. Nevertheless, entering the Archespheres of the First Realm, as Daly explains in *Pure Lust*, it is possible to 'dis-cover' the Arch-image (Daly, 1984, 85 f.) [12]. The Christian tradition's arduous attempts at extinguishing the Archimage did not succeed. The Archimage shines through in Mary. The 'mind-molders' (Daly's notion) could not prevent the Archimage from being translucent in Mary. Daly invented the word Arch-Image to name this phenomenon: i.e. the Archimage shining through in Mary despite manipulation (Daly, 1984, 92).

Daly suggests that Mary should be radically reconnected with the Archimage to counterattack the Protestant erasure of Mary and the Catholic usurpation of Mary. This needs to be done because the Mary image is still powerful. Although it has been distorted, it has also inspired women towards acts of knowing and passion (Daly, 1984, 94-95). Refutation of Catholic doctrines about Mary proves necessary. Daly looks at the recent Marian dogmas as "mythic paradigms disclosing and foretelling

---

12. Archimage: the Great Original Witch in every woman and Elemental creature; a Metaphoric form of Naming the one and the many; Active Potency of Hags, etc. Daly, 1984, 86-87, further 89f.

reality" (Daly, 1984, 109). The doctrine of the Immaculate Conception, for instance, sets forth the image of Mary as model rape victim (Daly, 1984, 104-106). Already from the very first beginning of her life Mary has been denied a self-determining existence. She is silenced and totally subdued. It prepares her for further rape at 'The Annunciation'. "Already violated at her conception, Mary affirms at the Annunciation her need of male acceptance" (Daly, 1984, 106). The Immaculate Conception, proclaimed in 1854 on December 8 by Pope Pius IX also functions as the starting point of female tokenism: a strategy that makes women stand up against each other. Tokenism is the procedure of selecting some women for so-called promotion thereby incorporating them in the male-created world and making them harmless. This system gives token women the idea of exceptionalism and empties them of autonomous intellect and will. 1854 should be seen as prophetic: a warning against a false inclusion of women within so-called male professions (Daly, 1984, 107-116).

In *Gyn/Ecology* similar ideas are developed in connection with the Virgin Birth (Daly, 1978, 83-87). Mary becomes totally estranged from her "Power of parthenogenetic Goddess" (Daly, 1984, 106) and thus becomes very useful as model in a patriarchal framework. The Virgin Birth shows Mary as little more than "a hollow eggshell" (Daly quoting A. Dellenbaugh, 1978, 83). Women are denied creativity. The perception of autonomous female transcendence, which Daly wants to promote, is unlikely.

The Assumption, proclaimed in 1950, bears as much witness to the phallic sublimation as the Immaculate Conception did. Daly reads the Assumption as a mythic paradigm of nuclear disaster: just like Mary's bodily Assumption seems to be a triumph over death, so is nuclearism presented as a restoration of hope for life. Daly also warns that we should realise that the proclamation of the Assumption in 1950 was of no help for women: As Mary went up, women went down. The fifties were a time when women had to return to the kitchen after a time of productivity outside the house during the Second World War (Daly, 1984, 124).

These cheerless analyses of the Marian dogmas have a reverse side: they also reveal something of Elemental Being. They are broken metaphors of Translucent Transcendence (Daly, 1984, 113-129). The Immaculate Conception can function as "a Metaphor evoking the Parthenogenetic Powers in women" (Daly, 1984, 113 f.) -- Daly can only maintain this, if the Immaculate Conception referred to the conception of Jesus, which however, is not the case: the Immaculate Conception refers to the conception of Mary -- while the Assumption can function as "a freewheeling Metaphor of Elemental reality" (Daly, 1984, 129). In the Assumption the Arch-Image intercepts and transmits messages of Wild be-ing.

Daly's crusade ought to be viewed from its own perspective. Daly steps outside pre-arranged frames and follows her own aims. Her major project is to develop a mode of thinking that agrees with women's experiences and a language that names women's religious experience. It looks as if Daly uses the existing philosophical schemes and incorporates available images. She invests them with new meaning. I contend, however, that Daly's oeuvre must be read as a quest, a quest that makes use of philosophical and imaginal tools. This quest is expressed in evocative language and images that enable women to spiral to the Elemental Being in every woman. The quest is not an easy one and every traveller must overcome many obstacles.

If one reads Daly's books as an evocative and provocative quest, one soon discovers and realises that a true historical interest will not be satisfied, even though Daly makes use of historical elements as stepping stones or examples. Daly does not talk about the historical Mary or about the historical situations evolving around the image of Mary. She points out the devastating effects of the Mary image, but her remarks are of a rather general nature, and they are often questionable. Daly wants to clear away stumbling blocks in order to discover a Mary who enables women to continue their quest. Her language has a mythical touch: the stories Daly tells aim at changing women's lives.

It is in this context that we have to understand Daly's identification of Mary with the Goddess. This is not a counterimage for the Christian male God or some kind of static entity. The Goddess is, according to Daly, "the ultimate reality, divine spark of being", the one who "affirms the life-loving be-ing of women and nature" (Daly, 1978, xi). The Goddess is present and alive in the ancient Mother Goddess, Arachne the Spiderwoman, the Cosmic Mother, Athena, the Triple Goddess, Hera-Demeter-Kore, Eire-Fodhla-Banbha, Thetis-Ampitrite-Nereis, Eurynome, the Minoan Snake Goddess. The Goddess was/is also perceptible in Mary even though considerable efforts have been made to subdue her. Mary provides a window through which certain aspects of religious reality can be seen.

Daly's books are fascinating. They have a fairy tale-like quality and have a provocative and evocative strength. One wonders, however, whether Daly's interpretation of Mary is not too bold. Is it possible to disconnect Mary from her Christian roots? Can we de-contextualise Mary?

7. C. Ochs, C. Mulack, and others: Mary, faded Goddess

Other authors similarly play with the idea that Mary is the reemergence of the Goddess. The context in which they use this idea is very different from Daly's strict frame, however. In her book *Behind the Sex of God*, Carol Ochs identifies Mary as the Goddess. A comparison with four characteristics of the major Goddesses makes this clear: the Goddess is the mother of the God; she has a special relationship with the male God as source of being, consolation and protection; the Goddess is the bride of the God and as such serves as an exemplum for human matrimonial relations; she is Virgin; and she mourns the dead: she is the mater dolorosa. The Goddess is addressed with several other titles: Queen of Heaven, source of salvation, source of all sustenance. All those elements are reminiscent of Mary. Ochs declares that, regardless of the Church's incessant attempts at denying Mary any godlike status, Mary was worshipped as a deity, and "all women took on some aspect of her deification." (Ochs, 1977, 74)

The same intention guides Christa Mulack's book, *Maria. Die geheime Göttin im Christentum*. A profound study of the four Mary dogmas reveals, according to Mulack, that Mary is the hidden Goddess of Christianity. Mulack thinks that the mere existence of four dogmas concerning Mary (i.e. Virgin Birth, Theotokos, Immaculate Conception and Assumption) proves that the Goddess reveals the feminine side of the divine (Mulack, 1985, 22-23). These dogmas disentangle, under the inspiration of the Spirit, the presence of the female side of human nature. Mulack's thesis is that Mary is the christianized version of the 'pagan' mother religions: Mary is the triumph of the feminine. Manifold reasons, however, prevented the Goddess from being recognised.

Naomi Goldenberg, on the other hand, rejects the figure of Mary even though she connects her with the Goddesses. Her thesis is that "it would be better for women to contemplate the images of the great Goddesses behind the myth of Mary than to dwell on the man-made image of Mary herself" (Goldenberg, 1979, 76).

These authors all have different interpretations of the Goddess. Mulack sees Mary as Goddess as the female side of the divine. It seems as if for Mulack, and others along with her, somewhere somehow a pantheon existed/exists where Gods and Goddesses are fighting among each other, trying to peep out of the window so that the earth can see them. The ideal situation is when male God and female Goddess can be seen together at the same time. At that moment complete divinity, both male and female, is shown. So far, this situation has never been reached. These authors give us a mixture of psychological, mythological, theological, and historical ingredients in order to restore Mary for the women of today. It is clear why these authors proclaim Mary to be a Goddess as, in their scheme, it is necessary to find room for the divine female. Their position, however, becomes completely unintelligible, if one does not accept their theo/thealogy. It is remarkable that these authors do not consider the idea that Mary could be meaningful as a 'mere' human being. It is astonishing that she could only be considered worth talking about if she were divine.

We notice that most authors seem to agree that the Goddess is manifested in a multitude of names, images, and myths. This agreement is not unproblematic. The use of the term 'Goddess', 'Mother Goddess' as a collective noun is not a simple affair. The term serves to denote various things. It is applied to the Venus of Willendorf and to hundreds of statues found all over the world, to Demeter and Diana, to Isis, and many others. According to the knowledge and preference of the authors, Paleolithic, Greek, Egyptian, North-European elements, are jumbled together regardless of the differences in time and culture. The term 'Goddess' covers them all. At first sight it may even look as if the mixture is homogeneous enough: every ingredient after all is female and is, in one way or another, connected with the divine. After closer inspection, however, it reveals itself as a real hotchpotch. Too many different and differing elements are brought together under one term. Is the fact that we encounter a constant factor of 'female' and 'divine' a sufficient reason to state that it is 'all the same' or the manifestation of one Goddess? I contend that it is not. Isis functioned in a culture and society and theology completely different from that of the paleolithic fertility Goddesses. Even the acceptance of the existence and functioning of these Goddesses is problematic and raises many doubts. See for instance the discussion around the existence of Goddesses and matriarchies in the volume *The Politics of Women's Spirituality* (Spretnak, 1982, 541-561). The anthropologist, S. R. Binford, states that the 'humbug' about the Mother Goddess and former Matriarchal Greatness is founded on beliefs and not on facts. The existence of the 'Goddess' becomes plausible only after acceptance of such beliefs. Binford's article attacks these ideas and denounces them as nonsense. Even though Binford's article is lacking here and there in subtlety, I agree with her main ideas. To put it less bluntly: until now, no evidence has been produced that supports the existence of matriarchies and the prevalence of the mother-goddess religion. The material at our disposal gives rise to conflicting hypotheses. So far there is no sufficient reason to accept the existence of matriarchal empires in which women were in power under the guidance of the Great Mother, and neither is there a solid reason to reject the idea unconditionally. If one wants to compare the different Goddesses, one not only has to bridge the gap in time, but also the difference in cultural context, societal structure, religion[13]. The mere comparison of titles, functions, or characteristics is insufficient. As a consequence it seems that the term 'Goddess' becomes

13. Concerning the problems and complexity of comparative religion see the article of F.J. Porter Poole, *Metaphors and Maps*, 1986. See also A. R. Sandstrom (1982) who questions the possibility of comparing Tonantsi and the Virgin of Guadaloupe. His answer points to a more complex analysis than can be found in the works quoted.

meaningless: it covers a multitude of things and becomes a general term that has no specific content. Talking about 'the Goddess' only leaves question marks.

A meaningful statement about the common entity, if any, of these Goddesses can only be made after a careful study of these Goddesses in their own context, and after the establishment of their relation to this context. Furthermore the dictum "Analogie ist nicht Genealogie" (S\ ll, 1984, 122) remains valid. It remains an arduous task to come to a general theory that links these Goddesses together. The authors mentioned here can be accused of neglect, of neglecting to explain the proper status of their discussion of the Goddess and consequently of Mary: is it historically weighted, or psychologically, or what exactly?

8. M. Kassel: Mary, female archetype

Many authors link Mary with the 'Ur-Mutter', the 'Magna Mater', the so-called mother-goddesses of pre-patriarchal societies. In order to connect Mary with these mother-goddesses, they often make use of the Jungian theory of archetypes and the collective unconscious. Maria Kassel explicitly elaborates on this in her article in Concilium, *Mary and the Human Psyche* (Kassel, 1983). Kassel presumes that the worshipping of 'Mary'[14] in different countries and centuries is not simply the adoration of the historical mother of Jesus. It rather reflects a fundamental mentality that is universally human. The attention given to Mary seems to point to the need for the female archetype, particularly in Christianity. Kassel's interest is how this archetype functioned in and for the Church. She starts from the contention that archetypes "represent processes of psychological differentiation and form the stages of the human race's development of self-awareness" (Kassel, 1983, 74). In what way did/does 'Mary' help people to become themselves?

The picture of 'Mary' with her divine son is not an accidental image. In mythology this picture is wellknown. It represents the psychological process of a human being becoming conscious. The all-embracing feminine principle, as embodied in Mary, adjusts the unconscious collective. The divine child represents the psychologically whole human being: the one who finds a balance between unconsciousness and consciousness.

In the Catholic Church 'Mary's' presence provided a continuous link with the primeval feminine. Furthermore, she represented the unconscious in order to counterbalance the tendency to emotionlessness. For

---

14. Kassel parenthesises 'Mary' because she refers to her archetypal function.

women 'Mary's' virginity is liberating: it shows the way to autonomy. On the other hand, splitting and individualisation took place. The 'great mother' was split into the bad 'Eve' and the good 'Mary'. 'Eve' and 'Mary' were no longer considered archetypes but were connected with historical persons. It was not difficult to transpose Eve's and Mary's qualities to individual women: women are bad (Eve) and they should all be virgins (Mary). Women are not any longer allowed to be human beings but have to be archetypes. Kassel asks:

> "... the question can also be raised of the extent to which socially relevant phenomena in the Catholic Church are connected with the representation of psychological development in the image of the 'great mother' -- for example, celibacy turned into a law and the education of priests in all-male groups, (...)" (Kassel, 1983, 78).

How can 'Mary' enhance the humanisation of Christians? It could be that the recent distancing from 'Mary' is the voice of an evolution away from the archetype of the feminine in its projected condition. It could also be a backsliding. Kassel concludes with some 'utopian' remarks: how 'Mary' could influence future developments. Men should outgrow the 'son-stage' by integrating the 'anima' in their psyche. Women should grasp the chance of virginity: that is, promote a conscious autonomy.

> "The new human being who is both healed and healer thus emerges from the joining of the feminine potentiality of the human psyche with the potentiality that comprises the conscious totality and is thus divine" (Kassel, 1983, 80).

Kassel's article can only be appreciated if one decides to go along with the Jungian theory about archetypes. It determines the entire interpretation of the Mary phenomenon and its meaning for women and men today. Jung himself was an ardent adherent of Mary and he reacted enthusiastically to the proclamation of the dogma of the Assumption of Mary. He pronounced the dogma to be the triumph of the feminine divinity. This made Jung rather popular in certain feminist circles. Neumann's book, *The Great Mother* (Neumann, 1955), falls in line with the 'Goddess-movement'. In *The Great Mother*, Jungian depth psychology is applied to explain the function of the Goddess. Without critically evaluating the Jungian theory, many feminists find a confirmation of their own ideas in this book[15].

Turning back to Kassel's article we notice that she conceives of Mary as an element in the process of becoming a whole human being.

15. For a feminist critique on Jung, see N. Goldenberg (Goldenberg, 1976; 1979; 1985).

Myths and stories about Goddesses and about Mary reflect the coming into being of human self-awareness, individually and collectively. Mary as archetype is part of a psychological theory.

9. M. Warner: Alone of all her sex

An extended account of the myth and the cult of the Virgin Mary can be found in Warner's book *Alone of All Her Sex*. Reading this book is plunging into a multitude of stories, images, pictures, symbols, etc. Mary, or as Warner often names her the Virgin Mary, has known a long and fruitful history, a history that has not yet come to an end. Warner remarks how amazing it is that Mary has known such an overwhelming popularity. She assumes this can be explained by the fact that Mary is the mediator between earth and heaven. Every human being knows through Mary that she/he belongs to God's creation. Furthermore, Mary is the perfect human, she is a reflection of how humanity should or can be. Here we encounter a paradox: "in the very celebration of the perfect human woman, both humanity and women were subtly denigrated" (Warner, 1976, xxi). One cannot disregard that Mary stands 'alone of all her sex'. The phrase, 'alone of all her sex', pervades the entire book as a refrain. Time and again it becomes clear that in every century, in all aspects Mary was an exception, an out-standing figure.

Warner's programme is to illuminate the history of a people and the beliefs they produce. The myth of the Virgin reflects their story and their beliefs. As a consequence Warner does not want to describe why people long for a mother (Freudian approach) nor does she want to clarify why people in a certain culture and time have produced a particular image. Mary is a constant presence in the history of Western attitudes to women, but she appears under several masks. Warner picks out five themes: Virgin, Queen, Bride, Mother and Intercessor. Her treatment of these themes is breathtaking: she runs back and forth through history, but devotes much attention to the Middle Ages. This is not surprising as this period can be described as the heyday of the Marian cult and devotion.

The title 'Virgin' has no singular, eternal meaning. Warner notices a change in interpretation from virgin birth to virginity, from religious sign to moral doctrine. As a consequence, Warner concludes, a mother Goddess like the Virgin Mary was transformed "into an effective instrument of asceticism and female subjection" (Warner, 1976, 49). It therefore is no wonder that Mary has been interpreted as the second Eve. Eve, a sexual and thus evil creature is opposed to Mary, the Immaculate. Purity, in patristic thought, is not a mere technical and physical question. The devotion to Mary cannot be understood outside this context of 'dangers of the flesh' and its link with women. A virgin body becomes the supreme image of wholeness, holiness. A 'hopeful' message for women is announced: virginal life reduces the special penalties of the fall in women (Warner, 1976, 72). Women are asked to deny their sexuality, but even then, the sublimity of the Virgin is beyond women's reach.

A similar phenomenon relates to Mary's Queenship, which cannot be disconnected from the Assumption (first called Dormition). Mary is safeguarded from the dissolution of the grave. Her purity guarantees her passage out of time into eternity. Once more, Mary is put upon a pedestal and enjoys an exclusive role, a role other women had better not dream about.

The nuptial imagery, Mary as bride, is also called in to prove Warner's thesis. The love-imagery used in this context is one of love in heaven, love deferred and as a consequence love denied (Warner, 1976, 133). In Mary, earthly love is discredited and men's eyes are turned to heaven (Warner, 1976, 148). Mary more and more is "the feminine perfection personified; and no other woman was in her league" (Warner, 1976, 159).

The 'mother' theme is another sample of the debasement of women. Mary's consent to the incarnation has turned into a most unsatisfactory and oppressive expression: "Let it be". This phrase has been equalled with feminine submissiveness. "Let it be" has not been uttered as an expression of cooperation between God and the world but has too often been interpreted as a Christian ideal of humility applied to women (Warner, 1976, 177). Similarly the theme of Mary breast-feeding Jesus has been used to underpin the biological determination of women and to reject medical means to overcome their biological destiny (Warner, 1976, 192-205). Mary rises higher and higher on the pedestal. It culminates in the doctrine of the Immaculate Conception. This doctrine teaches that the ideal cannot be incarnate in a creature who is like everybody else (Warner, 1976, 237-252). Another example of this polar thinking is reflected in the opposition of Mary and Mary Magdalene. Even though the (inadequate) tradition of Mary Magdalene tries to recount that no one is beyond reach of grace, it above all gives an idea about Christian images of women: a woman is a virgin or a whore (Warner, 1976, 225-235). However, there is also a ray of light: in the figure of the Mater Dolorosa Mary is very close to the people for she shares the sorrows of everybody and her tears are part of the universal language of cleansing and rebirth (Warner, 1976, 220-223).

Mary's intercessory function seems to be appreciated in a positive way by Warner. It is constructed according to the anthropomorphic model of salvation used in catholicism: Mary is the mother of all sinners and she mediates between them and God. It is nevertheless questionable whether the mother role is one of intercession. It fits extremely well in the Christian ideal of womanhood. Mary can obtain salvation through Christ: she is subordinated, a gentle woman who fulfils her natural role, i.e. motherhood. The domestic dominion is reinforced. A tension between theory and cult-practice is noticeable, however. Mary absorbs the functions of her son (Warner, 1976, 275-330).

Warner concludes her book with the remark that Mary is "the instrument of a dynamic argument from the Catholic Church about the structure of society, presented as a God-given code" (Warner, 1976, 338). In Mary motherhood is venerated, but sexuality is debased and womanhood is narrowed to submission. Warner still recognises in Mary a glimpse of the Goddess. It is not the most pretty image of the Goddess, but better this than no Goddess at all. She concludes:

> "But it should not be necessary to have a Goddess contrasted with a
> God, a divinity who stands for qualities considered the quintessence
> of femininity and who thus polarizes symbolic and religious thought
> into two irreconcilably opposed camps" (Warner, 1976, 338).

This is an important conclusion, but a rather odd one, coming at the end of this book. Indeed, Warner every now and then refers to the idea of Mary as a Goddess[16], but her major interest is focused on the way the Mary myth functioned in the Church and how it related to the image of women. She does not systematically deal with the godlike character of Mary. She refers to the practice of Mary tending to become a Goddess, but she does not explicitly go into the consequences of this tendency. Her conclusion does not seem to connect with the rest of the book. Warner could have come to this conclusion without having written 'Alone of All Her Sex'. Her book is nevertheless important[17] because she shows how the history of Mary has been ruled by images, images that correspond to the society in which they functioned. The book points to the complexity of developing the discourse about Mary: there is not one Mary but a multitude of images.

---

16. E.g. how the idea of Mary as Magna Mater was guided into meaninglessness because of the ideas of chastity and female submission (147); the parallel between Goddesses suckling their children and Mary suckling Jesus (193); Mary as Mater Dolorosa can be connected with the fertility Goddesses (221); cosmological symbols, elements of classical sky-goddesses are applied to and transformed in the Mary-cult (256).

17. The book is marred by certain mistakes, however. See the review by J.L. Nelson, *Virgin Territory* in Journal of Religion and Religions, 1977.

10. P. Schine Gold: The Lady and the Virgin

Another work with a historical angle is *The Lady and the Virgin* by Penny Schine Gold. It studies images, attitudes, and experiences in twelfth-century France. This book is interesting in that Gold has shifted her thesis from the position that "twelfth-century idealizations of women, rather than indicating a positive trend in attitude and experience, could be seen instead as expressing a negative view of women contemporary with increasing strictures on women's experience" (Gold, 1985, xv-xvi) to "a recognition that the images express not one attitude but many, that the experience of women, even of the women of the noble elite, was diverse and sometimes contradictory, and that the relationship between image, attitude, and experience is not always direct or causal" (Gold, 1985, xvii).

Gold compares secular and religious images, religious and secular life. The Virgin Mary is the example of religious imagery. That the twelfth and thirteenth centuries witnessed an increasing interest in the Virgin is not enough evidence for any interpretation of the attitudes toward women. It is necessary to excavate the particular aspects that were emphasised (Gold, 1985, 43-44). It is impossible to make one-to-one correspondences between actual women and literary characters (Gold, 1985, 1-42). It is even more difficult to understand whether the figure of the Virgin Mary had anything at all to do with ordinary women. In the *Chanson de geste* -- the literary genre examined by Gold -- an understanding of the complexity of attitudes towards women is possible when basic patterns of interaction between women and men can be discerned. Where Mary is concerned, very often her singularity is emphasised, even though she is held out as an example to women. Gold concludes this chapter:

> "Gothic images of the Virgin, even more prolific and more focused on the Virgin Mary herself, serve to underline existent cultural norms of humility, submission, and tenderness, with the exception of the short-lived Triumph of the Virgin image that emphasised equality and power. Yet the later images also express an ambiguity similar to many of the prayers and theological writings discussed above: Mary shares the qualities of humility and tenderness with ordinary women, while she is also portrayed in a unique relationship with Christ as his bride, his mother, and his queen" (Gold, 1985, 74).

Gold offers a varied, complex, and ambivalent characterisation of twelfth century imagery of women. She surveys religious life of women in monasteries and studies the property relations. Time and again she discovers:

"The tendency to define women relationally to men rather than independently (with the exception of widowhood) keeps women in the system but on the periphery, connected to the center, but not at the center. It is this ambivalence of inclusion, but inclusion usually in secondary roles, that is deeply characteristic of female imagery and of female experience, in both the secular and religious spheres" (Gold, 1985, 144).

The word *ambivalent* is the key-term in the description of the situation of women in twelfth-century France. Images and literature more likely reflect men's concerns than that they convey anything about women. It is difficult to find out what women really experienced and how they reacted towards this ambivalence. Gold warns that we should contextualise the experience of these women: our measuring rod should not be equality but the hierarchical society and its concomitant values.

Once more we find a study that confronts us with the difficulties that arise when we discuss Mary. *The Lady and the Virgin* has special attention for the complicated interaction of images of women and women's lives. It offers a new perspective on some critiques of feminist theologians on the Mary image. It is no longer possible to hold on to the simple idea that women are denigrated in Mary. The relation between Mary and women is more complex.

11. B. Corrado Pope: Immaculate and Powerful

In the volume *Immaculate and Powerful*, Barbara Corrado Pope presents an article that has modest pretensions. Her aim is not to elaborate a general theory about the enormous popularity of, and the devotion to, Mary, but to study one particular area and period and discover what elements induced the rising popularity of Mary. She focuses on the modern Marian devotion as instigated by the manifold apparitions in the nineteenth century, and tries to trace back the purely human history that determines it. The French pilgrimage movement that expressed both political discontent and religious fervour is one of the factors that receive Pope's attention. The threats from the modern world made pious people turn back to the one person who always offered comfort in the hour of need: Mary. Mary's popularity, however, cannot be isolated from the political situation in France and in the Catholic world. The Pope tried to re-establish his grip on the world. To get the support of the laity, devotion of an affective kind was promoted. "That is, they chose to direct rather than to condemn or ignore emotional and potentially subversive religious impulses in order to maintain and increase Catholic influence" (Pope, 1985, 183). The unifying symbol of Mary also served the fervent French nationalists under the

Third Republic. Especially the Assumptionists were involved in this. The pilgrimages to Lourdes were partly an instrument to enforce conservative nationalist feelings.

Lourdes was more: it was also "motivated by sincere religious belief and spiritual hope" (Pope, 1985, 189). Mary, on the one hand, is the symbol of the one who transcends all classes, and regional and local differences. She enhances a community feeling: everybody comes together in front of her shrine. On the other hand she is also the figure with the special privileges, who can give help to the faithful.

One question remains to be answered: "Can we see in the Marian revival a resurgence of the 'feminine principle' or a 'feminization' of religion or culture?" (Pope, 1985, 193). It is remarkable that during the nineteenth century everything that had to do with religion was handed over to women. This, however, did not have the consequence that the male hierarchy lost control. They determined to what extent female symbolism could be applied and how. The veneration of Mary was indeed something special and could be a source of female pride. But it turned a blind eye to fertility and sexuality, so much part of women's lives. The nineteenth century Mary also shows little autonomy, and neither did her apparitions call for social transformation. Altogether, a not very cheering example for women.

Looking back on her article, Pope concludes that "the old saying, 'As Mary goes, so goes the Church', should be reversed. Rather we have learned: 'As the Church goes, so goes Mary'" (Pope, 1985, 196).

Pope's article is limited but very precise. Its strength lies in the meticulous research[18] that ends up in some carefully formulated conclusions. Pope's starting point is a specific situation, namely nineteenth-century France, and she looks at the forces that guide and determine this situation. She wonders whether we are confronted with a resurgence of the 'feminine principle'. Her study shows that this question cannot be answered with a simple 'yes' or 'no', but that it is influenced by a variety of aspects that have to be accounted for.

18. A similar research can be found in the book of S. Michaud (Michaud, 1982). In *Muse et Madone* she sketches the way women were perceived and what images of her existed.

12. Evaluation

This overview shows a confusing image. The authors look at Mary from different angles and their goals are different. Halkes tries to fit Mary into Christianity: she can overcome the one-sidedness of patriarchal religion as memory of the Goddess and as positive image for women. Ruether looks at Mary from an ecclesiological viewpoint and presents her as model for a new Church. Schüssler Fiorenza identifies Mary as a myth that has to be disentangled from its patriarchal roots. Johnson emphasises the symbolic character of theological statements about Mary. Kassel sees Mary as the archetype and grants her major psychic importance. According to Daly and other authors Mary is a distant reminder of the Goddess and as such introduces an era where women find the divine in themselves. Warner interprets Mary mainly as an image that debased women. Pope looks at Mary as a phenomenon that has to be interpreted in the context of a culture and time eager for power. Schine develops a similar line of thought. We find differing opinions about one and the same reality.

We can, however, detect one aim that all authors have in common. They all want to uncover the oppressive elements that pervade the Mary image. The authors do not apply the same methods for achieving this, nor do they operate from the same mind set. Warner, Pope, and Schine Gold want to liberate the historical images of Mary and women in providing us with detailed historical analyses. All other authors operate within a religious framework. Daly, Ochs, and Mulack try to create a new religious language. They step beyond the boundaries of the traditional religions. Daly makes a radical step in leaving behind her all patriarchal religion, while Mulack oscillates between Christianity and Goddess religion. All other authors, Radford Ruether, Halkes, Schüssler Fiorenza, Gebara and Bingemer, and Johnson continue developing the Christian tradition. They seek for ways of liberating Mary within the particular tradition in which she has been generated. Two important questions arise from the authors that we have read: 'is it possible to use 'Mary' outside the context of the Christian tradition?' and 'what is the significance of the history that the image of 'Mary' has known?'

When we consider 'Mary's'[19] history over the centuries a pattern consisting of different images emerges, images that fit in with the time and the community in which they exist. Warner's book illustrates this rather well: the shifts in the images of Mary cannot be disconnected from the religious, economic, political and cultural situation. Even titles that are used over several centuries do not always cover the same content. The

---

19. 'Mary' in this case denotes the Mary-images.

so-called constant elements do not seem to be particularly constant. *Alone of All Her Sex*, Pope's article *Immaculate and Powerful* and Schine's *The Virgin and the Lady* indicate that developing discourse about Mary is not an easy task. They point at the historicity of each and every image of Mary.

Any pronouncement about Mary must realise that it presupposes an image, or several images that are set in a historical context. It will be necessary to analyze this historical context. Even though Radford Ruether pays attention to the history of Mary, this only seems to serve the purpose of discarding this history and turning back to the biblical roots. Irrespective of the question whether it is possible to neglect the influence of history, one can wonder whether a dogmatic approach of Mary, any dogmatic approach is possible. Several authors suffer from historical inaccuracy: Daly for instance presents a rather stereotypical image of the functioning of Mary for women. Gold's study shows that the thesis 'Mary stands alone of all her sex' must be modified in the light of the ambivalent interplay between image and society, ideas and attitudes.

The book of Gebara and Bingemer has shown us the importance and necessity of a contextualised approach. They have pointed out to us that we must analyze the interplay of the several elements in the hermeneutical field. How can we talk about Mary? How can we choose between all these different proposals? Is it merely a question of preference or are there any criteria that enable us to make a choice? What is Mary: a myth, a symbol, a cultural given, a theological concept, an archetype? Can Mary function in any context? Can she be involved in the same way in the Christian tradition as in Goddess religion? This first chapter leads us to the question: what are the conditions for arriving at an interpretation of Mary that is liberating for women? There are indications that an approach focused on the interpretative process and with special attention for the historical context could contribute to the discussion about the place of Mary in feminist theology.

In the next chapter I want to propose an approach to Mary in a frame of symbolic imagination. The idea of symbolic imagination is the screen through which it becomes possible to 'read' Mary. The term 'symbolic imagination' is used to emphasise the imaginal character of Mary as a symbol. The symbolic character of Mary arises from the obvious and immediate reference to a historical woman named Mary -- as E.A. Johnson says -- with simultaneous reference to something else. It is clear that the reference to the historical Mary has to do with facts that can be ascertained. No wider pronouncements can evolve from this. Every imaging of Mary, verbal or by other means, indeed starts from the reference to the historical person, but this imaging itself points to something different.

Johnson, in limiting herself to the symbolic character of theological statements about Mary, can state that

"they reach their intended and theological referent when interpreted finally as statements about the Church, the community of faithful disciples, of which she is a member and in which she participates" (Johnson, 1985a, 313).

If Mary taken as a whole -- viewed as the collective noun covering all images instigated by the historical Mary -- is regarded as a symbol, it becomes more difficult to offer a clear view of what the symbol is referring to. In order to tackle this problem successfully, we will have to provide a systematic consideration of what a symbol is.

The question raised at the beginning of this chapter "How can women conceive of Mary in a liberating way?" has been modified to the question "How can women interpret Mary in a liberating way?" The former question implied the possibility of working towards a new interpretation of Mary. The latter shifts attention from Mary to the activity implied, i.e. the activity of interpretation. In the next chapter, in dealing with symbols, the process of interpretation will be crucial.

Chapter 2

A Feminist Model of Interpretation

Introduction

The annotated presentation of feminist authors who have written about
Mary[1] in the first chapter has left us with a feeling of discomfort. A multitude of interpretations of Mary are possible and there are no immediate
indicators for valueing one particular interpretation more than another.
Preference for a specific interpretation seems to be connected with the
position chosen. To let the matter rest here is intellectually not satisfying.
We need a clarification of the process of interpretation that is taking
place in the discussions of Mary. The question 'How can we talk about
Mary?' demands an analysis of the process that takes place when 'we' and
'Mary' come together.

In the previous chapter I hinted at the importance of E.A. Johnson's
article about interpreting viewed theological statements about Mary as
having a symbolic character. I endorse her train of thought but I want to
widen her proposition so as to include everything concerning Mary: not
only theological statements but also devotional aspects, paintings should
be considered as having a symbolic character insofar as they convey
something about Mary. In this chapter I will develop a systematic reflection on symbols. The main author that I will consider here will be Paul
Ricoeur. Throughout his oeuvre he has paid a considerable amount of
attention to symbols. Other authors and positions will be briefly mentioned before expounding Ricoeur. We will follow Ricoeur because in his
work he starts from the thinking about religious symbols, which is important in connection with Mary. As Clark writes, for Ricoeur

> "the point at issue is not the dismantling of the theological super-
> structure, but the kind of value ascribed to the enigma that remains.
> The paradox is central to Ricoeur's whole treatment of the symbol:
> although it is endowed with rootedness in the mystery of being, this
> is precisely what it withholds" (Clark, 1990, 32).

---

1. From now on, when I write Mary I refer to the entire complex imagery and history
that has evolved from the historical person Mary.

Ricoeur is interesting because he shifts towards a hermeneutic inquiry that emphasises contextual conditions of thought.

Ricoeur will lead us to the subject, understanding itself in confrontation with the symbol. Being is for Ricoeur "une manière d'exister qui resterait de bout en bout *être-interprété*" (Ricoeur, 1969, 15). The 'we' and 'Mary' in the question 'How can we talk about Mary?' come together when interpreting Mary as a religious symbol. This 'we', however, is not unproblematic. Feminist theory has provided us with the insight that every subject is gendered. Furthermore we are confronted with a paradoxical situation: on the one hand we can say that in general the subject is in crisis, while on the other hand this is the first era when women structurally and otherwise claim their subjectivity. How can this be combined? Our attention will be drawn to the 'female subject'. In this discussion the main author will be Rosi Braidotti, surrounded by a chorus of opposing and supporting voices.

It will be clear that in this chapter I am addressing issues at stake in feminist theorizing[2]. This chapter is a report of this dialogue and an attempt at knitting together several differing developments. In I. Images and the Female Form, I will present certain books that have attempted to link up women and images. I do not want to offer an overview of feminist approaches. I prefer to offer a sampling of books that seem to be promising. This presentation can be read as a prelude, an appetizer. It gives an idea of how women's studies deal with this topic and at the same time it points out some of the flaws and difficulties that may be encountered.

2. I view feminist theological research as a project that enhances a dialogue with women's studies and 'malestream' theorising, but which is accountable to the women-and-faith grassroots movement. I am strongly opposed to a disconnected 'ivory tower' kind of feminist theology.

1. Images and the female form

"No pictorial subject is more determined
by a complex web of cultural interests
than visual narrations of the female
body; such images are not susceptible to
simple naturalistic interpretation"
M. Miles

Introduction.

The presence of 'images' in a feminist study is no novelty. Naomi Goldenberg noted:

"It is important to note that whenever a feminist critic might appear on my spectrum, she is always concerned with problems of imagery. This concern usually expresses itself by attention to questions about the gender of images presented in religious texts and rituals - for example, why many male images are esteemed and why many female images are degraded" (Goldenberg, 1979, 14).

These questions run as a continuous thread through the books presented here. Marina Warner in *Monuments and Maidens* (1985) tries to answer these questions by turning to the concept of allegory. In *Immaculate and Powerful* (Atkinson, 1985) the central notions are gender, culture, and religion, while *Gender and Religion* (Bynum, 1986) embroiders on these concepts and tries to deepen the understanding of religious symbols. We will take a closer look at these volumes as we evaluate these approaches.

1.1. Monuments and Maidens.

In the discussion about images and what images can best convey ideas and feelings, M. Warner's book, *Monuments and Maidens* can not be overlooked. Warner draws our attention to the remarkable fact that we encounter the female form in many places. When you walk in the street you will see statues of female bodies representing justice, liberty, virtues, vices, the elements of nature, etc. In myths female bodies give rise to glorious ideas and deeds. Warner illustrates her point with an enormous number of examples, ranging from the statue of liberty in New York, to Margaret Thatcher, and Pandora's box. Warner identifies this use of the female figure as allegory, i.e. saying something which conveys one meaning, but which also says something else. Her book is an attempt to explain "a recurrent motif in allegory, the female form as an expression of desiderata and virtues" (Warner, 1985, xix). The female form functions

> "to lure, to delight, to appetize, to please, these confer the power to persuade: as the spur to desire, as the excitement of the senses, as a weapon of delight, the female appears down the years to convince us of the message she conveys" (Id., xx).

Warner especially wants to throw light on the paradox that can be found in the representation of concepts in the female figure: the female figure seems to resemble the concepts presented, e.g. liberty, justice, etc., but such a resemblance is mostly not traceable in the actual world of women. Warner nevertheless affirms that

> "a symbolized female presence both gives and takes value and meaning in relation to actual women and contains the potential for affirmation not only of women themselves but of the general good they might represent and in which as half of humanity they are deeply implicated" (Id., XX).

This seems to be somewhat in contradiction with the previous idea. The book hopes "to throw some light on the plural significations of women's bodies and their volatile connections with changing conceptions of female nature" (Id., xix).

The book contains three parts. First of all Warner explains why she tackles the question of allegory even though this seems to be -- at first sight -- an outmoded subject. She shows its topicality by exploring the meaning of the Statue of Liberty in New York, the exuberant architectural ornaments of Paris, and a cartoon of Margaret Thatcher. They respectively stand for American democracy, the history of France, and the political drama of Britain under the first female Prime Minister.

The second part of the book explores the connection between allegory and the female form. Abundant examples illustrate this section. The third -- and to me the most interesting -- part describes "the varied premises that structure allegorical female figures, and the ideas that underpin their appearance both in text and image" (Id., xxii). It describes the contradiction between the female body perceived as the passive recipient of divine/male energy and as at the same time endangering men. An example of this is Pandora, who is made to bring disaster into the world. The female body also presents the perfect vessel for unchanging ideas, in contrast to actual women's bodies that are constantly moving and never perfect. The model of this is the Sieve of Tuccia. Tuccia, a Vestal Virgin proved her chastity by carrying a sieve filled with water from the Tiber to the temple of Vesta. The sieve has become a symbol of ideal integrity. A sieve that does not leak, says Warner, is probably as impossible as the ideal female body as a container for high and virtuous meanings is impossible. Finally the female body represents the contradiction between motherly love and erotic attraction, see e.g. the Slipped Chiton: a woman portrayed with a dress or tunic slipping from her shoulder, sometimes revealing a naked breast. The naked female breast suggests at once motherly love and affection and erotic attraction, as contrasted with an Amazonian exterior. The Slipped Chiton "is a most frequent sign that we are being pressed to accept an ulterior significance, not being introduced to the body as person" (Id., 277).

The reason Warner wrote this book is that:

> "Allegories of the female form inform and animate many of the myths which have, in constant interplay, enriched and reinforced, maintained and reshaped our present identities as the inheritors of classical and Christian culture; whether they may save us from pollution and from death, we cannot tell. We cannot escape being what they have made us enough to see with such clarity and objectivity. But we may think they can; for we continue to speak them, see them, make them, live with them, almost unwittingly, as if we did trust the order they construct to hold out some promise. This book seeks to unfold how that promise is conveyed by the bodies of women" (Id., xxii-xxiii).

The major ideas of the book are that the female form is more likely perceived as generic and universal, apt for symbolic use. This is enhanced by the addition of devices: improbable nudity, heroic scale, wings, etc. These figures hardly relate to living women. The male form tends to emphasise the individual who is represented, even when a generalised idea is conveyed. The female body has been the recipient of all possible male fantasies and fears and consequently also of female fantasies and fears. The representation of all these longings and terrors in the female form has influenced the conception of femaleness and women's behaviour. "A constant exchange takes place between images and reality" (Id., 37). Warner seems able to point out where one of the disconnections between female allegory and real women took place: in the centuries following the Middle Ages "the disjunction between women and the positive ideas they traditionally represented in allegory was increasingly stressed" (Id., 199). She sees this for instance in Mary, who was capable of taking on a plurality of identities. This ends when she is encapsulated in a complex symbolic field that allows contradictory elements. Jesus, on the contrary, never loses his identity as a single personality[3].

Warner explains that "it is because women continue to occupy the space of the Other that they lend themselves to allegorical use so well" (Id., 292). All allegorical use of the female body seems to have evoked the strong powers that nations needed to fight for their lawful liberation. The equation of male with culture and female with nature is cause and foundation of this use of the female form. "Otherness is a source of potential and power, but it cannot occupy the centre" (Id., 293). Nakedness is one of the most prominent means of representing this otherness. It shows an elusive other who seems to be living in a natural state and who is uncorrupted.

> "The many women who are wounded by the continual public use of women's bodies today diagnose correctly that women are thereby reduced to objects of desire. (...) The female form can excite that desire to sell soap, drink, cars, butter, aeroplanes, holidays, whatever. Her desirability, taken for granted, gives its light and its energy to the product. Women are expected to identify with the subject in the image; men to experience desire without such mediation. To condemn altogether the applied erotic power of the female body entails denying an aspect of the human condition; the task we have to take up, as women who inhabit these centres of energy and as men who respond to their charge, is how to tap it and make it fructify" (Id., 320-321).

Warner concludes:

> "but the changing representation of woman in text and image circles around the unanswered question, What is she? And like a magnet twitching back from its like pole, it can never come to rest with an unchanging definition" (Id., 331).

The female form is omnipresent. Many different meanings are given to it. It seldom expresses who woman is. It is difficult to recover the integrity of the female body as allegory, as it has been (mis)used for ages. Reaction and rejection alone however do not bring any solution. Warner wants us to broaden the limits of understanding of the female. This can happen through "the creative energy of imaginative empathy, to draw us in the subject of a figure, make us feel inside the body on whose exterior we have until now scribbled the meanings we wanted" (Id., 332). The old

---

3. Warner's argument is rather unclear at this point. The idea that the disjunction is dated in the centuries following the Middle Ages is not convincingly argued. Furthermore, it is questionable whether Jesus has never lost his identity as a single personality.

fantasy figures that have been subjected for so long now raise their voices "and they are saying, Listen" (Id., 334).

Warner's book raises interesting questions, acute observations, and plentiful examples. Her choice of the allegory as all-explanatory principle, however, is neither convincing nor very clear. She acutely shows the complexity of the presence of images in people's lives: the confusing and sometimes contradictory messages they convey, the asymmetrical status of images of women and images of men, etc. The abundant examples are well-chosen and sometimes serve as eye-opening illustrations. But she does not make use of modern paintings or sculptures and pays no attention to how women are represented in contemporary art. The reader of this book constantly has to suppress uneasy feelings that Warner's interpretations might be reversed. There seems to be some degree of arbitrariness in her interpretations. An example of this is furnished by the statue of a naked, reclining woman in the town where I was born and raised. Everybody knows this statue by the name of 'Fat Mathilde'. The name suggests an individual, and I remember wondering as a child whether the 'real' Mathilde was still walking in the streets of this town and what her real name was. Years later a quiz asked people to give the official name of this statue. This started a massive search in the archives to find that name, which turned out to be: The Sea. On the one hand, Warner's thesis that the female figure is suited for allegorical use is confirmed by this, on the other hand this example shows that in its specific context this statue was not perceived as 'The Sea' but as an individual: a voluptuous woman named Mathilde. The ambiguity in Warner is due to her use of the concept of allegory. Defining allegory as 'saying something which conveys one meaning but which also says something else' lacks precision and clarity. It is necessary to indicate how that 'one meaning' and how that 'other meaning' is determined. Warner's book is very suggestive, but it does not define and therefore gets lost in ambiguities.

1.2. Immaculate and Powerful

One of the most titillating women's studies in religion publications of recent years remains *Immaculate and Powerful* (Atkinson, 1985). This volume assembles a variety of articles, written by women who participated in the Harvard Women's Studies in Religion programme. Unlike so many other collections, this volume succeeds in presenting articles that form a unity. They all examine religious images in various cultures and times. They all consider these images as inextricably linked with the social institutions in which they are being used. The starting point for the volume is that religious images cannot be denied an important role in "shaping cultural patterns and social structures" (Atkinson, 1985, vii). A blind spot in research has been the understanding of the exact nature of that role. When women's lives and experiences are put in the spotlight, it becomes obvious that religious images and social roles cannot be disconnected. As a consequence, the category of gender -- more specifically gender in relation to race, culture, class -- is a central tool of analysis in this volume. Gender, culture, and religion are the keywords to the analyses of women's experiences in this collection.

The central thesis of this volume is

> "that the area of intersection of religion and culture provides a fruitful nexus for exploring women's lives. (...) Religion can provide women with a critical perspective on and alternatives to the conditioning they receive as members of their societies. (...) Not only can religion make available tools with which women may create a degree of spiritual, political, and personal autonomy not provided by secular culture, but it also inevitably forms part of women's cultural conditioning" (Id., 2).

The essays illustrate this thesis. They have their own specific methodological preference. They do not work within the traditional framework of histories of ideas presupposing that subjects are informed by or congruent with the dominant ideas of the societies in which they exist. The

> "essayists infer that ideas must be interpreted in the context of lives in which they occur. They demonstrate that people's daily lives, their relationships, and the commitments and pressures with which they lived and died constitute the only accurate context for understanding their religious ideals and symbols" (Id., 12-13).

The articles in the volume painstakingly analyse small areas where the intersection of religious symbols and social reality can reveal something of women's lives and experience. Clarissa Atkinson for instance analyzes the story and visual images of Saint Monica, the mother of Augustine of Hippo. She became the example of the good mother. Atkinson shows how this 'good mother' is modelled on the phantasies and desires of clerical men. Women's own experience has been left out of the official story, or has simply been "sucked up" (Id., 5) to bring credit to male institutions. Dolores Williams brings to the fore the narrative style and resources of black women and links these with the enterprise of feminist theology.

The approach developed in this volume constitutes at the same time the volume's strength and its weakness. The option of analysing small, specific, limited fields is legitimate and is a conscious methodological choice. The article of Pope (see for an extended review chapter 1 p 38-39) shows what excellent results this approach accomplishes. At the same time, however, the volume claims to provide more than a mere analysis of those well-described fields. It also presents a general theory saying that women work creatively with the images with which they are presented. As a consequence religious symbols and imagery are both oppressive and liberating. This is the presupposition that at once guides the analyses and must be proved by the analyses. This is a circular argument. The question: 'how can it be that images provide room for creative elaboration' is not even asked.

The volume lacks a reflection on the specific characteristics of images/symbols[4]. I do not want to imply that the articles only provide examples of how symbols/images work. Through their meticulous approach, they do indeed reveal the specific working of images/symbols and show how in different circumstances and times this can be different. Yet, a dialogue with a more explicit theoretical framework about the functioning of images/symbols would have been useful.

1.3. Gender and Religion

A volume closely related to *Immaculate and Powerful* is *Gender and Religion: On the Complexity of Symbols* (Bynum, 1986). The book is the product of the faculty of the Comparative Religion Program at the University of Washington which offers a variety of cross-cultural studies. The articles

> "attempt to show, in various ways, the complexity of gender as a symbolic system - in its relationships to the social order, in its poly-semic meanings, and in its variation with the perspective of the per-ceiver" (Bynum, 1986, viii).

The first chapter of the volume is most nearly concerned with the questions I am dealing with in this present chapter. Chapter 1 gives an insight into the theoretical discussion of the complexity of gender as a symbolic system. I will present it in detail as it forms the theoretical basis for the other articles. I commented on the lack of theoretical reflection in the volume *Immaculate and Powerful*; *Gender and Religion* on the other hand offers a more reflected basis for its articles.

In the introduction, *The Complexity of Symbols*, Caroline Walker Bynum stresses the importance of the contribution made by feminist scholars to studies in religion. Whatever stand one takes in the debate about the discarding of all male symbols or the reinterpreting of the

---

4. Note that very often the distinction between image and symbol is unclear.

traditional religions[5], gender has become an inevitable category in the study of religion. *Gender and Religion*

> "is intended to respond to the present situation of scholarship by explaining what it means to take gender seriously in studying religion and what it means to take religion seriously when asking questions about gender. This book is about gender *and* religion" (Bynum, 1986, 2).

Two insights provide the foundation for the articles: human beings are gendered and religious symbols point beyond daily experience. This means that religious experience is undergone, and its study undertaken by gendered people, i.e. women or men. This experience differs given the society at which one is looking, or in which one is participating. In their view of religious symbols the authors feel related to Ricoeur who explains that religious symbols are more than signs, they are 'polysemic' (V. Turner). The book suggests that

> "gender-related symbols -- symbols that, at one level, signify maleness or femaleness (and symbols never merely signify) -- do not simply determine the self-awareness of men and women as gendered nor do they simply reflect cultural assumptions about what it is to be male or female. Gender-related symbols, in their full complexity, may refer to gender in ways that affirm or reverse it, support or question it; or they may, in their basic meaning, have little at all to do with male and female roles (...) It is not possible ever to ask How does a symbol -- *any* symbol -- mean? without asking For whom does it mean?" (Bynum, 1986, 2-3).

The authors definitely do not want to elaborate on knowledge of women's religious behaviour, nor do they want to deal with the question of male dominance. They neither offer a delineation of the cultural and sociological conditions for gender ideology, nor do they contribute to the discussion between reformist and revolutionary feminists[6]. The questions that are asked are: How do religious symbols relate to genderedness? What are the differences in perspective? How do symbols render meaning? The authors lean upon those French feminist theories (Bynum, 1986,

---

5. This is the division between so-called revolutionary and reformist theologians. See A. Carr, 1982.

6. The boundaries established here refer to existing discussions and volumes.

12-13)[7] which do not try to explain causes but pay attention to the fact and the experience of genderedness and the question: How can we talk about women's experience? They also make use of the phenomenological symbol theory as expressed by Ricoeur.

The choice of Ricoeur is due to his interpretation of symbols as "opaque, oblique, and analogical" (Bynum, 1986, 9). In contrast with Clifford Geertz who sees symbols as models, for Ricoeur "it is not the case that the symbol points out a meaning; it 'gives rise to thought'" (Bynum, 1986, 9). They both consider symbols as pointing to a beyond, but for Geertz this beyond mirrors the world, for Ricoeur the beyond is open-ended. As a consequence meaning is "appropriated in a dialectical process whereby it becomes subjective reality for the one who uses the symbol" (Bynum, 1986, 9). V. Turner's idea of polysemic[8] symbol is being used by the authors of this volume "to signify an emphasis, first, on the multivalent quality of images and, second, on symbol using as an active process of appropriation" (Bynum, 1986, 10)[9].

The suggestions made about genderedness in the final chapters by Bynum, Toews, and Hawley imply a modification of this theory of symbol. Their articles add the idea that experience is gendered: gendered symbols may be experienced differently by the different genders. Hawley advances this idea in his article about poetry written to Krishna. He compares poems written by Mira, the most influential poet of North India (16th century C.E.) with the poetry of Sur, an almost contemporaneous male poet who takes on the female voice in his position as gopi (i.e. a woman tied to Krishna in an illicit liaison). Hawley shows how the poems of the woman-gopi differ from the poems of the man-gopi. Bynum demonstrates how gender imagery in the Middle Ages did not signify the same thing for women and men. Toews analyses the appropriation of the Oedipus myth in the psycho-analytical movement. He discovers a distinct female

---

7. This rather casual reference to 'French feminism' is suspect. One immediately wonders: what kind of French feminism? Furthermore the reception in the U.S. of for instance 'difference', 'sexual difference' has not been unproblematic. An excellent account of this is given by Alice Jardine in *Gynesis* (1985).

8. polysemic: multivocal: a symbol can have several meanings; a symbol is ambivalent, i.e. the specific context determines the meaning of the symbol.

9. One can wonder whether the theories of Turner and Ricoeur are as compatible as the authors of this volume seem to think. To answer this question a comparative study of Ricoeur and Turner is required. At the beginning of his work Turner for instance defines the symbol in the context of ritual activity: ritual symbols are "the smallest units of ritual which still retain the specific properties of ritual behaviour" (Turner, 1968, 239). Is this the definition that Bynum has in mind? It seems that she -- and the articles in this volume -- do not hold on to this strict definition of the symbol. In his later work, Turner does not offer a definition of the symbol. We must keep in mind that Turner did not write about individuals, but about social events (see Boudewijnse, 1991).

56

perspective. He suggests that "the time has come to pay closer attention to the ways in which they (i.e. women and men, E.M.) also have made, and continue to make, themselves" (Bynum, 1986, 314). Having read (and written) these articles, Bynum concludes that:

> "We may need to adapt for women the processual or dialectical elements in Turner and Ricoeur. That is, we may need to modify their models of how symbols mean by incorporating women's tendency to emphasize reconciliation and continuity. The symbolic reversals so important to Turner as a component of ritual may be less crucial for women than for men. The synthesis of objective referent and subjective meaning, which Ricoeur thinks is achieved in the user by the symbol, may be for women less a dialectical process than an acceptance of, a continuous living with, paradox. (...) In other words, the phenomenological emphasis of Ricoeur on the process by which the symbol is appropriated may need to be expanded by the phenomenological emphasis of French feminism on genderedness until we have a more varied and richer notion of the experiences of symbol-users. By taking female symbol-users seriously, we might evolve an understanding of symbol itself in which paradox and synthesis take an important place beside dialectic, contradiction, and reversal" (Bynum, 1986, 14-15).

Bynum is aware of the fact that these findings have the status of suggestions. Premature theorizing is dangerous. The conclusion is formulated very carefully. The authors stress the complexity of symbols and therefore feel no urge to affirm that new rituals are easily created nor that radical excisions of traditional symbols will have predictable results. Still, this "cautious, academic conclusion" (Bynum, 1986, 15) gives occasion to more radical conclusions such as: "traditional symbols can have revolutionary consequences" (Bynum, 1986, 15), and "varied experiences of men and women have been there all along" (Bynum, 1986, 16). It will not be necessary to replace male- or female-referring symbols but the opening of new symbolic modes is the task ahead.

No indication is given of what these 'new symbolic modes' are. It seems this volume ends in a mist. The strength of this volume is the emphasis on a thorough reflection on symbols. A rereading of Ricoeur remains necessary, however, that does not stop at *The Symbol Gives Rise to Thought* (1972)[10] but incorporates his later work as well. Ricoeur has continued thinking about symbols and has incorporated this in a larger system. Justice to Ricoeur and to theorizing from a feminist perspective requires a reading also of his more recent work, as it 'gives rise to thought'. Furthermore it is necessary to reflect upon the idea of gen-

10. Bynum only refers to this article and to *The Symbolism of Evil* (1967).

deredness. Bynum seems to feel able to summarise the entire discussion and at the same time to answer some complicated questions by a reference to 'French feminism' (see also my remark note 7). This rather casual remark complicates the issue as it is not clear what or whom Bynum actually is referring to. It will be necessary to establish very clearly the theoretical backgrounds of the debates in the next paragraphs, to outline the crucial questions, and to make an attempt at conceptualisation.

*

* *

The three volumes we have read have first of all pointed out that the interplay between images, symbols and reality is very complicated and needs a precise instrumentation for analysing. Secondly they have demonstrated that the concept of gender is crucial. Thirdly the necessity of analysing small areas has been shown. The fourth area of interest is the place of the subject in the interplay of symbols and social reality. These studies, however, are lacking in systematic reflection on the concepts they use. Two concepts are at the core of our analysis: symbol and interpreting subject. In what follows a systematic reflection on these two crucial concepts will be offered.

2. Symbolic imagination

Introduction.

Looking at Mary, we noticed, confronted us with a reality that is not pictured with a simple stroke of the pen. Mary is more than the figure about whom the gospel gives us such little information. She is the powerful Mother, Queen, Virgin, Sustainer, Comforter, Miracle Lady. This is not a question of 'either-or'. Mary incorporates all characteristics -- sometimes contradictory and conflicting -- that have been ascribed to her. This already seems miraculous. According to time, place, and audience we cannot deny she truthfully embodies 'something' meaningful and appealing. The word 'something' with its open and unspecified content is appropriate in this context. Nowadays Mary is perceived as an ambiguous figure. The interpretations span a wide range of possibilities. No consensus can be found regarding who Mary was or what she stood for in the past or today.
    One of the main problems concerning the interpretation of Mary stated in the conclusion of the first chapter, concerns the neglect and lack of clarity about the theoretical status of Mary. Authors rarely take full

account of the observation that Mary is an historical illusion, an image that has been embraced by different ages and cultures. This point is duly noted but at best relegated to the footnotes. I have argued that we had best conceive of Mary as a symbolic image. What exactly this means will become more clear in the following pages. I will start with an associative train of thoughts about images and symbols.

2.1. Images and symbols: a first exploration

Contemporary culture and science give a lot of attention to language. Language is supposed to be the centre of the constitution of the subject. Freudian therapy is one example of the core position of language. "Without language, no experience of one's own identity" (Vandermeersch, 1978, 114, my transl.[11]). Twentieth century philosophical debate is centred around language. Lacanian thought focuses on verbal utterance. Verbal abilities are valued very highly and the power of the word cannot be underestimated. "The master of the language is the master of us all" (Wittgenstein, quoted in Miles, 1985, 22). This quote is very popular in feminist circles. It is used as an incitement for women to take hold of and participate in (verbal) discourse[12]. It is an example of how language is not only seen as structuring and organising the lives of individuals but also of how it structures power among people. Those who are at ease with language are considered to be powerful. I experienced the striking power that is given to words while participating in and guiding a Dutch women's group. I did not properly realise what was really going on because they were able to communicate very fluently about what occupied their minds. Unconsciously I had concluded that if they were able to verbalise things acutely, this meant they were in control of the situation. Words however in this case only served as 'disguise'. Only when they were asked to evoke images that empowered them did their real concerns become visible.

When we look at our immediate environment, it becomes clear that words are not the only forces guiding our lives. We are constantly bombarded with an overwhelming amount of visual impulses, visual impulses that try to convey a message. The streets are decked out with advertisements, newspapers try to attract our attention by publishing spectacular photographs, television brings a constant flow of visual information, films

---

11. Zonder taal is er geen beleving van de eigen identiteit.

12. The term "discourse" means: 'talk, converse; speak or write at length on a subject'. It has received a different meaning in Foucauldian theory where it has come to mean: written or spoken texts about a specific theme that can be joined in a social perspective. Discourse generates power (da Costa, 1989, 26).

provide us with pictures that engrave themselves upon our retinas. Some of these visual images are captivating. We soon realise that we select, more accurately that a selection of images stays in the mind. We nevertheless cannot grasp the influence they exert on our actions and ways of thinking. Images steal in without our being aware of it. We feel amazement when their influence is made conscious. Some time ago I was talking with a friend about how much we adored ageing actors who had the courage to show their signs of age on the screen. We were happy to find that there was more to be seen than the smooth-skinned puppets who commonly populate the movies. At first I considered our remark as merely expressing the hope that films would bring us more 'real' people. Subsequently I discovered that something else was going on: we had been influenced by the overpowering mass of quasi-perfect persons that so many films put on the screen. Even though we thought of ourselves as critical people who *know* that people in real-life are not perfect, those perfect people had nevertheless had a normative influence on us. Though we were aware of the unrealness of those persons, they had left us with an idea of what we ought to look like. Only the sight of an alternative could comfort our sense of failure of not measuring up to the ideal. It showed us that being wrinkled and older could be beautiful as well. Words, telling us that the norm of the young slim person is arbitrary and very questionable were not enough. *Seeing* the alternative was more convincing. This example shows that visual images unconsciously settle in the mind. They can act as sedatives, but they can also shock. They can open the eyes to new perspectives.

In this example we have moved from visual images to images in the mind. The image of the 'perfect person' is a configuration of unnameable elements in our mind. The feminist theologian Nelle Morton says: "I became convinced that we live out of our images; not out of our concepts or ideas" (Morton, 1983, 31).

2.2. Symbols: theoretical reflection

These first somewhat naïve and associative thoughts need further reflection and correction. In the next step I will try to clarify what images and symbols are. The ideas of Paul Ricoeur are crucial for my approach of images and symbols. Ricoeur defines the symbol as a movement from primary meaning to latent meaning. The act of interpretation is central in living with symbols. This interpretative act cannot be limited to symbols as isolated entities but takes place within contextualized situations in which the subject is placed before intermediary elements that call for interpretation. These are the ideas we will explore in Ricoeur's work. Before doing this, I will present some other approaches to symbols: this will enable us to situate Ricoeur within the broader context of symbol-theories, and it emphasises his contribution to the discussion. As there exists a vast amount of literature about symbols, I limit this presentation to some general positions. Susanne Langer and Lonnie Kliever are especially helpful in this presentation. I will start with the account of Susanne Langer[13] in *Philosophy in a New Key* and *Philosophical Sketches*.

If asked to characterise the human race many people will answer: 'human beings are language users'. When you come to a country where you cannot speak the native language and you do not find a common foreign language, it often feels as if you are partly stripped of your humanity. This is a very general statement that leads to a second question: 'what is using language'? It seems obvious to connect language use with the ability to communicate. This however is not specifically human: animals also communicate. Well-known example are deer who warn each other when danger is near, or dogs who bark when someone enters their territory. Communication does not seem to be the most striking human ability: human beings share it with other living beings. The intuition that some connection has to be made between language and humanity is not a wrong path to explore, however. This path is only a dead-end if language is defined as communication. Even though language is used to communicate, this is not its main characteristic: communication is the outcome of using language. The specificity of human language is that it is a process of symbolisation. Symbolisation, however, is not only linked to language. Things can be grasped in a symbolic way that is not discursive. The phrase: 'being human equals using language' should be corrected. A more appropriate statement is: 'essential for humanity is its capacity to symbolise'. Symbolisation is an act essential to human thought.

> "The symbol-making function is one of man's (sic) primary activities, like eating, looking, or moving about. It is the fundamental process of his (sic) mind, and goes on all the time" (Langer,1980, 41).

It is the way in which human beings express themselves.

Language cannot assert exclusive rights on the process of symbolisation. The disclosing, revealing power of language, i.e. its capacity to express and to mediate the experience of the self as self, is not always sufficient. Other forms are necessary to express the self as self, forms that

---

13. I follow Susanne Langer as she has made an important contribution to the discussion and reflection about symbols, seen in the context of philosophy in a new key. She claimed that the philosophical study of symbols "perhaps holds the seed of a new intellectual harvest, to be reaped in the next season of the human understanding" (Langer, 1980, 25).

are non-discursive. Visual forms stimulate us in formulating, articulating thought. I would like to stress that 'visual' in this case does not explicitly refer to the materially visual but also includes mental visual forms. Visual forms are especially useful when one wants to express 'inner feelings'. Language seems powerless in this domain. This inner realm is often depicted as not rational. It only seems irrational, however, because discursive symbols do not have the capacity to name it (Langer, 1964, 79).

> "Rationality is the essence of mind, and symbolic transformation its elementary process. It is a fundamental error, therefore, to recognize it only in the phenomenon of systematic, explicit reasoning" (Langer, 1980, 99)

The idea that thought is rooted in the body is important for feminist thought, it is an impulse to a way of thinking that does not disconnect mind and body.

According to Langer the main difference between discursive symbolisation and visual forms lies in the capacity of visual forms to present their determining relations simultaneously. She contends that the constituents of a visual structure can be grasped in one act of vision. A visual structure therefore has the possibility to convey thoughts that cannot be expressed in a discursive way. A non-discursive symbol is composed of elements that do not independently convey meaning. Whereas the meaning of ultimate single words can be defined, this is not possible for, for instance, the lines that mark the curve of a nose. As a consequence, the visual representation of an object will be more close to it than its verbal representation. The discursive description of an object is more elaborate than the information we receive at once when we see a visual representation. This visual representation is able to convey a great deal of information all at once. It has the capacity to compress elements and make them more intelligible by contracting them and reducing them to one denominator. It informs the spectator about the relations between the different constituents in a way that words cannot. This presentational symbolism can be defined as non-discursive and untranslatable; it does not directly convey generalities and can only be understood through the meaning of the whole[14].

14. The claim that 'the constituents of a visual structure can be grasped in one act of vision' should be explained. Art historian E. Gombrich says that "to see at all, we must isolate and select" (Gombrich, 1982, 15). We can never see everything simultaneously. Human vision is selective and unconsciously chooses elements. That is why symbols are used: "thanks to their economy of elements" (Gombrich, 1982, 16) symbols have the capacity of recall.

It is time to return to the definition of the symbol. We could easily lose our way in a morass of theories, but I will try to distinguish certain approaches and argue my choice of one in particular. Suzanne Langer described the symbol-making process as fundamental for human beings. This is important as it points out that symbolising belongs to human life and that every human being is involved in it. Her statement nevertheless leaves us unsatisfied in that it does not give a clear definition of what symbols are. If everything is symbol, nothing is symbol. We will have to turn to other authors in order to find more precise descriptions of what symbols are. In common parlance the word symbol does not apply to the means by which human beings construct their universe of perception and discourse. It is rather used to explain that 'something stands for something else'. This common use of the word symbol is fruitful but needs refinement. Furthermore, it will be necessary to concentrate on religious symbols. If we nevertheless followed Langer first, it was because in her extremely broad description and definition of symbolisation she has pointed out the double track we have to follow of discursive and non-discursive symbolisation.

Several symbol theories have been constructed, which represent different approaches. Lonnie Kliever, whom I will follow here, has pointedly analysed several strands of symbol theories in an article in *Union Seminary Quarterly Review* (Kliever, 1972). I present this article in order to delineate the choices that exist in other symbol theories. Kliever goes so far as to allege that symbol use and symbol meaning are at the core of contemporary (that is 1972) religious research. The author finds agreement among scholars about the dismissal of religious literalism but can hardly point at any positive unity. Kliever distinguishes between the commonly accepted schools of reductionistic and realistic symbol systems and adds a third approach, which he names symbolic formism. These three approaches presuppose different things about religion. Kliever says that Paul Tillich described symbolic reductionism as a negative theoretical position. Those belonging to this school deny the presence of any transcendent reality in symbols. Religion and religious symbols obtain their strength and power from external factors: it is either a necessary stage in the human evolutionary process (e.g. A. Comte) that can be left behind as soon as the next phase is reached, or religious symbols are considered to be projections of essential things in life (e.g. Freud, Feuerbach, Durkheim). Religious symbols must be overcome in order to obtain truth. The reductionist school has shown that it is impossible to disconnect religious symbols from their functional interweaving and entanglement with daily life and thought.

The symbolic realistic school contains in its theoretical positions a criticism of the reductionistic school. Its adherents are not satisfied with the reduction of religion to its human origin and function. Reductionistic theories in their view overlook the transhuman aspect, which, according to the symbolic realistic school, is a fundamental characteristic of religious symbols. Symbols mediate the transcendental ground of existence. The term 'realism', according to Kliever, refers to three elements: 1. there is a transcendent reality beyond religious symbols that is disclosed and denoted by them; 2. religious symbols can be judged true or false; 3. religious reality can only be expressed in a symbolic mode.

Symbolic realists do not agree about the role of religious symbols in religious experience. Some (e.g. Bultmann, Ramsey, Macquarrie, etc.) contend that the function of religious symbols is limited to representing the divine. They presuppose a pre-symbolic experience, an experience that logically precedes the symbolic. Even though symbolisation affects religious experiences, symbols will always remain an echo of the experience. Others (R. Niebuhr, Tillich, Jaspers, Polanyi) claim that religious symbols represent and mediate ultimate reality. Religious experience is possible only by means of a symbolic system. "The reality *beyond* the symbol is experienced *in* the symbol" (Kliever, 1972, 99).

The third school distinguished by Kliever is symbolic formism. Its authors (James, Cassirer, Langer) criticise the others for their distorted view: their point of departure is the objectivistic idea that symbols should be anchored and verified in a reality outside themselves. Symbolic formists emphasise that there are symbolic systems that do not represent an ontological reality but that represent symbolic realities. Imaginary as they are, these are influential and formative for human existence. "Because of the stress on the formative power of imaginative language in all human experience, I call this third approach *symbolic formism*" (Kliever, 1972, 100). The human being is seen as "animal symbolicum", i.e. a creature that has the capacity to transcend its immediate surroundings and experiences. Different symbol systems constitute human existence. Symbolic formism does not deny that these symbolic universes could be real. Reality, however, is not an objective ontological entity but is shaped by meaningful human experiences. Different real meaningful worlds exist. The jewel in the crown, however, is the day-to-day world of experiences and socialisation. This world is the foundation of and creates the possibility for, other created worlds.

> "... the task of personal and social existence is to live and move freely within and between multiple realities which are anchored but never confined to the everyday world. Precisely this task transposes the question of the truth of imaginative constructs to their satisfactoriness in relation to the everyday world. By this measure there can be no uniform or absolute truth, but discriminating and

relative judgments can be made about competing imaginative constructs" (Kliever, 1972, 101).

Religion is one of these many imaginary worlds.

Kliever ends this article with the rather trite remark that symbolic formism is still developing and that symbolic realism probably will remain popular among those interested in religion. Symbolic formism is nevertheless of interest because it offers answers to questions raised by the reductionist strand that could not be solved by the realists.

Kliever's framework helps us to understand the background against which discussions about symbols should be understood. I am not prepared to follow her option for symbolic formism, however. I want to maintain that religious symbols disclose a transcendent reality that can only be expressed in a symbolic mode. The verification of these symbols cannot, however, be sought in that transcendent reality, as we can only get to that transcendent reality through symbols. We can only try to understand how those symbols inform our lives. It is with this question that Paul Ricoeur can help us.

2.3. Paul Ricoeur

> "L'énigme du symbole n'est pas que le bateau
> représente une femme, mais que la femme
> soit signifiée et que, même pour être
> signifiée au plan de l'image, elle soit
> verbalisée"
> P. Ricoeur

Ricoeur attempts to offer a definition of the symbol that is neither too narrow nor too broad. He avoids the position of Cassirer -- and I would add S. Langer -- that says that "Le 'symbolique' désigne le commun dénominateur de toutes les manières d'objectiver, de donner sens à la réalité" (Ricoeur, 1965, 20). Neither does he want to characterise symbols as analogy. The former position conceals the distinction between *univoque* and *multivoque* expressions. The latter, i.e. that one is carried through the first meaning towards the second meaning, does not entirely cover what Ricoeur understands to be a 'symbol'. For him a symbol is "toute structure de signification où un sens direct, primaire, littéral, désigne par surcroît un autre sens indirect, secondaire, figuré, qui ne peut être appréhendé qu'à travers le premier" (Ricoeur, 1969, 16). In other words: "Symbol is the very movement of the primary meaning that makes us share in the latent meaning and thereby assimilates us to the symbolized, without our being able intellectually to dominate the similarity" (Ricoeur, 1968, 194).

The act of interpretation is crucial: "(...) il y a symbole là où l'expression linguistique se prête par son double sens ou ses sens multiples à un travail d'interprétation" (Ricoeur, 1965, 26). Without interpretation, there is no symbol. Interpretation and symbol are organically linked. Interpretations, however, will never be exhaustive. The symbol joins two dimensions of discourse: the linguistic and the non-linguistic[15]. It is impossible to categorise all the semantic possibilities of a symbol. An endless exegesis is necessary (Ricoeur, 1976, 53-57). One of the most famous sentences in this regard is: "Le symbole donne à penser" (Ricoeur, 1965, 46). "Le symbole donne; mais ce qu'il donne, c'est à penser, de quoi penser" (Ricoeur, 1960, 324). Thought is evoked, provoked by symbols.

Ricoeur describes what symbols are more precisely by distinguishing and differentiating them from similar structures. First of all a symbol is a sign as it is directed at something beyond itself. It differs from a sign because it holds a double intentionality. There is an analogical relation between the first or literal meaning and the second meaning. The analogical correspondence is not between signifying word and signified thing but between first meaning and second meaning.

> "(...) the symbol in fact is the very movement of the primary meaning which makes us share the hidden meaning and thus assimilates us to the thing symbolized, without our being able to get hold of the similarity intellectually" (Ricoeur, 1972, 314).

Secondly the symbol differs from the allegory. The allegory is hermeneutic while the symbol precedes it: "the symbol yields its meaning in enigma and not through translation" (Ricoeur, 1972, 315). Furthermore, Ricoeur's interpretation of the symbol varies from symbolic logic. He does not stop at a mere formalist relation between primary content and secondary content. Ricoeur's symbol is essentially bound up with content. Finally, the symbol must be distinguished from myth. Myth is a symbol developed into narrative form.

The interpretation of symbols is accompanied by three major problems: First of all we are confronted with the opacity of the symbol. The symbol is in an analogical way rooted in materiality but is at the same time opaque. Secondly, symbols are contingent. Why are these specific symbols used and not others? Thirdly, the interpretation of symbols remains problematic, we can not offer an unproblematic interpretation (Ricoeur, 1969, 313). We are trapped in a hermeneutic circle in which "il faut comprendre pour croire, mais il faut croire pour comprendre" (Ricoeur,

---

15. Langer sees symbols as discursive and non-discursive, Ricoeur says symbols join the discursive and non-discursive level together.

1960, II, 326). This description of symbol does not give access to a true and controllable meaning. We have to go through a seemingly endless chain of interpretation acts. Does Ricoeur leave us here with an absurd conclusion? It looks like it at this point: we are caught in an eternal web of interpretation.

Many authors leave Ricoeur at this point, probably contented with the idea of eternal exegesis of symbols, and do not add the insights of his later work. If we indeed leave Ricoeur at this point, we seem to arrive at a pointless but continuing process of interpretation. A Sisyphean project? Our core question should be: how is this interpretation taking place? Our task is to unravel this process of interpretation, or in other terms the 'production of meaning'. Ricoeur has attended to this in his books *La métaphore vive* (MV) and *Temps et récit* (TR). They modify and especially refine his previous theory. Ricoeur's attention and scope is enlarged by an attention to metaphors (MV) and narrative function (TR). The former book deals with reference and truth, while the latter concentrates on new configurations that are made of the pre-comprehensible order of acting through fiction. In *Du texte à l'action* (Ricoeur, 1986, 11-35) Ricoeur gives a summary and overview of his own work. He retraces his steps by moving from his latest work on narrativity and narrative functions to his earlier books. He characterises his occupation with intrigue[16] and metaphor as studies that deal with fundamental issues about sense and reference. The tradition in which he moves rotates around three axes: reflective philosophy, Husserlian phenomenology, and hermeneutic phenomenology. His epistemological notions can be summarised as:

> "Il n'est pas de compréhension de soi qui ne soit médiatisée par des signes, des symboles et des textes; la compréhension de soi coïncide à titre ultime avec l'interprétation appliquée à ces termes média- teurs" (Ricoeur, 1986, 29).

This threefold mediation is the core of Ricoeur's oeuvre. Mediation through signs refers to the primacy of language for all human experience. Symbolic mediation concerns the 'double sense' expressions. Ricoeur rebukes as too narrow his own former point of view of hermeneutics as interpretation of symbols. His arguments are:

---

16. "L'intrigue est l'ensemble des combinaisons par lesquelles des événements sont transformés en histoire ou -- corrélativement -- une histoire est tirée d'événements. L'intri- gue est le médiateur entre l'événement et l'histoire" (Ricoeur, 1986, 14). In English the word 'emplotment' is used: to effect a mediation between events and certain universally human 'experiences of temporality' (White, 1987, 172-173).

"D'abord, il m'est apparu qu'un symbolisme traditionnel ou privé ne déploie ses ressources de plurivocité que dans les contextes appropriés, donc à l'échelle d'un texte entier, par exemple un poème. Ensuite, le même symbolisme donne lieu à des interprétations concurrentes, voire polairement opposées, selon que l'interprétation vise à réduire le symbolisme à sa base littérale, à ses sources inconscientes ou à ses motivations sociales, ou à l'amplifier selon sa plus grande puissance de sens multiple" (Ricoeur, 1986, 30).

Hermeneutics can no longer be defined as mere interpretation of symbols. Symbols are a step between the general recognition of the linguistic character of human experience and the more technical definition of hermeneutics as textual interpretation. Furthermore it undermines the idea of intuitive self-knowledge as it forces one to work through the symbols a culture provides.

The third mediation is through texts. Discourse reaches a triple semantic autonomy in texts; "par rapport à l'intention du locuteur, à la réception par l'auditoire primitif, aux circonstances économiques, sociales, culturelles de sa production" (Ricoeur, 1986, 31).

The hermeneutical field resembles a three-layered texture. The first layer consists of the fundamental linguistic character of human experience, the second layer is fabricated of the symbolic and the top layer is constructed by texts. Symbols are the hinge between signs and texts. The subject envisaged by Ricoeur is complex and not immediately transparent. "Se comprendre, c'est se comprendre *devant le texte*[17] et recevoir de lui les conditions d'un soi autre que le moi qui vient à la lecture" (Ricoeur, 1986, 31; idem, 54). This understanding is explained and analyzed in Ricoeur's writings about mimesis[18]. We have to keep in mind that "écrire-lire (...) n'est pas un cas de dialogue" (Ricoeur, 1986, 139). It is not simply an act of exchanging information, nor is it speaking and answering. In the act of writing a text the reader is absent, in reading the text the writer is absent. We can only understand the subject dealing with a text to be a subject that is involved in mimetic activity.

The central notion of mimesis has been extensively elaborated in *Temps et Récit*. Mimesis, as Ricoeur presents it, is more than mere imitation or reduplication. It is an act of synthesising, i.e. bringing things together in a story, joining acts, aims, causes in a plot, and is a crucial aspect of subject-activity of a human-being-in-the-world. New conjunctions are made, new perspectives are given awareness. Or as IJsseling says in and through mimesis reality appears on a different level (IJsseling, 1990,

17. Text is all discourse fixed by writing.
18. The complex backgrounds and use of mimesis can be found in S. IJsseling, 1990.

18). Mimesis is the central faculty in the constitutions of these new configurations. Ricoeur distinguishes three levels of mimesis:

> "L'enjeu est donc le procès concret par lequel la configuration textuelle fait médiation entre la préfiguration du champ pratique et sa refiguration par la réception de l'oeuvre. Il apparaîtra corollairement, au terme de l'analyse, que le lecteur est l'opérateur par excellence qui assume par son faire -- l'action de lire -- l'unité du parcours de mimèsis I à mimèsis III à travers mimèsis II. (...) Nous suivons donc le destin d'un temps préfiguré à un temps refiguré par la médiation d'un temps configuré" (Ricoeur, 1983, 86-87).

Mimesis I spans the structural, symbolic, and temporal pre-knowledge of an action. In order to be comprehensible an intrigue must be carried by intelligible structures. The pre-given rules must be known. "Comprendre une histoire, c'est comprendre à la fois le langage du 'faire' et la tradition culturelle de laquelle procède la typologie des intrigues" (Ricoeur, 1983, 91). Narrative and action are connected with one another. They are linked in a relation of presuppositions and a relation of transformation. All narration presupposes a familiarity with the terms in which the story is told. These terms receive a meaning in the sequential chaining up of the intrigue, and thus they render meaning.

The symbolic context is always present. It is "une signification incorporée à l'action et déchiffrable sur elle par les autres acteurs du jeu social" (Ricoeur, 1983, 92). The symbolic system provides actions with a first frame of interpretation. A specific act can only receive an interpretation in a specific context. Symbols introduce a notion of normativity as they bring order and direction in people's lifes. Ethical neutrality is out of the question.

The temporal character takes care of the conceptual system of an action and its particular temporal dimension. Ricoeur defends a rupture with a linear representation of time and presents an analysis of *'l'intra-temporalité'*. In turning to the idea of a triple present, a present of future things, a present of past things, and a present of present things (Augustine), Ricoeur wants to clarify the exchange that the action effects between the temporal dimensions. It is "sur le socle de l'intra-temporalité que s'édifieront conjointement les configurations narratives et les formes plus élaborées de temporalité qui leur correspondent" (Ricoeur, 1983, 100).

In short, mimesis I is about "précomprendre ce qu'il en est de l'agir humain" (Ricoeur, 1983, 100).

Mimesis II is the mediator between mimesis I and mimesis III. It opens the territory of the "comme si" (Ricoeur, 1983, 101). Mimesis II mediates on at least three levels: First of all between individual events and the entire story[19]. Single events are organised in such a way in the story that they are no longer a mere enumeration but they become a configuration. It presents the events in an intelligible combination, in such a way that one can always ask: 'What is its theme?' Secondly, mimesis II joins heterogeneous elements (agents, aims, means, interactions, etc.). Thirdly, it mediates the temporal characters. Mimesis II, the act of *'mise en intrigue'*, combines the chronological and the non-chronological dimensions of the story. The chronological dimension characterises the story as a sequence of events, the non-chronological dimension is the configuration that transforms the events into a story.

The mediating function of mimesis II towards mimesis III can be labelled as schematisation and traditionality, resting on a game of innovation and sedimentation. Innovation, schematisation, and imagination are intricately linked concepts. Schematisation is to be understood in the Kantian way of productive imagination: it is the faculty constituting a generating frame for rules. This schematisation is active in a history that can be characterised as tradition. Tradition is "la transmission vivante d'une innovation toujours susceptible d'être réactivée par un retour aux moments les plus créateurs du faire poétique" (Ricoeur, 1983, 106). Sedimentation and innovation are the core activities of the settlement of a tradition.

Mimesis III marks the intersection of the world of the text and the world of the listener or the reader (Ricoeur, 1983, 109). It corresponds with what Gadamer names 'application'. It refers to the reader or the listener in whom the entire mimetic activity is taking place. "Le texte ne devient oeuvre que dans l'interaction entre texte et récepteur" (Ricoeur, 1983, 117). The transmission from mimesis II to mimesis III happens through the act of reading. Again, schematisation and traditionality occupy a central place. On the one hand, the paradigms that have been handed down structure the expectations of the reader and help her/him in recognising the rules and the genre of the story. They enable the reader to follow the story. On the other hand, it is in the act of reading in which the configuration is happening and that actualises its capacity to be followed. Following a story is actualising while reading (Ricoeur, 1983, 116).

19. In French the word 'histoire' contains the double meaning of story and history.

*
* *

To recapitulate here what has gone before: we first established the sym-bol-like character of Mary and then sketched several schools of thought about symbols and more particularly about religious symbols. Our next step was to opt for one approach, i.e. P. Ricoeur. We chose this author not only because his theories have been used in the field of women's studies but especially because he gives us a meticulous analysis of what symbols are. His analysis does not stop at that point but reaches further. He reviewed his own theory and redraws it into an encompassing philos-ophy. Symbols are no loose ends, nor do they lead a disconnected life. They are a component of a more elaborated system that makes the sub-ject into what it is[20].

Ricoeur's major point is that symbols are part of a story and only as such are they symbols. According to its place in a story a symbol points to something else. The context in which it is set is determinative. A symbol without context, without story simply does not exist. Ricoeur enables us to move on in our quest of an interpretation of Mary. As symbol she can only be understood in a context, she does not operate individually but receives and gives meaning within a mimetic elaboration. There is a prob-lem, however, insofar as Ricoeur more and more seems to insist on the predominance of texts. In the associative first paragraph I stressed the importance of 'images', things we see, things we see in our mind that influence us. This 'visual' aspect must receive more attention. As I already noted while presenting Johnson, theorizing about theological statements about Mary as being symbolic is only part of the picture. It is necessary to bring the image dimension into the arena. This is what we are going to attempt in the next paragraph.

2.4. Symbolic imagination

"Historical hermeneutics must develop a method that includes the use of both texts and images if the worlds of historical people are to be under-stood" (Miles, 1985, 12). Images are given an important place in the pro-cess of gaining insight and knowledge. Lonergan's statement: "Images are necessary for insight" (Lonergan, 1957, 8) establishes the relation between seeing and understanding: 'in-sight' implies that something must be in sight in order to give insight, seeing from within. The double association of image with something 'visual' and as related to imagination is especially

---

20. We must remember this definition when we arrive at the project of R. Braidotti, see p. 78-83.

revealing when dealing with Mary. She has initiated an incredible amount of visualisation and she has seldom been absent from the imagination.

Images have obtained a bad reputation owing to their use in empiricist theories and behaviourist psychology (Ricoeur, 1986, 214). Several definitions are circulating. Ricoeur (1986, 215) distinguishes four major descriptions. First: the arbitrary evocation of absent things that exist elsewhere; secondly: portraits, paintings, etc. They possess their own physical existence but they have to *tenir lieu* the things they represent; thirdly: what evokes non-existent things; fourthly: illusions, i.e. representations that for an exterior observer or reflector are addressing non-existing or absent things but which are real objects for those immersed in them as real objects.

Theoretical reflection about images emphasises several aspects: Images are said to provide representations of the nature of reality and the range of human possibilities that intimately inform the emotional, spiritual, and intellectual lives of individuals (Miles, 1985, xi). They

> "are not only capable of connoting the things from which our sense-experience originally derived them, (...), but they also have an inalienable tendency to "mean" things that have only a logical analogy to their primary meanings" (Langer, 1980, 145).

Images help us to find a way in the enormous flood of impressions that comes to us. A multitude of impressions overwhelm every human being. In order to survive, a structure needs to be imposed on these manifold impressions. Images provide us with a first framework for this chaos. They structure the impressions in a primitive abstraction. "(...), they are our spontaneous embodiments of general ideas" (Langer, 1980, 145). Images have the capacity to confront the viewer in a new way with elements that are not foreign to her (Miles, 1985, 30). They have the power to combine and to organise things in such a way that they not only give access to what is already known but open a window to new ways of seeing.

> "An image is not just a picture in the mind's eye but a dynamic through which one communicates publicly or which communicates oneself. An image *is* its functioning -- whether it operates consciously or deep in the unconscious; whether it operates in an individual or in the body politic" (Morton, 1985, 131).

This characterisation of images is no longer connected with the classical reference to the Latin *imago* and *imitari*. This reference engendered a conception of the image that defined it as "a substance like something analogous to an icon, a picture, a figure, (...)" (Pruyser, 1983, 3). In contemporary thought images are far more characterised by their evoca-

tive power. The term evocation frees the term image from a static definition. It stresses a process that opens manifold possibilities and suggests
limitless opportunities.

The process-like character of images perceived as evocation finds a
better description in the verb to imagine. The stress has been shifted from
'having images' to 'imagining'. It denotes a

> "mental process that has considerable freedom of action and a great
> deal of self-sufficiency to produce with much spontaneity and inven-
> tiveness an immense variety of images, with very little likeness to
> any models with which reality has ever confronted us" (Pruyser,
> 1983, 6).

Imagination uses sense data but goes a step further and transcends them.
The image is "a function of a freely acting perceiver who shapes and
forms the 'stuff' presented to his (sic) senses. The emphasis shifts from
image to the activity of imagining" (Pruyser, 1983, 9). "The role of imagination is to lead us beyond what is present to our senses towards the
realization that there is something signified by the things before us, something which we can grasp in a way, but cannot express." (Warnock, 1976,
61). This leads us to the Ricoeurian level of Mimesis II where productive
imagination is said to play an important role in the game of innovation
and sedimentation of a tradition (Ricoeur, 1983, 102-109). "Avant d'être
une perception évanouissante, l'image est une signification émergente"
(Ricoeur, 1986, 219). Imagination is:

> "un libre jeu avec des possibilités, dans un état de non-engagement
> à l'égard du monde de la perception ou de l'action. C'est dans cet
> état de non-engagement que nous essayons des idées nouvelles, des
> valeurs nouvelles, des manières nouvelles d'être au monde"
> (Ricoeur, 1986, 230).

In bringing together Ricoeur's theory of the symbol as mediating
element in a mimetic field of interpretation and the activity of imagination we have constructed a frame for understanding Mary. We are,
however, left with a further problem: the interpreting Ricoeurian subject
must be more fully specified. This is the step we take in the next paragraph.

3. Women as symbolising/imagining subjects

Introduction

At the end of this chapter we are left with the question what we can do with symbols, how we can converse with them, how we can 'use' them. Where do women come in? Ricoeur's symbol theory has shown us that a shift has taken place from the object of symbolisation to the symbolising subject. Theories that concentrate on images show a move from image/-images to the act of imagination. We notice a focus on the imagining subject, similar to the one on the symbolising subject. I suggested that we should reflect on Mary as a symbolic image. Ricoeur also drew attention to the importance of the context in the process of interpretation (mimesis). He integrates his thinking about symbols in a wider perspective of who and what the self as self is. We must read Ricoeur carefully and critically. We already insisted on emphasising images. Another criticism is that his theory lacks a gender perspective. We should not take the idea of a symbolising, contextualised subject for granted but undertake a serious modification and correction of this idea by starting from a gendered subject. Our purpose in the rest of this chapter is to reflect upon the possibility of a female subject and on the context of women's lives.

Women's studies research as presented in I. Images and the Female Form has shown a similar concentration on the imagining subject. Its main focus was gender analysis. This has proved to be at once its strength and its weakness. It offers little theoretical background. A gender analysis gives a description of and insight into the object of symbolisation/imagining, but hardly provides any indications concerning the imagining/symbolising subject. I want to elaborate this in what follows. If the subject is important in the process of symbolisation it becomes necessary to know who this subject is. Speaking about that subject as a woman is more complicated than at first sight appears. The problems vary from the simple question whether the subject in (Western) philosophy has not always been a male subject to the question whether it is even possible to talk about a woman as subject. The feminist debate continues.

3.1. Human beings: woman or man

It is impossible to continue speaking about man, or human beings as if this does not raise several fundamental questions. Human beings are born in bodies that are female or male. This sentence must be corrected: human beings *are* their female body or their male body. The 'small biological difference' cannot be set aside as a mere biological fact. This is an instance of reductionism that overlooks the many consequences of this small difference. The concept of woman is a problem: it is both central to feminist theorizing and impossible to work with as it is not possible to formulate it precisely (Alcoff, 1988, 405). Simone de Beauvoir, one of the founding mothers of feminist theorizing, in Le deuxième sexe[21] asks "what is a woman?". The factual situation, so runs her reasoning, shows that women and men are not alike. There are obvious differences. A general definition of humanity is unjust towards women. It denies women's specificity. De Beauvoir struggles with the observation that on the one hand women exist -- this cannot be denied -- but on the other hand no conceptions can capture her: neither her functions nor 'the eternal feminine' define woman. De Beauvoir attempts a description of woman by starting from what is or is not essential for human beings. According to de Beauvoir sexual difference is one of the contingent elements of our experience (Simons, 1984, 352). She stresses the lived experience -- this in accordance with the existentialist atmosphere she lives in (Vintges, 1989, 122).

I agree with Vintges in her article in Tijdschrift voor Vrouwenstudies when she points out several ambiguities in Le deuxième sexe:

> "On the one hand female corporeality is presented as passivity and as being entirely determined by the species. On the other hand it is a culturally constructed experience of the female body. On the one hand women's biological functions are seen as the historical cause of their social arrears, while at the other hand de Beauvoir contends that culture decides whether these are a social handicap. On the one hand women and men are exhibited as biological essences, while on the other hand they are conceptualized as social products" (Vintges, 1989, 124, my transl.[22]).

Still de Beauvoir seems to favour the non-biological interpretation of woman. Witness is the famous sentence: "On ne naît pas femme, on le devient"[23].

De Beauvoir's account leaves us with many questions. The fact that being a woman means being a female body, has not been given a satis-

---

21. I will not in extenso study 'Le deuxième sexe'. I will only highlight the elements that are important for my argument.

22. "Enerzijds wordt vrouwelijke lichamelijkheid als passiviteit en onderworpenheid aan de soort ten tonele gevoerd. Anderzijds betreft het hier een cultureel vormgegeven ervaring van het vrouwelijk lichaam. Enerzijds worden de biologische functies van vrouwen als historische oorzaak voor hun maatschappelijke achterstand gezien, anderzijds stelt de Beauvoir dat de cultuur bepaalde of die een maatschappelijk nadeel vormden. Enerzijds worden vrouwen en mannen als biologische essenties opgevoerd, anderzijds worden zij als sociale produkten opgevat"

23. This sentence has often been wrongly translated as: one is not born as woman, one is made one. See for instance M. Bal, 1990, 29.

factory explanation. She does not offer an answer to the question: who or what is that female body, woman? This question is not a simple one. It is at the heart of feminist theoretical debate. With Alice Jardine I would like to make the representability of women and its limits the core question of feminist theory:"Can or should feminism be something other than an attention to the *representation* of women (in several senses of the word)?" (Jardine, 1985, 63). Or in the words of Suleiman, who in *(Re)-writing the body* (Suleiman, 1986) characterises the quest of the women's movement as a reclaiming of the body and an appropriation of a voice to speak about the body. "Let woman speak her own body, assume her own subjecthood" (Suleiman, 1986, 8). This slogan did not receive an easy answer for

> "what exactly do we mean when we speak of woman as subject, whether of speech or writing or of her own body? Is there such a thing as a --(or the) -- subject? Is there such a thing as woman's body, woman's sexuality? Is there such a thing as woman, or, for that matter, man?" (Suleiman, 1986, 8).

Suleiman acknowledges that these questions were not invented by the women's movement but she claims that these questions received a new impetus by feminist thought. They remain urgent questions and many attempts have been made to put 'woman' into discourse, to imag(in)e 'woman'[24]. And Jardine continues

> "If gynesis[25] as process has most certainly always been marginally at work in the West, especially in religious and literary texts, in what ways are its more visible links to modernity subject to feminist analysis? Is feminist theory as a search for the female self (most characteristic of Anglo-American criticism) in complete contradiction with the, strictly speaking, antifeminist insistence in France on the liberating potentiality of losing the self? Might there be a way to imagine a new kind of feminist hermeneutics able to give up its quest for truth; capable of self-reflection on its own complicity with inherited systems of representation? If feminism is to remain radical and not become but patchwork for a patriarchal

---

24. Talking about 'woman' implies saying something about 'man'. This has been rarely given a thematic treatment in the women's studies project in an explicit way. 'Men' complaining about being excluded in women's studies research and books should keep in mind that talking about 'woman' implies saying something about 'man'.

25. Jardine uses the neologism 'gynesis', it means: "The putting into discourse of 'woman' as that process diagnosed in France as intrinsic to the condition of modernity; indeed, the valorization of the feminine, woman, and her obligatory, that is, the historical connotations, as somehow intrinsic to new and necessary modes of thinking, writing, speaking" (Jardine, 1985, 25).

fabric ripped apart by the twentieth century, what kind of alliances will it be able to form with the most radical modes of thought produced by that century? These are indeed a set of historical intersections" (Jardine, 1985, 63-64).

Our problem remains which way to go.

"The attempt to analyze, to separate ideological and cultural determinations of the 'feminine' from the 'real woman' -- seemingly the most logical path for a feminist to follow -- may also be the most interminable process, one in which women become not only figuratively but also literally impossible" (Jardine, 1985, 37).

This leaves us with the almost desperate cry: "What's a feminist to do?" (Alcoff, 1988, 421).

It is necessary to explain some of the concepts that constantly are at work in this debate. We encounter terms like difference, essentialism, culturalism, sex-gender, etc. I will try to clarify the different positions and move on to a possible direction that could be fruitful. Cooey distils two extremes:

"At one extreme, feminists, notably French, have taken what has come to be known as an 'essentialist' position. At the other extreme, feminists, usually American, have attributed the significance of sexual difference to cultural determinism, particularly as that is manifested by language" (Cooey, 1987, 18)[26].

Neither of these positions is tenable.

"Essentialism fails to account for the extent to which body and nature are culturally constructed. Cultural determinism fails to take seriously material existence at its most fundamental level, the human body itself" (Cooey, 1987, 18).

Cultural feminism takes the sex-gender dichotomy seriously: sex is that what is determined by biology, gender[27] is a cultural construct. Ac-

---

26. Alcoff (1988) makes a different distinction: she recognizes cultural feminists and post-structural feminists. Her definitions of these two positions differ from what is currently accepted. I will follow her article in the footnotes as it is interesting to see how different definitions can mar the debate.

27. In general, gender is understood to be the social organization of the relations between the sexes. Cf. J. Outshoorn, 1989, 13-17. J. Scott (1986) takes gender to be an analytical concept and provides an entire programme for gender analysis. See also the definition by M. Brouns (1989): gender is the structural principle or structuring principle in which maleness and femaleness are being constructed in relation to one another and are brought into action.

cording to Farmer, "our bodies and physical activities provide the foundation for the circumstances of our existence, but those material foundations are mediated by cultural sources of meaning and value"(Farmer, 1987, 3). Biology is constitutive of our existence, but we will never really understand the relation between biology and culture. Everything we say about it is already culturally mediated[28]. All we know about the body -- which is a biological entity but also a symbolic construct -- is mediated and interpreted through some form of discourse.

One of the positions that has given rise to much debate and even more misunderstanding is essentialism. It seems as if in feminist debates (and elsewhere) essentialism has been identified with biological determinism and/or ahistorical essences. Essentialism should therefore be avoided at all costs. Those who claim to be serious about essentialism are ostracized as "flirting with essentialism" (Hawkesworth, 1989, 547). Sexual difference and essentialism are said to be one and the same. As a consequence sexual difference is proclaimed a heretical notion as well. It is supposed to pin down women and men to never changing essences. Teresa Brennan broaches this problematic status of essentialism in the introduction to *Between Feminism and Psychoanalysis*. She gives a clear account of how essentialism received its current bad name. In English marxist feminist thought in the seventies 'change' was a central concept. Essentialism, i.e. those theories that presuppose something essential, something pre-given in human nature, were limited to 'theories that make an appeal to sexual biology'. The attack on this kind of essentialist thought was fed by the fear that: "If it was allowed in any context that there was something fixed in sexual identity, then that argument was open to abuse: if women were naturally more nurturant, then by the same logic, women could be naturally incompetent" (Brennan, 1989, 7). In the eighties Lacan was embraced as a non-essentialist thinker. Brennan shows that this adaptation of Lacanian thought brings many problems and has not been able to clarify the question of essentialism. The debate is obfuscated by an attempt to bridge political theory (Marxism) and psychoanalysis (Lacan).

28. Alcoff defines cultural feminists as those who have answered the question of female self-definition by questioning the definitions given by men. They argue, according to Alcoff, that male supremacist culture has defined women and distorted female values. Those should be restored (Alcoff, 1988, 406-407). "Cultural feminism is the ideology of a female nature or female essence reappropriated by feminists themselves in an effort to revalidate undervalued female attributes" (Alcoff 1988, 408). Alcoff contrasts cultural feminists with post-structuralist feminists who not only attack the definition of woman given by men but undermine defining woman at all. She finds both responses inadequate. Though I find her characterization of cultural feminists confusing, I appreciate her titillating responses to the questions we are tackling here.

The bridge is made of somewhat obscure material. Non-essentialism is valued, in both contexts, as unconditionally positive.

I think it is necessary to distinguish between sexual difference and essentialism. They do not necessarily belong together even though a connection is possible. We need to find a way to think about 'woman', and 'women'. The project of Rosi Braidotti, who shows that essentialism cannot be abandoned by feminists, offers a -- albeit tentative -- frame of reference from where we can think about womanselves.

3.2. The Politics of Ontological Difference

> "The move from questioning the presumed
> ahistoricity of sexed identities does not have
> to result in celebrating the carnival of
> diffuse and contingent sexualities".
> D. Riley

Rosi Braidotti starts her article *The Politics of Ontological Difference* with a very strong statement concerning feminist theory and sexual difference. She holds that feminism of sexual difference has little to do with a reactionary movement, but represents a positive affirmation of the ontological desire of women. In the volume *Men in Feminism* Braidotti, in an article with the provocative title *Envy: or With Your Brains and My Looks*, considers this ontological desire of women within the framework of a postmodern world. She points to the paradoxical situation that deconstruction and its removal of the subject manifests itself at the historical moment that women finally start to get access to language, power, etc. It is impossible to deconstruct a subjectivity one has never had, or that has at the most been called the dark continent. "In order to announce the death of the subject one must have gained the right to speak as one; in order to demystify metadiscourse one must first gain access to a place of enunciation" (Braidotti, 1987, 237).

The ontological desire of women refers to the affirmation that women posit themselves as subjects, or more accurately posit themselves as female subjects. This female subject is not a mere cultural product, nor a purely biology-manipulated creature, but a sexual and embodied subject that is a bio-cultural entity. Being a woman can and must be defined in terms other than 'not-man'. The core question for Braidotti is how to obtain equality without losing difference. She asks this question within the context of contemporary Western philosophical developments, in which any acquired notion of the subject is suspicious. How is it possible to reconcile the political necessity to posit oneself as female subject on the one hand with the problematic nature and construction of the subject on the other hand[29]? Starting-point is the acknowledgement of the factual and historical asymmetry of the sexes and its hierarchical structure. The political will to recognise the specificity of the female experience[30], to refuse the merger of sexual difference into a disembodied post-modern anti-essentialist subject, and to relate the debate about difference to the bodily existence and the bodily experience of women are basic to her project. Braidotti refuses to be drawn into the game that makes equality feminists and difference feminists into opponents involved in a never-ending debate. According to Braidotti, these two approaches are indissolubly linked. Difference becomes operative within the pursuit of equality[31].

Braidotti argues that a feminist theoretician who thinks about femininity and difference cannot afford not to be an essentialist[32]. Three premisses underlie her defense of essentialism:

> "That in order to make sexual difference operative as a political option, feminist theoreticians should re-connect the feminine to the bodily sexed reality of the female, refusing the separation of the empirical from the symbolic[33], or of the material from the discursive, or of sex from gender. Secondly, that this project is important as both the epistemological basis for feminist politics in the social, economic, political, and theoretical context of the postmodern and the postindustrial condition. Thirdly, that in thinking about sexual difference one is led, by the very structure of the problem, to the metaphysical question of essence" (Braidotti, 1989, 93).

29. Alcoff refers to post-structuralist feminists who propound a negative feminism, i.e. a feminism that deconstructs everything. The dilemma is: "How can we ground a feminist politics that deconstructs the female subject?" (Alcoff, 1988, 419).

30. Riley's project for instance is entirely different from Braidotti's: her political stance is informed by pragmatism: "I'd argue that it is compatible to suggest that 'women' don't exist -while maintaining a politics of 'as if they existed'- since the world behaves as if they unambiguously did" (Riley, 1988, 112). Being an oppositional subject seems to be the best strategy even though it can become a trap. Riley brings together the philosophical position that denies the possibility of determining the term 'women' and the feminist will to use the term whenever it is necessary. "(...) feminism must be agile enough to say, 'Now we will be 'women' - but now we will be persons, not these 'women'" (Riley, 1988, 113). This position differs greatly from Braidotti's positive affirmation of the ontological desire of women.

31. See also Michielsens, 1990, 26-27.

32. Again I refer to the position of Riley who says: "For both a concentration on and a refusal of the identity of 'women' are essential to feminism" (Riley, 1988, 1). This seems to be similar to Braidotti but actually Riley takes a very different stance.

33. Margaret Whitford stresses that the problematic nature of the so-called 'masculinity' of philosophy is best characterized by pointing to the mechanisms of exclusion that are being used: "(...) the problem is that conceptions of rationality seem to have been based upon exclusion models" (Whitford, 1988, 111).

Braidotti advocates an ontological basis for sexual difference[34]. She maintains that it is possible that an anti-essentialist attitude is politically correct, but it is short-sighted when it comes to its conceptualisation (Braidotti, 1989, 100)[35].

The body is a major central concept[36]. It is seen as the structure where the biological and the social find a meeting-place; it is the inter-section between the socio-political field of the microphysics of power and the subjective dimension (Braidotti, 1989, 97). The question then becomes:

> "how to rethink the body in terms that are neither biological nor sociological. How to reformulate the bodily roots of subjectivity in such a way as to incorporate the insight of the body as libidinal surface, field of forces, threshold of transcendence" (Braidotti, 1989, 98-99)[37].

34. She realizes that the attempt to go beyond metaphysics has not yet had a decisive outcome (Braidotti, 1989, 93).

35. Alcoff formulates a similar point. She calls it "identity politics": "One's identity is taken (and defined) as a political point of departure, as a motivation for action, and as a delineation of one's politics" (Alcoff, 1988, 431-432). To me her point does not have the acuteness of Braidotti's ontological approach.

36. Riley contends that the body is not constantly a sexed body: "The body becomes visible *as* a body, and *as* a female body, only under some particular gaze -including that of politics" (Riley, 1988, 106). The category of the body is attractive to feminists, says Riley, as it is anchorage ground for sexual difference.

37. Morag Shiach in her comment on Cixous very pointedly expresses what many feminists feel or fear whenever the emphasis on the body as central theme appears: "Writing of the body, we fear appropriation at the point where, historically, we have been most vulnerable, and where we have been so ruthlessly placed" (Shiach, 1989, 155).
Naomi Goldenberg in her critique of the Jungian archetypes comes close to such an inte-grative theory that does not deny mind or body. She claims to offer insights that are not only applicable to Jungian archetypes, but also concern other "disembodied constructs" (Goldenberg, 1985, 55). Goldenberg's main claim against Jungian theory is that it "would have us believe that the contents of our minds -- our ideas, our motivations, and our fantasy images -- are controlled by forces completely divorced from flesh and physicality" (Goldenberg, 1985, 59). She points out that feminist theory has acknowledged and brought to attention the destructiveness of underestimating and repressing the importance of the body. It is damaging towards nature and towards women. As a consequence, feminist theory must be "firmly grounded in an understanding of the body's role in cognition" (Goldenberg, 1985, 61). She suggests that using psychoanalysis -- without closing our eyes to the sexism that pervades it -- is helpful to "think through the body" (Rich, 1976, 21). Goldenberg turns to Freud and outlines how his statement that masturbation and creative thought are inseparably connected (see Freud, Standard Edition, 23:300) shows how in his theory all psychological phenomena are derived from the body. "In Freudian thought, all of our notions, all of our images, all of our fantasies, and all of our ideals have their sources in our bodies" (Goldenberg, 1985, 67). Mental and physical lives cannot be separated but are intimately linked. The human body offers the key to the understanding of human imagination and cognition. Winnicott offers an excellent example of the importance of the body in psychoanalytic theory. He defines psyche as: "the imaginative elaboration of soma-

Braidotti makes a plea for a return to the metaphysical in order to close the false dichotomy between the biological and the political (Braidotti, 1989, 99)[38]. The argument runs as follows:

> "it is historically and politically urgent, in the here and now of the common world of women to bring about and act upon the enunciation of a common epistemological and ethical bond among us: a feminist cogito[39]. 'We' women, the movement of liberation of the 'I' of each and every women (sic), assert the following: 'I, woman, think and therefore I say that I, woman, am'. I am sexed female, my subjectivity is sexed female. As to what my 'self' or my 'I' actually is, that is a whole new question, dealing with identity. The affirmation of my subjectivity need not give a propositional content to my sense of identity: I do not have to define the signifier woman in order to assert it as the speaking subject of my discourse. The speaking 'I' is not neutral or gender-free, but sexed" Braidotti, 1989, 100).

Important in this quote is the emphasis on the commonality of women. 'We, women' is written down without diffidence[40]. Braidotti's 'we, women' does not imply that the mutual differences among women are neglected or enervated. As she already outlined earlier on in the article:

tic parts, feelings, and functions" (quoted in Goldenberg, 1985, 69). A definition that cannot be overlooked when imagery is the subject of study. "Symbols and images are, very simply, bodily feelings perceived pictorially" (Goldenberg, 1985, 69). As a consequence, imaginative work will always be the expression of physical feelings, drives, sentiments, and longings. Imaginative work of men will convey men's physical feelings, drives, sentiments, and longings.

38. Braidotti refers to the works of Luce Irigaray. It at first sight seems to repeat phallocratic thinking. The mimesis she performs is a strategic move, however, and aims at producing difference (see also Rina van der Haegen, 1989).

39. Discussions about a feminist epistemology very often emphasize a political episte- mology. Anne Seller e.g. balances between realism and relativism and hopes to reach a politically adequate epistemology. Her solution is to give the concept of "community of resistance" a central place. Truth cannot be found individually but manifests itself in a process of conversation. "This commitment to engage in conversation to find out what the world is like is a moral or political commitment to a community, to be with a group through growth and change. It involves in me an act of faith, not only of knowledge and politics as process, rather than achievement" (Seller, 1988, 180). Lorraine Code stresses the stories of individuals in the process towards truth (Code, 1988, 187-204).

40. The commonality of women is of major interest in contemporary feminist theory. How can this commonality be expressed without covering up the mutual differences? Riley warns against any discarding and critical analysis of 'Woman' if it is not accompanied by a similar attitude towards 'women' (Riley, 1988, 1). In feminist theology a strong protest has been voiced against the universalizing tendencies of Western, white, bourgeois feminist theologians. See e.g. K.G. Cannon, 1985; L.M. Russell, 1988 who attempt to give shape to these differences.

"Speaking 'as a feminist woman' does not refer to one dogmatic framework but rather to a knot of interrelated questions that play on different layers, registers, and levels of the self" (Braidotti, 1989, 94). Braidotti, however, contends that the sameness of sex of all women is, regardless of all differences, a sufficient and necessary condition to manifest a commonality, or even a bond among women that reaches farther than an ethics of solidarity and rises above a mere sharing of common interests[41]. It is necessary to make this bond explicit, as it is the foundation for potential and different representations of the shared differences of women. Thinking about this as a feminist is an epistemological position (Braidotti, 1989, 94).

Braidotti joins together biological and historical[42] explanations of what or rather who a woman is. These elucidations should not be used as opposites. It is clear that sexual difference is a social construction and is mediated by language, but it is also true that this construction is built around biological evidence.

> "'Being-a-woman', as the result of a construction of femininity in history and language, is to be taking (sic) as the starting point for the assertion of the female as subject. 'We' feminists can therefore adopt the strategy of defining as 'woman' the stock of cumulated knowledge, the theories and representations of the female subject. This is no gratuitous appropriation, for 'I, woman' am affected directly and in my everyday life by what has been made of the subject of woman; I have paid in my very body for all the metaphors and images that our culture has deemed fit to produce of woman. The metaphorization feeds upon my bodily self, in a process of 'metaphysical cannibalism' that feminist theory helps to explain" (Braidotti, 1989, 101).

41. I again refer to the articles of Code and Sellers for a similar line of thought. Riley argues that: "'women' is both synchronically and diachronically erratic as a collectivity, while for the individual, 'being a woman' is also inconstant, and can't provide an ontological foundation. Yet it must be emphasised that these instabilities of the category are the *sine qua non* of feminism, which would otherwise be lost for an object, despoiled of a fight, and, in short, without much life" (Riley, 1988, 2).

42. Riley refuses to make a choice between the position that claims that 'women' cannot be talked about and the position that women are a reality that will be defined by women themselves. She proposes "that 'women' is indeed an unstable category, that this instability has a historical foundation, and that feminism is the site of the systematic fighting-out of that instability -which need not worry us" (Riley, 1988, 5). This is not a dispersion of women's identity into nondescriptness but it is inscribed in and formed by historical discourse. Riley oscillates between the affirmation and the denial of the existence of 'women': "How can it be overlooked that women are a natural as well as a characterised category, and that their distinctive needs and sufferings are all too real?" (Riley, 1988, 3).

All prescriptions and definitions of woman belong to the historical essence of what it means to be a woman[43]. It is 'my' responsibility as woman to change the rules of discourse that have until now been responsible for this historical essence[44]. Braidotti's proposal needs to be readjusted, better specified. Alcoff refers to de Lauretis and her insistence on the inclusion of habits and practices in the construction of meaning (Alcoff, 1988, 431). I contend that Braidotti's notion of 'history' must be read as including habits and practices.

Braidotti gives a foundation, opens up the possibility for 'we, women' to effect changes. This is to be achieved by using sexual difference as a political strategy that gives women as a collective movement the right and the competence to define themselves. She makes an appeal to a 'community' formed by 'we, women', more specifically 'we, women acting as members of a feminist community'.

Recapitulating this chapter, we started with the question how we can conceptualise Mary. After a theoretical survey we proposed seeing Mary as a symbolic image and we concluded that the subject and the context are the crucial hinges in the functioning of images. This guided us to the question: Who or what is the female subject? Is it possible to talk about a female subject? How can you talk about it? To find an answer -- albeit provisionally -- to these questions we turned to the feminist discussion and chose the project of Rosi Braidotti, who makes a plea for a political use of ontological difference. She draws on the idea of a 'community of feminist women', the political movement of women that aspires to the liberation of the ego of every woman as epistemological centre.

4. Conclusion

At the end of this chapter, we have come to a point where several stepping stones meet. It is necessary to relate these stepping stones to Mary. We started with the idea of interpreting Mary as a symbolic image. In order to understand what this means, two authors were found helpful:

43. Riley rejects a history of ideas of women because it diminishes the full historicity of 'women'. 'Men' and 'women' are interwoven with a multitude of other concepts. The histories and historicity of those concepts need to be faced as well.

44. It is obvious that 'experience', one of the favourite topics of feminist theory, will play an important role. "Experience should have a role -the virtue of feminist philosophy, of women's philosophy, is not only in bringing the experiences of a group previously only dimly heard, or hazily interpreted through centuries of male bias, but in emphasising the whole idea of the need for experience in the first place. *But it must be treated carefully*" (Boddington, 1988, 220, my emphasis).

Paul Ricoeur and Rosi Braidotti. If we understand symbol in the way Ricoeur has explained, we see that the commonsense understanding of symbol as 'something standing for something else' is too simple. This implies that we cannot simply say that Mary stands for something else. In Ricoeurian terms a symbol is the movement from the primary meaning to the latent meaning. It is the process going from Mary, present in the Christian tradition, to a latent meaning that can never be expressed in absolute or definite terms. This is an ongoing process in which we become assimilated without ever being able to grasp the 'similarity'. The symbol unites the linguistic and the non-linguistic. In our discourse about Mary that about which we cannot speak is also present. The symbol is both rooted in materiality and is elusive. Mary is a historical woman, but a historical person that we know nothing about. All accounts about Mary are interpretations. The New Testament stories are interpretations about Jesus in which Mary is present in as far as she illuminates the stories about Jesus. Still, this unknown historical woman has given rise to a multitude of interpretations. Symbols are, according to Ricoeur, contingent. This seems to be illustrated by the almost total absence of Mary in Protestantism. Mary does not necessarily have to take a prominent position in Christianity.

At this point we can clearly see some of the problems Ricoeur has tried to solve in his later work. We are immediately confronted with the question about which Mary we must start from: a medieval Mary, the New Testament Mary, a Roman Catholic Mary, or a Greek Orthodox Mary. Can we talk about Mary as a symbol that has received and takes one interpretation? How does the ongoing interpretative activity take place? What are its boundaries? Can we see Mary separate from the context in which she is interpreted?

Ricoeur answers these questions by pointing out that, contrary to his own earlier approach, symbols cannot be seen as isolated facets of existence. He insists on situating them among the materials of interpretative existence. Understanding oneself is interpreting signs, symbols, and texts. A symbol is not any longer defined as merely the movement from the manifest to the latent meaning, but also as deriving its significance from the context in which it is situated. This explains the sometimes contradictory interpretations of a symbol. It means that we have to look at Mary-as-symbol as one of the building-bricks of a three-layered world in which experiences are mediated linguistically (signs), symbolically, and textually. It is impossible to fix one ultimate interpretation of Mary, as this functions within a context. Different and conflicting interpretations are possible because of the different contexts. This gives us a clue about the wide range of interpretations we have encountered in the first chapter where we saw that Mary could be the Goddess, redeemed humanity, part of political speculations and explanations, or myth, or still something else.

Our being in the world is an interpreting existence -- still according to Ricoeur. The interpretative activity has a mimetic structure. In a synthesising act the existing, present social field and the representational reception are carried to another level. Mary seen as symbol is set in a wider context, a story, that is there to be interpreted. The interpreting subject understanding her/himself confronting the story -- and we will have to determine in what story Mary is active -- is propelled towards another self, conditioned by the story. In interpreting the story new conjunctions are made that open up another level of reality.

In using the concept of symbolic imagination emphasis is laid on the aspect of imaginative action. The term 'image' carries a suggestion of evocative power. This power is contained in the verb to imagine and the activity of imagination. It refers to a space, moment, or state of 'trying-out'. It is a moment of testing without immediate feedback from the world. Mary conceived of as symbolic imagination seems to guide us towards a Mary who offers a space of (limited) freewheeling. All this means that whatever is said about Mary need not immediately have limiting normative implications. The concept of symbolic imagination provides the opportunity for exploration of possibilities and boundaries.

Ricoeur's interpreting subject is qualified by Braidotti. There is an *essential* difference if the interpreting subject is female or male. Making an appeal for a politics of ontological difference, she posits the female subject in order to underpin feminist claims. This subject is a bio-cultural entity, establishing a commonality among women. The sameness of the sex of all women is the foundation of any expression of differences among women. 'Woman' is "the stock of cumulated knowledge, the theories and representations of the female subject" (Braidotti, 1989, 101). This definition is a strategy of 'we', feminists. The interpreting subject that in Ricoeur's elaborations still was a formless subject, has now been specified as a female subject. This has several consequences: the reader, who at the level of mimesis three forms the nexus of the interpretative process, is not any reader but a female reader. We cannot parenthesise the sex of the reader, this is what we have to conclude from Braidotti. We even have to make use of sex as foundation for feminist claims.

We must look at how the terms in which any story is -- the level of mimesis I -- told are possibly different[45] for women and men. A careful analysis of the pre-knowledge is necessary because we cannot uncondi-

---

45. In the following paragraph, the word 'different' will be repeated ad nauseam. The term cannot be avoided as it is the key-word.

tionally start from the principle that there is one world of pre-comprehension, similar for both women and men. Mary has been contributing to the definition of 'woman'. This implies that the pre-comprehensive world in which Mary is embedded incorporates this 'woman'-defining aspect, an aspect that has different implications for women and men. This example clearly shows that symbols have no ethical neutrality, as Ricoeur explained. We need, however, to move one step further: the normativity introduced by symbols cannot be regarded as being the same for women and for men.

The activity of imagination as part of the mimetic undertaking (the mediation from mimesis II, sedimentation and innovation to mimesis III) enables us to understand how changes in the rules of discourse about how woman is defined can take place. This was an aspect of Braidotti's theory that left us in the dark: how can women change the rules of discourse? If we turn to the Ricoeurian hermeneutic circle we encounter, within the work of appropriating tradition, a moment of active synthesising that has been preceded -- not in time but structurally -- by a moment of imagination that enables innovation. This explains why and how change is possible.

Mary as an element of the definition of 'woman' must be analysed. Mary conceived of as symbolic imagination can bring about changes in this definition. In the next chapters, an attempt will be made to apply the theoretical and systematic conclusions of this chapter. This implies an analysis of the preliminaries of my specific field of research. The next chapter, therefore, will give an analysis of Mary in the nineteenth century in Flanders.

Chapter 3

Mary: A Nineteenth Century Heritage

Introduction

Taking the Ricoeurian scheme seriously and applying it to Mary demands an analysis of the history of Mary and its influence today. 'An analysis of the history of Mary and its influence today' is obviously a task that cannot be fulfilled. Offering an historical overview of Marian history and imagery is not the aim of the Ricoeurian paradigm. What we are asked to do is to disentangle the constitutive elements of our present-day existence in which religious symbols have a specific place. In this chapter I will focus on the constitutive elements in our speaking about Mary today at the end of the twentieth century in a secularized Western European context. In other words: I will take a close-up picture of the elements and mechanisms that determine the ways in which we express Mary today. Along the way it will become clear that our focus will have to become more precise and specific: I have chosen to zoom in on my own background. It consists of post-Vatican-II Roman-Catholicism, Belgium, and women's studies. These three elements are the framework of this chapter. I will move from a more general sketch to the Belgian situation. This chapter does not claim to fulfil all conditions a historical analysis must satisfy. Its aims are setting out certain lines that determine our ideas about Mary today.

The key to understanding Mary in a post-Vatican-II Roman-Catholic context lies in the nineteenth century. Mary is like a patchwork quilt: who or what she is, is a combination of images. Every century and age added another patch of cloth to the quilt. I contend that in the nineteenth century and the first half of the twentieth century, the quilt was completed. The fact that papal reluctance towards Marian maximalism had finally been overcome in the nineteenth century speeded up the finishing of the quilt. Looking at the nineteenth century means observing the completion of the Marian quilt. To say it in the words of M. Carroll:

> "From the perspective of say, 1960, an adherent of the Mary cult
> could easily have argued that the preceding century and a half had
> been a period of great advance in Marian devotion. The nineteenth
> century had witnessed three of the best-known of all Marian
> apparitions -those at Paris, La Salette, and Lourdes- and all three
> have given rise to important devotional practices. Then too, after
> nearly a thousand years of theological debate, the Church had
> finally committed itself irrevocably to a belief in Mary's Immaculate
> Conception by proclaiming that belief a dogma in 1854. The
> intensity of Marian devotion could also be seen in the fact that
> virtually every one of the several dozen new religious orders for
> women founded during the nineteenth century was dedicated to the

90

Virgin Mary. This upsurge in Marian devotion intensified in the twentieth century, (...)" (Carroll, 1986, 219).

The depiction of Mary has known a similar evolution:

"In the nineteenth century a strange development took place: there was a lack of tradition in religious art and for this very reason specialists in religious art came to the fore. They accepted a self-made canon and created types of Christ and Mary that continued to exist *until the Council*"[1](Schoonbaert, 1986, 17 -my emphasis and transl.).

More in general we can affirm what Michaud says about the nineteenth century and its relevance for today, especially for the image of women we have today:

"Par bien des racines, nous tenons encore à lui (i.e. nineteenth century, E.M.), quand ce ne serait que par ce simple fait que le temps de l'idéalisation de la femme est loin d'être véritablement résolu" (Michaud, 1985, 234).

Attacks against the Mary imagery are in the first place, though not always consciously, directed against this heritage. W. Beinert is firm about the importance of nineteenth century marianism for the understanding of contemporary feminist theology and its preoccupation with Mary:

"Die nähere Sichtung des Materials zeigt freilich, dass die Feministische Theologie und deren Mariologie historisch nicht zu lösen ist von der Mariologie des 19. Jahrhunderts, vor allem nicht der Romantik" (Beinert, 1988, 11).

My approach to the nineteenth century is not confined to the idea that it forms a closed entity, uninfluenced by previous centuries -- many of the examples given in this chapter do not exclusively belong to the nineteenth century. Nineteenth century Mariology and Marian devotion were moulded by the past. E. Henau (Danneels, 1988, 29-50) describes the image that the twentieth century has inherited, as an image of Mary that has been structured especially by the Counter-Reformation and its continuous influence on theology, piety and the dialogue -- or rather very often non-communication -- between the churches. This period can be

---

1. " Er ontwikkelde zich in de negentiende eeuw een zeer eigenaardig fenomeen: men miste elke traditie op het gebied van de religieuze kunst en precies daardoor ontstonden specialisten in religieuze kunst. Ze volgden een soort canon van eigen makelij en schiepen Christus- en Mariatypen die *voortleefden tot aan het Concilie*"

characterised as the era in which Mary was the distinguishing mark of Roman Catholics and in which Mary reached the same altitude as her son, or even sometimes rose above him.

The second half of the twentieth century can be characterised as an unravelling of the Marian quilt. Two possibilities remain open: the patchwork can start again, with the same patches but set in a different pattern, or a completely new patchwork can be set up with new pieces of cloth. In order to be able to make a decision, it is necessary to gain knowledge about the old quilt. I have chosen to look at the almost completed quilt we encounter in the nineteenth century, it is the quilt we are dealing with today.

I will stop at the beginning of the twentieth century, even though Marian maximalism expanded and culminated in another Marian dogma in 1950. I will not go into detail about this period as it is a continuation of the process started in the nineteenth century. New apparitions are at the centre of attention -- in Belgium we have the apparitions at Beauraing (1932-1933) and Banneux (1933) -- and another dogma is being prepared, voices are raised to make Mary's intercessory function a dogma. Generally speaking these events and movements are variations on the theme that was sounded in the previous century.

In sum, the reasons for turning to the nineteenth century are threefold: first of all I want to take a closer look at the mechanisms that structure Marian devotion. This can only be done if one turns to a specific time and area. Secondly, the nineteenth century remains problematic for feminist theology. Even more, the feminisation of the nineteenth century creates fields of concern for contemporary feminism. Thirdly, the quilting comes to a close in the nineteenth century.

The controversial position of Mary in recent feminist theological discussion asks for a closer look at the roots of the inherited image of Mary which people of the twentieth century are carrying with them. I contend that the protest against an oppressive image of Mary cannot be understood as long as it is not sketched against the background of the image of Mary that feminist authors have lived with. The claim of those authors to re-image Mary seems to be answered with an overly-intellectual response: the authors we encountered in the first chapter sense the discontent with contemporaneous Mary-babble and now try to provide an answer to this dissatisfaction. The question is whether their answers sufficiently reflect women's daily experiences. There is an important difference between what one knows and what one lives. As Nelle Morton wrote: "Those who respond with 'But I don't think of God as male!' are immediately putting the issue in the wrong place -- on the level of reason rather than on the level of alive imagery" (Morton, 1985, 151), we can mutatis mutandis say that those who 'know' that Mary has known a long history and therefore seem to be able to offer an appropriate answer to the questions about the place of Mary in women's lives today, overlook the active influence of recent Marian imagery on their own and those women's responses. Knowing that Mary has been given little space in the Bible does not change one's response to the overwhelming presence of Mary in Roman Catholicism.

We must be suspicious of broad historical overviews of the evolution in Marian depiction and imagery. These overviews provide us with a sense of relief as we see that Mary is an object of change and that seems to give us the liberty for transformation. This however is an intellectual response that does not take into account our response to "the level of alive imagery" (N. Morton). Furthermore, this attitude overlooks the fact that most twentieth century Western Catholics do not possess this information but mainly continue on the road paved by nineteenth century Catholics, or, maybe partly due to the lack of this information, simply reject what they see around them.

I will first of all sketch a picture of nineteenth-century Europe, and more particularly of Roman Catholic Belgium. I will try to provide the reader with some clues so that she can -- with some help of her imagination -- get a feeling of what being a Catholic in the nineteenth century meant. I will narrow my focus to Belgium, a newly constructed state that was predominantly Roman Catholic. This new country was the first to have a liberal constitution and Rome watched the country sharply. The small country absorbed a great amount of Marian devotional literature. The advantage of describing the Belgian situation is that until now it has attracted little attention in regard with Marian devotion. Most authors focus on France as some of the most important apparitions happened there. As Pope shows in her article politics made great play of those apparitions. The reception of the French apparitions in Belgium is less complicated as the political factor is less dominant. The apparitions are received more as religious happenings.

I will not only narrow my focus geographically, I will also limit the sources I am going to refer to. I will tell something about the approach of the theologians of Mary as it is laid down in Mariology, this by way of information. It shows the state of affairs surrounding theological reflection about Mary. My main sources however are the popular literature and, as its counterpart, the popular prints of Mary. It was these popular devotional books about Mary that informed the lives of nineteenth century people. The stories about Mary, the manuals for the children of Mary convey to us the message that these people received. What theologians said and wrote can hardly be considered to be what people listened to or read. The products of theologians were, and often are, shared with other theologians. "Attempting to explain religious phenomena by theological ideas is a category error that has been , repeatedly committed by historians and historical theologians (Miles, 1988, 6).

1. The European Catholic World in the Nineteenth Century

1.1. General climate

Apart from a few exceptions, the nineteenth century can be characterised as a period of little original Catholic intellectual labour and of great attention to devotional practices. Everywhere in Europe attempts are made to establish a reasonable co-existence between Church and State. A high wall is built between lay civil society and the ecclesiastical world. The same movement is noticeable on the intellectual level: the Catholic intelligentsia shows solipsistic tendencies. It is mainly concerned with its own everlasting and eternally true system. Its energy is reserved for the defence and the transference of this body of rules of faith (see de Bentier de Sauvigny, 1965, 166 ff.). Laurentin evaluates the nineteenth century as follows:

> "Tout le drame religieux du XIXe siècle est là. C'est une époque où une piété ardente et profonde se nourrit d'une littérature frelatée et d'un art déplorable" (Laurentin, 1968, 87).

A similar evaluation can be given of Marian iconography. In his book *Iconographie mariale* (Clément, 1908) Clément describes the evolution of nineteen centuries of Marian iconography. Arriving at modern times, he entitles the nineteenth and twentieth century as "'Copiage' et industrialisme", copying and industrialism. He says that a wondrous activity of magnificent Marian depiction might have been expected considering the great examples that nineteenth century artists had before them, and keeping in mind all the wondrous Marian events in the nineteenth century. But nothing of the kind happened. The connection between Mary and artistic activity established itself at a disastrous level. "Industrialism" was the call of the day and art could not avoid its influence. Classical and romantic artists only painted what they were asked to paint, any religious notion remained absent. The result was either the copying of the old, or a completely earth-bound presentation. A negative evaluation of nineteenth century religious art is not exceptional: M. Denis wonders how it is possible that the vivid spirituality of the nineteenth century could have produced such banal art. An interesting observation was made also by P. Claudel:

"c'est le divorce, dont le siècle passé a vu la douloureuse consommation entre les propositions de la Foi et ces puissances d'imagination et de sensibilité qui sont éminemment celles de l'artiste" (Schoonbaert, 1986, 16).

Several devotions flourish, for instance the Holy Heart of Jesus, the Eucharist, Mary, etc. In handbooks of Church history the evolution of the nineteenth century is usually described as an evolution towards a more emotional religious life[2]. External piety becomes normal (Jedin, 1962, 662-670). Part of it can be understood as a reaction against eighteenth century rationalism. Nédoncelle, a not unbiased twentieth century chronicler, describes the rationalist eighteenth century as an epoch of ongoing indifference to humanity and to the inner and transcendental universe. Human society is proclaimed divine and men's ultimate future is to be found on earth, an earth that will be reduced to a mechanical paradise. Religion will be superseded by ratio and the state; priests will be replaced by moralists and civil functionaries (Nédoncelles, 1936, 10). The romantic inhabitant of the nineteenth century tried to create a safe and secure Catholic society[3]. The model for such a society was found in the Middle Ages. The Middle Ages were presented as a homogeneous ideal society that was a religious paradise (Jedin, 1962; de Mayer, 1988, Raedts, 1990[4]). The nineteenth century ought to follow this medieval example. Marian devotion also reverts to the Middle Ages. In general we see here a search for motherly cosiness and security in an era of unworldly *Insellillusion* (Jedin, vib, 1962 265-315). The nineteenth century thus seemed to become a period of revaluation of the so-called soft values. The words of Lacordaire seem to underline this:

"Il y a sur la terre trois faiblesses, dit le P. Lacordaire, la faiblesse du dénuement, c'est le pauvre; la faiblesse du sexe, c'est la femme; la faiblesse de l'âge, c'est l'enfant. Ces trois faiblesses sont la force de l'église, qui a fait alliance avec elles et les a prises sous sa protection en se mettant sous la leur. Cette alliance a changé la face de la société, parce que jusque-là le faible avait été sacrifié au fort, le pauvre au riche, la femme à l'homme, l'enfant à tous" (Conférences de N.D. de Paris, année 1844, Paris, éd. 1907, 329, quoted in Nédoncelle, 1936, 104-105).

---

2. In 4.1. Women's Studies and the Nineteenth Century we will see that we could also call this an evolution towards a more feminine religious life.

3. Schoonbaert also situates the 'spiritual renouveau' in the middle of the nineteenth century against the background of a reaction against rationalism (Schoonbaert, 1986, 16).

4. Further on I will return to the position of the neo-gothic style.

Nineteenth century religiosity is focused on external reality: internal impulses must be translated into action. This ranges from good works (caritas, cornerstone of nineteenth century Catholicism, see Demolder, 1984, 125-136[5]) to exuberant devotions that take shape in pilgrimages, processions, etc.

> "Ce siècle bourgeois, individualiste et positif a compris mieux que beaucoup d'autres l'influence que peut avoir une âme chrétienne lorsqu'elle a découvert ses responsabilités dans le salut du monde, et jamais époque ne vit pareille floraison d'âmes ou d'instituts se vouant à l'apostolat du sacrifice" (Aubert, 1952, 465).

This externalisation furthers a Catholic réveil. Demolder's thesis is that at the same time the religious object changed. Not the 'infinite', or the 'absolute' was the goal. The attention was directed at intermediary objects that mediate the transcendent (Demolder, 1984, 133). Marian devotion in the nineteenth century must be understood from this background. It is not a single event but it is part of a wider set of behaviour and suppositions. It is important to realise that devotion to Mary existed together with manifold other devotions.

1.2. Marian apparitions

An important influence in nineteenth century Catholic society came from the apparitions of Mary. I do not want to immerse myself into the abundant literature that has been produced about apparitions. My only aim in mentioning these apparitions is to give an idea of the world in which the nineteenth century faithful lived. It was a world in which people were apt to accept apparitions as possible means of God's presence in the world and in which the Church was ready to confirm these apparitions.

RUE DU BAC

In 1830 Mary appeared three times (between July 1830 and January 1831) to a simple nun, Catherine Labouré (age 24), in 140 Rue du Bac in Paris. Labouré lived in the convent of the Sisters of Charity of St. Vincent de

---

5. In this article, Demolder tries to explain the nineteenth century religiosity. He sees the concept of caritas as central. Caritas is "an inner impulse that wants to be immediately exteriorised in good works" (Demolder, 1984, 125 -my transl.). His hypothesis is that the motives for this Catholic caritas can be explained as a combination of two factors: 1. it is an engagement in, and strategy to enter, nineteenth century civil society. As such it finds access to the humanistic ethics. 2. caritas is a typical exponent of nineteenth century religious feeling. This religiosity is a product of the remains of romanticism and of the loss of spiritual traditions. Nineteenth century spirituality is caught in the web of ascetical-moralistic ideals and exteriorization.

Paul where she had recently entered the novitiate. The Lady of the Rue du Bac has become known as the Virgin of the Miraculous Medal. When she first appeared to Catherine (July 18), she warned her that France would be endangered: the cross would be treated with contempt and blood would flow. This was a very political message[6]. Later apparitions (Nov. 27, and at least five more times until Jan. 1831) had a more religious character[7]. The Virgin appeared within an oval, standing on a globe. Her feet trod on a snake, which represented Satan. She was dressed in white with a blue mantle. Her arms were extended downward and out. From them radiated rays that symbolised the graces the Virgin would grant her devotees. Around the top of the oval ran the words "O Mary conceived without sin, pray for us who have recourse to thee". The vision asked that a medal be struck in this image[8].

A medal was minted from 1832 on and since then it has known enormous popularity[9]. This presentation of Mary became the norm: this was the way to depict the Immaculate Conception, this was the way Mary had ordered it herself.

LA SALETTE

In La Salette Mary appeared to two shepherds, Mélanie Mathieu Calvat[10] and Maximin Giraud. The fourteen year old girl and the eleven year old boy saw the vision on September 19 1846. They saw a weeping Lady who spoke to them. She first addressed them in French, then in patois. She summoned them to warn the people to stop blaspheming, to pray regularly and to attend mass. If not, famine and crop failures would strike them. She told them she had suffered for the sins of the world, but that she could no longer hold up the arm of her Son, which would fall on them in punishment. Then she told each child a secret. She asked them to pass on her message to everybody. The woman was seated, with her elbows on her knees, and her face in her hands. When the frightened children wanted to attack her, she rose and folded her arms across her

6. This message has been interpreted to predict the French revolutions of 1830, 1848, and 1871.

7. The first vision did not present the lady of the miraculous medal, but a seated lady whom Catherine at first seems to have considered to be St. Anne.

8. See R. Laurentin, *Catherine Labouré. Documents*, 2 vols., Paris, Lethielleux, 1976-1978; Id., *Vie de Catherine Labouré*, 2 vols., Paris, DDB, 1980.

9. Labouré's identity remained secret until 1876. It also must be noted that the medal did not exactly fit the description of Labouré. Labouré's vision also held a golden ball with a small golden cross.

10. Carroll (1986) mixes up the names on p. 149 as he mentions "Melanie and Mathieu". On the next pages he correctly names Maximin.

breast. She was dressed in white and gold and she wore a crown encircled with roses. Round her neck she wore a crucifix, a hammer and pincers. Throughout the encounter the Lady continued to weep.

LOURDES[11]

On February 11 1858, Bernadette Soubirous, fourteen years old and coming from a poor family, was gathering wood with her sister and a friend. In the grotto of Massabielle near the Gave she saw a Lady. She told her companions what she had seen. News of the event inevitably spread and soon hundreds of people attended at the grotto. In the next five months (until July 16, 1858), Bernadette, accompanied by a multitude of people, saw her vision another seventeen times. The Lady spoke eleven times. The Aquero, 'that' or 'her' as Bernadette called her, was beautiful, simple, young, wearing a white robe and veil and a blue sash. She had two gold roses on her bare feet, and carried a rosary. Bernadette described the Lady as being about her own age and height. The Lady identified herself as "the Immaculate Conception", "Que soy er Immaculada Concepciou", on March 25, the feast of the Annunciation. She called for repentance.

PONTMAIN

In 1871 five peasant children said that they had seen a smiling Virgin on a starry night (January 17) in north-western France. The Lady was standing in an oval and wore a deep blue robe covered with golden stars. On her head she wore a black veil and a golden crown, in her hands she carried a crucifix. A message was written beneath her feet: "But pray my children. God will answer you soon. My son permits himself to be moved" - "Mais priez mes enfants. Dieu vous exaucera en peu de temps. Mon fils se laisse toucher".

1.3. Ineffabilis Deus

The dogma of the Immaculate Conception, proclaimed on December 8 1854, has been extremely influential. The idea of the Immaculate Conception has known a long history and gave rise to many debates. The proclamation of the dogma apparently put an end to the uncertainty surrounding this question. Furthermore, it tried to reconcile theology and devotion. The dogma did not only have a theological aim, but it also served a political goal.

---

11. For an extended account of what happened, see Estrade (1899).

The way for the dogma was prepared by the study of Giovanni Perrone, Jesuit and professor at the University of Rome, who devoted a book (1847) to the question whether the Immaculate Conception could be defined in the form of a dogma. His point is that even though scripture does not furnish grounds for the Immaculate Conception, neither does it contradict it. The dogmatic definition could not be stopped. The initiative was now rested with Pope Pius IX, a faithful devotee of Mary. On the first of June, 1848, he installed a committee of nineteen theologians to investigate the possibility of formulating the dogma. In 1852, they produced a document in three volumes. Even though in November 1848, the Pope had been forced to flee from Rome, this did not prevent him from installing another committee, composed of cardinals, that was to further investigate the possibility of formulating the dogma. On February 2, 1849, the Pope sent out a letter, *Ubi Primum*, that asked the bishops to give their opinion about the dogma in question. Of the 603 bishops 546 gave a positive answer. Perrone was mandated to write a draft for the dogma. A new committee was empanelled on the tenth of May 1852. Their recommendations, written in a *Breve esposizione*, became the basis for the dogma. On 8 December 1854 the dogma was ceremonially proclaimed (Söll, 1984, 209-213, useful background information can be found in Martina, 1986, 261-286).

New about this dogma is that it is not a reaction to a form of heresy, but that it arises from the dynamics of faith of Roman Catholicism itself (Söll, 1984, 217). An appeal was made to the 'Factum Ecclesiae'. This concept implies that "die Begründung eines Dogmas mitsamt den Schrift- und Väterbeweisen erhält ihre Kraft in erster Linie aus der Tradition, Lehre und Praxis der gegenwärtige Kirche" (Söll, 1971, 214). This appeal is only theologically possible if it starts from the principle that the Spirit will not lead the faithful into error.

The dogma says that Mary was saved from original sin, from the first moment of her existence. Her life started with the grace of justification. Traditionally, original sin is the situation into which every human being is born. Augustine's idea that original sin is transmitted because children are procreated in concupiscence was a barrier to the idea of the Immaculate Conception as only Jesus could have been without sin through his Virgin Origin (Schoonenberg, 1962, 129-130).

The political background of the dogma is that the Catholic Church was desperately fighting against 'modern errors'. Already from 1849 on, the *Syllabus Errorum* that was to name the errors of modern time, was being prepared (Martina, 1986, 287-356). It seemed a good idea to connect the condemnation of the modern errors to the dogma of the Immaculate Conception. This dogma could serve as an antidote for modern rationalism, stepping stone of nineteenth century socialism. The dogma contradicted a boundless confidence in human nature in confirming the universality of the Original Sin. Rationalism is unacceptable, and the rejection of the supernatural must be condemned. The Pope decided in June 1853 to disconnect the dogma of the Immaculate Conception from the condemnation of the modern errors. The *Syllabus Errorum* was released on the eight of December (feast-day of the Immaculate Conception) of 1864 after extremely long preliminary investigations and consultations (Kenis, 1989, 458-493; about the reaction of the Belgian bishops see Aubert, 1955, 63-99).

2. Mary in Devotional Literature

Introduction

The nineteenth century is flooded with publications about Mary. Quantity and quality here do not go hand in hand[12]. Devotional literature is an important source of knowledge about popular reflections about Mary. We here find the ideas that were transmitted to the faithful community. The bibliography of nineteenth century publications from 1823 to 1913 contains the works I have used to extract the most important characteristics ascribed to Mary. Many more titles could be added to this list. Most books are, however, merely reiterative. I gathered the results under several headings: 1. Mary's virtues; 2. How to follow Mary; 3. Mary and the Trinity; 4. Mary and women; 5. Titles; 6. Mary's power.

2.1. Mary's virtues

Virtues are ascribed to Mary in enormous number. I will not pay attention to the frequency with which the virtues appeared in the texts, but will concentrate on the variety that was found.
Mary has a lively faith and she is obedient. Her entire being is devoted to God. Absolute fidelity and complete surrender to God are the high standards she meets. Pleasing God is her guiding principle. She knows a depth of meekness that is found in no one else. This is most praiseworthy as meekness is the greatest virtue of all. It is the foundation of all virtues. The purity of her opinions and the magnanimity of her love should be praised. Her abundant love embraces all people. It is founded on self-

---

12. "..., à partir de 1850 on assiste à une production littéraire abondante et généralement *de qualité*" (Rayez, 1977, 470). This is the one and only positive appreciative comment I have encountered about nineteenth century Marian 'theological' literature.

denial, compassion, and patience. Tenderness inspires her charity, which opposes Christ's justice. Mary's behaviour is characterised by mercifulness, amiability, and softness. Her opinions are pure and holy, she is very careful in her advice, and she is extremely modest. She is vigilant, and she never offends anybody. Her ideal was to be good to everybody, to honour old age, and never to envy her equals. She never disappointed her parents nor did she look down on those that are usually despised. She neither despised the weak nor did she denounce the poor. Nothing reprehensible could be found in her conduct, in her attitude, in her language, in her gaze, nor in whatever she did. She loved solitude and shunned the worldly-minded. She was simple and chaste, a Virgin in body and soul.

In short: Mary loved virtue, she did everything in honour of God, and she always acted in accordance with Jesus' teachings. She excelled in everything she did or was: in faith, hope, love, piety, modesty, godliness, solitude, purity, and holiness.

2.2. How to follow Mary?

A child of Mary must know that she is not on this earth to enjoy food and drink, beautiful clothes, pretty and useful needlework, honour or wealth, but to honour and serve God. The imitation of Mary can find expression in prayer and in a chaste life. A chaste life means showing self-restraint, even in regard to permissible pleasures and permissible pleasure resorts. One needs to guard against a lust for reading and dancing. Prayer and religious practice, confessions and eucharist will be the keywords in a life of imitation of Mary. Chastity will be the source of all happiness in life and death (Kerbosch, 1893).

Salvation is connected with love of God and love of one's neighbour; forgiveness; devotion; prayer; communion; the eucharist; purity; work; obedience; the apostolate; vocation; the Church and devotion to Mary. This last element will guarantee that one obtains from God what one is asking for (van Volkxem, 1903). "être pure" is one of the most cherished ideals (Le plus précieux trésor, 1906). "Let Mary govern your life. Let her lead you to Jesus! She wants only one thing: the glory of her son and your happiness"[13] (Bartels, 1908).

The day of a child of Mary runs as follows: 1. get up at a regular hour; 2. the first act of the day is to make the sign of the cross, the first thought of the day must be to offer one's heart to Jesus and Mary, the first words ought to be "Jesus, Mary, Joseph"; 3. dress modestly, and while doing so preferably have pious thoughts; 4. next kneel and pray, thinking

---

13. "Laat derhalve Maria uw leven besturen. Laat haar u tot Jezus voeren! Zij wil slechts ééne zaak: de glorie van haren zoon en uw geluk!"

about the difficulties the day will bring; 5. try to find a good moment for meditation; 6. when leaving the house, make the sign of the cross; 7. try to go to mass as often as possible; 8. say the Angelus three times a day; 9. read a short spiritual text; 10. have some pious thoughts during the day; 11. at the end of the day: say your prayers kneeling down and examine your conscience; 12. go to sleep at a regular hour (Manuel, 1868,19-20).

In one sentence: think about Mary all the time, in everything you do (Anriemma, 1890).

2.3. Mary and the Trinity

"Salut, ô vous que Dieu, dans ses décrets éternels, choisit pour amante et pour mère!"(Victor d'Anglais, 1836, 7). Mary is daughter of God the Father, mother of God the Son, and bride of God the Holy Spirit. The key to everything is Jesus Christ, he is beginning and end of creation. Mary, together with Jesus Christ, reigns over all that is created. Jesus and Mary are inseparably united in the Father's plans: Jesus could only become son of humanity through Mary. The heavenly Father, Christ and Mary cooperated to fulfil divine salvation. Jesus and Mary are one and the same flesh, one and the same spirit, one and the same love. The Holy Virgin is intimately connected with the Holy Trinity. Mary is daughter and bride of the Father, daughter in a natural way, bride on the spiritual level. She is the mother of the Son, and the temple of the Holy Spirit. After Christ, she is the one who is most close to God. The difference between Christ and Mary is the nature of this intimacy. In Christ this is a personal unity. God is in Mary and, in a certain way, makes her participate in the progeniture of the Son. The grace offered to Mary is the example and the warrant of the grace offered to the angels, to humanity and to all creatures. Mary's soul is the perfect example for all pure spirits, her body typifies what our bodies ought to look like.

As the light of the moon depends on the light of the sun, so Mary depends upon Jesus. "She is clothed with the sun" (de Ségur, 1868, 55). The sun is the Creator with his gifts of grace. In creating the earth God wanted to depict Mary. From the beginning, God intended to portray Mary and Jesus in this creation (de Ségur, 1868).

Mary is in nature a daughter of Adam and Eve, but in grace she is daughter and bride of God (de Ségur, 1868, 88). It was her Son who created Mary. "De même que Dieu l'avait engendré de sa propre substance, Marie le conçut et le forma de son sang le plus pur[14]. Elle est

---

14. This reflects the ancient idea that the child was formed from the menstruational blood of the mother.

par privilege, à l'égard du Verbe Incarné, ce que le Père éternel est, par nature, à l'égard de ce même Verbe!" (Coppin, 1891, 85-86).

Through Mary grace has reached us, it is she who conceived Jesus. She is lofty in heaven, above the angels and the saints, very near the Trinity. In heaven she reigns as a queen. Jesus is father and Mary is mother (Manuel, 1894, 300). There is holy identity and mutual accordance between the holy Hearts of Jesus and Mary: on earth they are united in tender love, generous diligence, pain and woe, in heaven they are united in happiness and magnificence (*Handboek*, 1898, 242). Mary is characterised as co-redemptrix and co-adjutrix.

No greater triumph, after that of the Son, than the Assumption of Mary. In heaven a throne has been prepared for Mary on the right-hand side of her Son. She owes this place to her titles of Co-redemptrix, Queen of Angels and men, and Mother of God. God, the Father crowns Mary with power, linking her with her son's power; God, the Son crowns her with science and wisdom; the Holy Spirit crowns her with charity. The Trinity also honours Mary as Virgin, martyr, and doctor (Catherin, 1902, 352-354). Mary's influence on the heart of her son is without limit (Id., 359). "Le ciel, voilà le but de vos efforts, le terme de toutes vos aspirations. D'ailleurs le ciel est votre patrimoine, puisque votre mère en est la reine." (Id., 359). Mary opens the way to heaven for all the faithful and she also offers her power to intercede (Id., 359).

"God is a good Father, but he wants everything or nothing" (E. Faguette, 1902, 15). It is very difficult to reach God, the Virgin Mary is much more open, she can be intercessor (Ibid.). Devotion to Mary is one of the guarantees of obtaining from God what one wants (van Volkxem, 1903). Mary, like Jesus, conquers, rules, orders (Daems, 1904). "Marie est la réconciliatrice de Dieu et des hommes, en donnant au monde le Prince de la Paix" (D'Hoop, 1907).

2.4. Mary and women

> The highest plane of honour
> Ever achieved by woman
> is your lowest plane,
> So deep below are they:
> From the beginning of the world,
> Yes until the last day
> Not one of them can reach your
> glory or praise

(verse of a song in *Het nieuw Scherpenheuvels trompetjen*, 1835, my translation[15])
Concerning chastity:

> "Many christian virgins speak often, and without fear, to persons who are no angels. If they claim to be on the alert while doing so, I will answer that the devil is also on the alert to corrupt them. A virgin, who loves praise, will not be indifferent to those who praise her. In this matter of purity there is much to be feared; for the very reason that one does not fear enough. One not to love the dangers that one loves, and that one loves them is shown by the care taken to conceal them to oneself. (...) (*Navolging*, 1893, 37 my transl.)[16].

De lof van Maria, 1855, 15 ff. praises Mary and tries to bring the people to Mary. The way to get to know Mary is to think about everything that is praiseworthy in woman. Every perfection is found in Mary, and no woman can compete with her. She exceeds every woman in divine and moral virtue. Mary is praised because of her virginity, her fertility, and her chastity. No woman, may she be good and chaste, wise and virtuous, can ever be equal to Mary. Next to Mary, every woman looks imperfect[17].

> "Tell me, young daughter, do you follow Mary? Mary who was not able to sin, and who did not have to fear anything in the world, she fled from it, and feared to act in it; but you, who are so inconstant, as frail as a reed, and so very easily seduced, you dare to seek the world ..." (*Sermoenen*, 1865, 20 my transl.).

15. Den hoogsten trap van eer Die ooyt vrouw heeft betreden, is uwen leegsten trap, Zoo diep staen zij beneden: Van't begin des werelds af, Ja tot den laetsten dag, Niet een die uwen roem of lof beryken mag.

16. "Vele christelijke maegden spreken dikwils, en zonder vrees, met persoonen die geene engelen zijn. Indien zij zeggen dat ze ondertusschen waken om op hare hoede te zijn, ik zal haer antwoorden dat den duyvel ook waekt om haer te verderven. Eene maegd vooral, die den lof bemint, zal niet lang onverschillig zijn voor dien die haer zal prijzen. In den stoffe van zuyverheyd heeft men alle redenen van vreezen; om de reden zelve dat men niet genoegzaem vreest. Men tracht te veynzen de gevaren, die men bemint, niet te beminnen, en het bewijs, dat men ze bemint, is de zorg die men heeft om zich de zelve te verbergen. (...) (Navolging, 1839, 37) It is remarkable that in a book that numbers 336 pages, the 6 pages that are devoted to chastity are explicitly addressed to women; in the rest of the book Mary is talking to "my son".

17. In this book I found an entire chapter devoted to the "most holy breasts of Mary" (chapter 23, p.87-91). It contains sentences like:"Beschouwen wij met de oogen des geloofs en der godsvrucht den kleinen Jesus en zien wij hem nu eens met zijne poezele armtjes den hals zijner moeder omvatten, nu eens met tedere en vleyende lonkjes de borsten zijner moeder vragen, nu wederom haer al verrukkende kusjes toereiken (...)"(89)

"Especially persons of the female sex, and even more so virgins, should not appear in the world, unless out of true necessity, and with honourable aim "[18] (Arias, 1867, 135)

God created Adam and Eve. Jesus and Mary are a couple intimately linked with these very first human beings. The bond does not, however, imply equality, thus woman is made out of the rib of man. The scheme can be pictured as follows:

earth ----- Adam   Eve (before the fall)
heaven ----- Christ   Mary (Mary is Jesus' helpmate, she is not
                      identical but alike (de Ségur, 1868, 70-71).

Mary speaks to young women:

> "Qu'est-ce donc, ô ma fille, que ce corps que tu aimes tant, dont tu flattes les instincts déréglés jusqu'à l'exposer avec évidence au danger de le damner? Regarde-le dans la fosse et tu reconnaîtras qu'il n'est que fange et poussière" (Bayle, 1870, 15). "Tu commets le péché, ma fille, et tu n'en ressens aucune horreur ... (...) Comment donc, ô ma fille, toi qui n'oserais pas offenser des rois, qui ne sont que des hommes, oses tu offenser ce Dieu tout-puissant (...)?" (Id., 23).
>
> "Oh ma chère fille, mortifie maintenant ton corps, réprime ses instincts déréglés, tu lui rendra service. Garde-toi par ton obstination à favoriser ton corps, de forcer Dieu à chasser en enfer ton corps et ton âme, après avoir fait tant pour te mériter le ciel." (Id., 61).
>
> "Ma fille, tu caresses ton corps, tu le nourris, tu le satisfait en tout, et tu ne réfléchis pas qu'en le traitant de la sorte, tu le rends plus capable d'être la proie des feux de l'enfer. Oh! si tu ne connaissais ce qui là-bas est préparé aux âmes sensuelles et quels atroces tourments elles y souffrent, tu repousserais à l'instant tout ce qui peut mettre en danger ton salut éternel." (Id., 65).

On the other hand it is also glorious to see how humanity is elevated to heaven. It is a triumph for humanity that one of Adam's daughters, which we all are, rises above angels. The one most near to God is a mortal person, a person of flesh and blood. We should be greatly honoured by this. This is said in connection with the pronouncement of the Immaculate Conception of Mary which makes her Queen in Heaven[19] (Guillermin, 1893, 70-71).

---

18. Maar het betaamt bijzonderlijk aan de personen van het vrouwelijk geslacht en nog meer aan de maagden, van in de wereld niet te verschijnen, zonder eene ware noodzakelijkheid, zonder eenig eerbaren einde

19. It is remarkable that humanity, not womanhood, stands central here; positive statements reflect on all people. Negative ones are relevant only to women.

It is an obligation for everybody to follow Mary, but even more so for women: women owe everything to Mary. This is entirely clear when one looks at how women are treated in pagan societies. Women had no rights there, were not persons but things, pieces of property (Id., 73). Where Mary is honoured, women will be honoured! How could women should not be honoured as it is owing to a woman that humanity is saved, etc. (Id., 76).

Mary is described as sitting on the high throne (*Manuel*, 1894, 298) "La femme a reçu de Dieu, et c'est là une des raisons de sa grandeur, la sublime mission d'entretenir dans la société l'esprit de dévouement et de sacrifice" (Catherin, 1902, 16).

Woman is man's companion, but she has no real authority, she has to obey the head of the family (Id., 14). Through charity the christian woman has to bring unity, peace, and harmony to the family (Id., 44). Being called mother means bearing a title of honour (Id., 66). Like Mary, women should breastfeed their children (Id., 71). It is especially the whole truth about Mary that has repercussions for christian women. Mary did not live an extraordinary life. Her greatness lies in her conduct as mother and housewife: everything she did, she did to honour and praise God. Christian women should remember this: in the eyes of God nothing is big or small. Everything is precious in God's eyes (Id., 363-366). The best way to show Mary your love is to imitate her (Id., 375). "Do not become a slave of fashion, coquetry, and flirtation" (Edelin, 1904, 233-235).

2.5. Titles

The following were encountered: Heavenly Queen, Pure Virgin, Mother of Charity, Mother of Divine Grace, Holy Virgin, Mother of God, Most Holy Virgin, Lilyflower of the Heavenly Courts; Glorious Virgin; most Blessed Virgin; Queen of the Patriarchs (Jesus king of the patriarchs); Eastern Gate (cf. Salomon); Pleasure-garden of God; Star of the Sea; Gate of Heaven; Mother of human beings; Queen of angels; Mother of Divine Grace; Mother of the Creator, Pure Mother; Chaste Mother; Mother always Virgin; Mother without blemish; lovely Mother; admirable Mother; Mother of the Saviour; prudent Virgin; venerable Virgin; praiseworthy Virgin; powerful Virgin; clement Virgin; Mirror of justice; Seat of wisdom; Cause of our joy; spiritual Vessel; honorable Vessel; Vessel, sign of devotion; Mystical Rose; Tower of David; Ivory Tower; Golden House; Ark of the Covenant; Morning star; Salvation of the infirm; Refugee of sinners; Comforter of the afflicted; Recourse of Christians; Queen of the Prophets; Queen of the apostles; Queen of the Martyrs; Queen of the confessors; Queen of virgins; Mysterious Star; Sovereign; Immaculate Virgin; Sweet Queen of the Heart of Jesus;

firstborn Daughter of God; Advocate; Liberator; Queen of the Church; Mater Salvatoris.

2.6. Mary's power

Blessings and grace pour forth from Mary's hands. Her favours are accorded to us all, without exception, we can all go to Mary without fear (*Eenen dienaer van Maria*, 1855, 359 ff.). She is source of hope for sinners; source of consolation and joy. Mary is the mother of grace, through her we are children of God (de Ségur, 1868, 96). She has absolute power over sin, immense authority over her son; intercessory power; motherly power with her son; Jesus can not deny anything to Mary. It is she who will render assistance to the sinner, she is a pledge of eternal bliss. She rules the heart of her son, she shares in God's power.

2.7. Conclusion

With my twentieth-century eyes I see here a picture of Mary that I can only describe as: boring, dull, inhuman. I cannot help but wonder: "how on earth -- and this expression can be taken in a quite literal sense here -- could people feel inspired by this puppet they could even never imitate, even though this was the message that was continuously drilled into them". I wonder especially how women could turn to this incredibly bloodless creature. However this may be, what is at stake here is not how I perceive this creature now, but how people in the nineteenth century could have perceived it in their own day. Before I can answer that question I will have to look into other factors that dominated that specific society. In the next pages I turn to iconographical material, and to the general ideas about women. I will conclude this part with a summary of the specific image of Mary encountered in the devotional literature.

Mary is presented as an extremely virtuous person with whom nobody can compete. She is holy and as such she has received a very special place in the Roman Catholic pantheon[20]. Even though the authors of the texts continuously affirm arduously that Mary is not to be situated on the same level as the trinity, one cannot dismiss the feeling that Mary is very often seen as the fourth partner of the quaternity. The laborious attempts to explain the difference between Mary and Jesus are significant here. The very fact that the authors apparently cannot presuppose that everybody can see clearly how the hierarchy should be

---

20. I know that the term "pantheon" may provoke dissent in this context. I am, however, deliberately using it, as the texts show that there is considerable doubt about the place of Mary: is she human, godlike, angel, or something else? Who can really grasp this?

pictured gives rise to the suspicion that this was indeed something of problem.

The remarkable fact remains that Mary is represented as the figure to whom everybody has access. She is the bridge between the faithful and her son, and God. Her perfect outward appearance and her inimitable conduct seem to be no barrier. We have to keep this accessibility in mind. This will be an important factor in explaining her success.

The texts have also indicated that there was a very special bond between Mary and women. It was, however, limited to the question of chastity.

3. Marian Iconography in Belgium

Introduction

Written sources provide us with a great deal of information about religious life in the nineteenth century. The contents of the large numbers of popular devotional books enabled us to give a first description of nineteenth-century Marian devotion. It is, however, also necessary to bring in the visual aspects of Marian devotion. After all, "Western christianity reveals a continuous integration of visual imagery in christian worship and piety" (Miles, 1985, 4-5). Or in the words of Dupront: "Était-il possible d'apprehender les fondements anthropologiques de la vie de religion du monde occidental, sans tenir compte du langage des images qui en demeurent le support, l'enseignement, à tout le moins le cadre?" (Dupront, 1987, 100). The study of this visual imagery gives us additional information that can confirm what the texts say, but can also present a different view (see Miles, 1985, 41-62 about fourth century christianity). "Historical hermeneutics must develop a method that includes the use of both texts and images if the worlds of historical people are to be understood" (Miles, 1985, 12)[21]. The presence of Mary is an outstanding example of the thesis that: "Historically in western christian societies, images provided representations of the nature of reality and the range of human possibilities that intimately informed the emotional, spiritual, and intellectual lives of individuals" (Miles, 1985, xi). Mary has been depicted in many different ways. Nineteenth century believers were accustomed to

---

21. Miles' book *Image as Insight* is a plea for the study of sources other than the written sources in order to get access to the history of people who were not language users. This does not exclude the study of texts but criticizes the exclusive orientation towards texts. Miles' insights are of particular interest for historical women's studies.

many visual representations of Mary. The apparitions and the dogma of the Immaculate Conception confronted them with new problems, however: how exactly should they visualize this Mary? There was already a tradition of the depiction of Mary as Immaculate Conception, but the dogma made the question urgent. I will concentrate on the use and spreading of devotional pictures. They were imminently present in the life of nineteenth century believers.

How should Mary be imaged? Was she old, young, blonde, auburn, tall etc.? These questions exercised people's minds in the nineteenth century, especially where the iconography of the Immaculate Conception was concerned. There exists a long tradition of Marian paintings but the question of how to portray Mary receives a new impulse when the order to make the miraculous medal has been given. The importance of this order is that it has been given by Mary herself. Can one ignore Mary's own order? And what must Mary look like on the medal? Is not it rather difficult to depict her as Catherine Labouré herself does not seem to have seen one image? Anyway, the floor is open to debate[22]. I will first of all give a sketch of Belgian Catholicism in its nineteenth century setting before turning to the debate on how Mary could be depicted.

3.1. Belgian Catholicism

The nineteenth century is characterised by political instability and constitutional experiments. The Church now has to deal with a pluralistic society. It becomes one of the parties in the political game. Its opponent very often is liberalism. It is difficult to formulate a strict definition of liberalism, as it was less a definite ideology than a movement based on a feeling that was rooted in freedom. Freedom of the human being is fundamental. Government must protect this freedom, and the constitution must guarantee this fundamental freedom (Lamberts, 1972, xi-xii). Belgian Catholicism occupies a unique place in nineteenth century Europe. This appears especially in the very construction of the state and its constitution. A pact between Catholics and Liberals provided an unequalled situation: in order to obtain a Church free from state interference, Catholics joined with the liberal ideas of freedom. This was a rather contradictory situation as those ideas were rooted in rationalism, a train of ideas that was not favoured by the Church as it was feared to

---

22. In 1987-1988, the Marian year, a poster of a fifteen year old girl presented as Mary made feelings run high in the diocese of 's-Hertogenbosch (The Netherlands). 'It is a disco-girl', 'she is too sexy' were the comments. Others said that she linked up with the young people's world of experience and that this poster at least might bring them back to Mary. Nothing new under the sun?

result in relativism and indifferentism. The Catholicism that understands the necessity of dialogue with liberalism is often called a *Catholicism of facts* (Demolder, 1984, 109). The Catholic Church wanted to regain the position it had lost since Napoleon's concordat. Cardinal Sterckx was convinced that the Belgian government would not be able to govern without reckoning with Catholic influence. The bishops regularly came together in conferences: Belgium was the first country where a conference of bishops assembled. The bishops did not only put religious affairs on the agenda, but also participated in the political debates. "Bills were discussed with the bishops before being treated in parliament" (Boudens, 1984, 340 -my transl.). This may seem to be a controlling attitude, but this control had a positive background. The bishops, and especially cardinal Sterckx, helped securing the belgian construction against Roman interference. "La liberté comme en Belgique" (Demolder, 1984, 111) was praised in Europe.

Soon problems arose between liberal Catholicism and ultramontanism[23]. The delicate balance did not lead a happy and lasting existence[24]. Belgian ultramontanists wanted to establish Catholicism in every facet of society (De Mayer, 1988, 9). They tried to do this by putting their mark on the outward appearance of society. They for example wanted people to see that they were walking in Catholic streets as the buildings had a typically Catholic outlook. I will go on describing nineteenth century Belgian Catholic society from the position of the religious art that was supposed to mark Belgium as a Roman Catholic country.

3.2. Nineteenth Century Art

Nineteenth century religious art[25] must be looked at in the context of a search for identity. As the Roman papacy tries to secure its own right to exist, similarly on a local level Roman catholics try to consolidate their position. The nostalgic reflex, which often makes twentieth century fundamentalist believers revert to the nineteenth century 'wholly Catholic'

23. Ultramontanism: those who wanted complete independence of the Catholic Church in society. Another central issue was the supernational character and Roman Centrality of the Church. Ultramontanism even knew theocratic tendencies whereas it wanted to expand the power of the Church over temporary society. (About the complexity of Ultramontanism see Lamberts, 1972)

24. A brief but clear introduction to nineteenth century Europe and Belgium can be found in Demolder, 1984, 108-112.

25. I do not intend to discuss the meaning of the term 'religious art'. The notion 'religious art' is used here within the strict sense of art that is intimately connected with Christianity, even Catholicism.

society, also motivates the nineteenth century faithful. They found an all-catholic world in the Gothic era. The attempt to stimulate a revival of medieval values has been called neo-gothicism. The Middle Ages represented a monolithic religious society for the nineteenth century Roman Catholic. Gothicism and Christianity were perceived as one. This perception was nurtured by Chateaubriand's *Génie du Christianisme* (Van Cleeven, 1988, 29).

We have to understand the enterprise of neo-gothicism within the context of a society on the move. Pope (1985) explained the importance of the political situation for the acknowledgment of the apparitions in France. In Belgium we saw how liberalism was influential and how Catholics tried to improve their position. One of the means to solidify Catholicism was literally to leave a mark on the outward appearance of that society. This was possible through the penetration of neo-gothicism in art. The spreading of this 'neo-style' was furthered by the foundation of the Saint Lucas schools in 1887[26]. Around 1850 the ultramontanist traditionalists in Belgium declared neo-gothicism to be the most eminently becoming style for a Catholic réveil. Neo-gothicism can be defined as a conscious recapture of the gothic forms of the middle ages (van Cleeven, 1988, 20). It is not an independent style, but rather one aspect of nineteenth century art, and it does not exist in a 'pure' form. Neo-gothic artists make use of other styles as well. The recapture of the medieval gothic style was supplemented with new techniques, e.g. the application of cast iron (van Cleeven, 1988, 20-21).

Van Cleeven distinguishes different periods in the neo-gothic style: early neo-gothicism (1800-1850), which is imbued with pre-romanticism and romanticism; and high neo-gothicism (1850-1914), which is dominated by realism (van Cleeven, 1988, 23-55). Early neo-gothicism can be subdivided in two periods: the earliest is 'le genre troubadour' (1800-1830), which must be situated in a period of self-investigation of a culture that is influenced and changed by the French revolution and industrialisation. Neo-classicism and neo-gothicism are its results. Nature serves as its ultimate legitimation: "(...) the theoreticians of the gothic style point to the analogy between gothic vaulted construction and the intertwined branches of the forest" (van Cleeven, 1988, 24, my transl.). This evolves into 'le style à la cathédrale' (1830-1850). Romanticism obtains a firm footing, authoritarian regimes (Napoleon, Willem I) disappear, and nationalism, liberty, social equality, etc. flourish. Neo-

---

26. An account of the Saint Lucas schools and neo-gothicism can be found in De Mayer, 1988. This book focusses on the St. Lucas schools but at the same time provides us with abundant information about neo-gothicism in Belgium.

THE NEW GROUP Presents:

S E R V I C E M E N

Written by **Evan Smith**
Directed by **Sean Mathias**

With **Olivia Birkelund, Eric Martin Brown**
Heather Matarazzo, Steven Polito
Anthony Veneziale, William Westenberg

Set: **Derek McLane**
Costumes: **Cathy Zuber and Alejo Vietti**
Lights: **Jeff Croiter**
Sound: **Fabian Obispo**
Production Stage Manager: **Valerie A. Peterson**
Production Supervision: **Peter R. Feuchtwanger and**
Gregory Cushna
Public Relations: **The Karpel Group**

Performances begin March 13 - Limited Engagement!
Tues – Sat at 8pm, Sat at 2pm, Sun at 3pm

The New Group / Theatre @ St. Clement's
423 W. 46th Street (Btn 9th/10th Avenue)
Tickets $25 - $35
Call Ticket Central 1-8PM Daily at 212-279-4200

The New Group, 154 Christopher St., 2A-A, New York, NY 10014
tel 212.691.6730   fax 212.691.6798   www.newgrouptheater.com

Photograph © Pat Milo Studio/Mar-Age Press

Nigel Pounde
99 Clairemont Avenue
#118
New York, NY 10027

Scott Elliott, Artistic Director/ Elizabeth Timperman, Producing Director
Andy Goldberg, Associate Artistic Director/ Jill Bowman, General Manager

SERVICEMEN

WRITTEN BY EVAN SMITH   DIRECTED BY SEAN MATHIAS

gothicism gains a religious interpretation as gothicism becomes connected with christianity. Gothicism has a "mysterious, religious, christian effect" (Demanets, 1847, 28, quoted in van Cleeven, 1988, 30). Picturesque elements are mere additional options. An aestheticism of the sublime in this period has to satisfy the criterium of severity and grandeur. New techniques, products of industrialism, are eagerly used, especially cast iron.

Neo-gothicism remained present in the next period that can be labelled high neo-gothicism. The first phase of this period is dominated by an archeological approach (1850-1885). Society became aware of the incapacity of industrialisation to solve and prevent problems. Tolerance declined and the existence of several neo-styles together now became problematic. The scene is now set for 'the battle of styles': neo-classicism or neo-gothicism. In Belgium, ultramontanists tried to use neo-gothicism for their own purposes. Neo-gothicism becomes an overall concept: everything, according to its own function, could be embedded in neo-gothicism. A return to the original materials and techniques was favoured.

From around 1865 till 1885 neo-gothicism can be named reformed gothic: the archaeological data are more and more subjected to contemporary interpretation. 'Art' has a didactic and moralizing character: it serves the bourgeois interests. "Les tours de nos cathédrales et les flèches de nos hôtels de ville dominent encore les pignons de nos banques et les cheminées de nos fabriques" (de Haulleville, 1867, I, quoted in van Cleeven, 1988, 42). Neo-gothicism was successful as a style celebrating the hey-day of regional prosperity. As such it could develop independently from ecclesiastical authority.

Late neo-gothicism (1885-1914) is an epilogue. Society finds the stability it formerly lacked and the Church tries to find access to contemporary society. The climate is more relaxed. Neo-gothicism is no longer at the centre of artistic activity but it continues being practised[27].

3.3. A Belgian Bishop and the Depiction of Mary

One of the most elaborated texts on the iconography of the Immaculate Conception in Belgium was written by bishop Malou of West Flanders. Cardinal Sterckx before him, in 1854, had already written a small

27. Schoonbaert e.g. typifies nineteenth century religious art inspired by the neo-gothic style as practised in the Saint Lucas schools as, "devout academism": "Waar in de profane kunst de artistieke bezieling gedoofd werd door navolging, werd in de religieuze kunst zowel de artistieke als de religieuze bezieling gedoofd. Daarom spreken we van *devoot academisme* en niet van religieus academisme. De devotie verschijnt hier immers als een erosie van echte vroomheid." (Schoonbaert, 1986, 16-17 -my underlining).

dissertation *De modo pingendi Sanctissimam Dei genitricem Mariam, sine labe originale conceptam, brevis disquisitio* (the text can be found in Aubert, 1955, 94-99) in which he commented on the depiction of the Virgin Mary as immaculately conceived. He cannot find a special or privileged way of depicting the Immaculate Conception but he advises to represent the Immaculate Virgin displaying humility as well as splendour. She should be wearing a royal crown, a white tunic and a blue mantle. The depiction should indicate that Mary stands above all human beings and that she has conquered evil. A triumphal arch of angels surround her, and the Trinity who has preserved her from original sin are shown above her.

Malou, a student of Perrone, wrote a much more elaborated text on the depiction of the Immaculate Conception: *Iconographie de L'Immaculée Conception de la Très-Sainte Vierge*, 1856. He had made some important interventions during his stay in Rome when the dogma of the Immaculate Conception was being prepared. He stressed the prefiguration of Mary in the Old Testament (on Malou, see Cauwe, 1964, 433-462; 1984, 357-364). Some doubts arose whether this element had to be encompassed in the dogma. Malou explained that the Old Testament texts had to be read in the light of the interpretation of the church fathers. Consequently, the biblical texts separately did not provide apodictic proof for the dogma. Emphasis was put on tradition and the interpretation of the bible by church fathers and ecclesiastical writers (Cauwe, 1984, 362-363). In 1857 he published two volumes on the Immaculate Conception: *L'Immaculée Conception de la Bienheureuse Vierge Marie considérée comme dogme de la foi.*

Presenting his ideas at some length gives a fairly good idea of the problems that arise in the portraying of the Immaculate Virgin, at the same time highlights the concerns of a nineteenth century bishop. We should note that there are several 'classic' types of picturing the Immaculate Conception. Kolb (1984) distinguishes three types: all three represent Mary standing. The first type depicts Mary with folded hands (the ear-dress Madonna, the Madonna from Lourdes and Fatima). The second type shows Mary with a lily in the right hand, while the left hand is stretched out to the praying people or is devoutly held in front of her chest (most common in baroque Madonna's). The third type is that of the Madonna with both hands reaching out to the praying (Mary of the Miraculous Medal) (Kolb, 1984, 870-873).

Malou says that the definition of the dogma of the Immaculate Conception has heightened in the faithful a need for images, medals, and representations. Artists feel uncertain about the task of providing an image of the Immaculate Conception that illuminates the mystery. Malou wants to give some guidelines to help those artists. He takes upon his shoulders the task that the Council of Trent has outlined, i.e. that bishops have to guard the images the believers see (XXVth session). Until the proclamation of the dogma, no traditional type of representing this mystery has been developed. The predilection of the painter and of the faithful prevailed.

One of the first recommendations Malou makes is that there should be conformity to Church usage. The Church, he says, reveals the mysteries through forms and symbols that God has used to communicate with the faithful.

> "Les faits surnaturels, les vérités spéculatives qui appartiennent à un ordre de choses invisible et insensible, ne peuvent revêtir à nos yeux que les formes sous lesquelles Dieu les a présentées lui-même à notre esprit ou à notre imagination. C'est là une règle générale dont l'iconographie chrétienne ne doit jamais s'écarter" (Malou, 1856, 5-6).

A good image is like a good definition: it must represent the mystery and nothing else. The Immaculate Conception is characterised by the hidden action of grace. Malou prefers the symbolic option (as opposed to the historical way) to depict the mystery. The symbolic image is suited to express faith in the Immaculate Conception, to explain the effects of grace, and to represent the Immaculate Conception in the person of the Virgin all at once. The mystery of original, everlasting, and perfect holiness becomes real and alive in the representation of the Immaculate Conception.

Malou gives an extensive account of how the Virgin and her surroundings should look. The Virgin should be perpendicular, "like dawn rising at the horizon, announcing the arrival of the sun" (Malou, 1856, 24). Her feet should touch the globe: grace operates in and for the world. Most likely she will be about fourteen or fifteen years old, her age just before the annunciation. The youthfulness of her body will be a symbol of youth and beauty of the soul. Her figure should be of a noble and modest beauty. It is a beauty granted by God, a beauty that reflects the inner beauty of the soul. Her eyes are lowered or turned up to heaven. Her hair can be black or brown, for the most part covered by her veil. Elaborate hair styles are out of the question. Her hands are folded in prayer. Very often Mary is portrayed with naked feet. Malou fulminates against this outrageous habit: why shouldn't Mary be wearing shoes if she is fully clothed[28]? The right way to picture the Virgin Mary's feet is the following: her right foot, shod and partly covered, peeps from under her

---

28. Malou obviously does not realise that traditionally naked feet mean humility.

garments and rests on the head of the serpent, ready to crush it. The left foot does not need to be seen. Mary's clothes have to measure up to the general rule: they must have a real significance. She is to be dressed in a wide dress that covers her body completely, and a cloak draped around her. A veil should cover her hair as a sign of purity and modesty. Under no condition must her clothes draw the attention. The preferred colours are: white because it expresses virginity of soul and body; blue for the cloak because it has a mystical significance and reminiscent of heaven; gold for the stars.

Another chapter deals with the attributes of the Immaculate Conception. Malou considers it not a very good idea to present the Trinity: it is sufficient to picture the Father because the sanctification, usually the privilege of the Spirit, is in this case due to the Father. Neither should the child Jesus be depicted[29]. Angels can be present but in their right place, i.e. around her feet, never higher than her arms. Mary radiates forth spiritual superiority. About the stars and the sun Malou says the following:

> "Le soleil, la lune et les douzes étoiles, appartiennent à la représentation symbolique de l'Immaculée Conception, non seulement parce qu'ils font partie du type de la femme mystérieuse, c'est-à-dire, de la Sainte Vierge, mais encore par des raisons spéciales. Ces astres sont là pour rappeler, commes créatures lumineuses, que Marie a été comblée des lumières de la sainteté parfaite; ils sont là comme créatures célestes, pour attester que Marie, par son origine privilégiée, appartient au ciel; ils sont là,

---

29. The argument of Turner and Turner (1982) that in the nineteenth century "the emphasis began to shift to Mary herself, as an autonomous figure who takes initiatives on behalf of mankind, often intervening in the midst of the economic and political crises characteristic of industrialized mass society" (Turner & Turner, 1982, 145) seems to be confirmed by the strong emphasis of Malou on depicting Mary without child. This conclusion however does not hold against the data of the wider context. First of all, Malou's point is not a general one, but one specifically applicable for the depiction of the Immaculate Conception. Turner & Turner's argument would hold, if first of all the nineteenth century was exclusively oriented towards the Immaculate Conception. This is not the case. And secondly if the nineteenth century had introduced the autonomously acting Mary. This again is untrue. One influential and well-known example is the medieval legend of the *Beatrijs*. It tells how Mary takes the place of a nun who has a love affair lasting several years. Mary acts autonomously in this legend, there is no intervention from any person of the Trinity. Furthermore our reading of the devotional texts showed that these autonomous actions of the nineteenth century Mary are always relative. Nineteenth century devotional authors interpreted her behaviour in a hierarchical way: what Mary does cannot be disconnected from the Trinity. As such, her actions do not have any real power unless they refer to the next plane. Turner & Turner's remark should be rewritten: they should de-emphasize the fact that Mary's autonomous actions are a new fact and they should connect this so-called autonomous attitude with the hierarchical structure in which it is exercised.

comme représentant tous les astres du ciel, pour rendre hommage à
la plus pure et la plus sainte des créatures" (Malou, 1856, 70).

A royal crown, a sceptre and a throne are unnecessary attributes
according to Malou. The mystery of the Immaculate Conception is
completely devoid of any idea of sovereignty, power, and protection. What
indeed is essential, so says Malou, is the infernal serpent. The mother of
God, the co-redemptrix is imaged with the serpent. The serpent can be
green, red, or black, and it must hold the apple in its mouth. The rose,
symbol of Jesus Christ or God, is not a necessary attribute so it is better
not to use it in the image of the Immaculate Virgin. Light and darkness
are allowed as respectively innocence, wholeness and purity, and as a
contrast to the centre of light: Mary.

Another element of concern is the use of symbols, legends and
inscriptions. Symbols are allowed, but they should be directly related to
the Immaculate Conception. Those derived from scripture are preferred.
Some possibilities are a lily amidst thorns, a mirror without blemish, the
moon and the sun, the city of God founded on the holy mountains, the
most holy Tabernacle, the rainbow shining through the clouds. For
legends and inscriptions the same guidelines should be followed. One
general rule is: do not exaggerate.

3.4. Devotional Prints

3.4.1. SOME THEORETICAL REMARKS.

I want to take a close look at one particular means of representation of
Mary in the nineteenth century, i.e. devotional pictures. "Religious
popular prints are tools for religious education, these resources were and
are printed for varying edifying purposes" (Stalpaert, 1976, 15, my
transl.[30]). They help to stimulate and to promote religious life. Jesuits
take the lead in using devotional prints for educational means. Post
sounds a critical note here:

> "as so often in history, there is in my opinion, also in this case,
> question neither of the enlightening illustration or teaching of the
> illiterate, nor of uncontrolled and spontaneous popular art. Indeed:
> pictures that are not commissioned, serve no interests, are not
> controlled, represent no strategies and functions are hardly
> thinkable. But it is highly questionable whether teaching and

---

30. "Religieuze volksprenten zijn gebruiksvoorwerpen bij het godsdienstonderricht,
deze hulpbronnen werden en worden nog steeds gedrukt met een variërend stichtelijk doel
..."

enlightenment here take on important place in these strategies and functions" (Post, 1988, 251, my transl.[31]).

Post contends, in agreement with Schrade and Schenda, that most religious images were accessible only to an elite (Post, 1988, 251). It seems to me that this position must be readjusted when it comes to nineteenth century depictions of the Immaculate Conception. As I will show further on, the collection I have studied ranges from menus to diplomas, made for different occasions and different people. This points to a widespread presence of images of the Immaculate Conception in nineteenth-century Belgium.

Post distinguishes several functions of religious images: two clusters can be formed. A. decorative; aesthetic; memorative; illustrative-didactic or pedagogic. B. interpretative; propagandistic; representative; empathic; 'Kultbild'. Most of the material I have studied can at the least be seen as decorative and memorative. Post presents two methods to study the material, indicated respectively as iconographic and iconological. This refers to the work of Panofsky and Warburg. Panofsky, in *Meaning and the Visual Arts*, actually distinguishes three phases: pre-iconographical description; iconographical analysis; and iconological interpretation (Panofsky, 1987, 51-87). The pre-iconographical description is an enumeration of the recognition of the world of pure forms as carriers of primary or natural meanings (Panofsky, 1987, 54). Iconographical analysis is a description and classification of images and their identification (Panofsky, 1987, 54; 57). Iconology is the labour of interpretation (Panofsky, 1987, 58). "We deal with the work of art as a symptom of something else which expresses itself in a countless variety of other symptoms, and we interpret its compositional and iconographical features as more particularized evidence of this 'something else'" (Panofsky, 1987, 56). It is this last level that interests me.

I will have to devote some time to the description of the pictures I am going to deal with, but the real aim of this chapter is how to interpret them. The ideas of Dupront (1987) can be helpful on the interpretative level: Dupront elaborates on the function and presence of religious art and devotional prints. His theory helps to situate the devotional prints that I will describe later. Dupront contends that the use or the rejection of images in a collective religious experience reflects fundamental and

---

31. "zoals zelden in de geschiedenis, is ook hier mijns inziens noch sprake van illustratie of didactiek van het ongeletterde volk, noch van ongestuurde en onbevangen kunst van het volk ('volkskunst'). Inderdaad: beelden zonder opdrachten, belangen, controle, strategieën en functies zijn nauwelijks denkbaar, maar of didactiek en illustratie nu deze strategieën en functies inhoud geven is zeer de vraag"

existential choices (Dupront, 1987, 100). "L'image, dans sa massivité quantitative, s'avère découvreuse impudique des secrets d'âme" (Dupront, 1987, 102). Religious images carry a psycho-sacral force. Images show things. Even though they at the same instant reveal things, they also remain silent. They are immobile, but also animating. In one way or another, they are able to reveal a fundamental image that expresses what is being said to the pious. "Aux différents niveaux de cette culture, l'image matérialise la parole, non pour la pétrir en objet, mais pour la délivrer à la vue" (Dupront, 1987, 103). The image gives the words a presence and structures a relation between what is made present and the pious. What is evoked is eternal and timeless.

Images, according to Dupront, do not appear without reason: "Toute création d'image répond à un besoin" (Dupront, 1987, 108). Every analysis of religious images will have to look for the needs the images respond to. Is the image an illustration of a dogmatic enunciation, is it a celebration, is it meant to be educational, etc.? One also has to reckon with the limits of the artist: s/he belongs to a tradition, to a specific school, etc., has to comply with the wishes of the commissioning instance. Post has argued that prints must be studied within an historical and art-historical context. It is important to understand what kind of pictorial language is being used (Post, 1990). The prints we are going to look at are situated within the neo-gothic pictorial language that we have explored.

3.4.2. PRINTS: EXAMPLES[32]

I will limit the description of devotional prints to the prints of the house of Vande Vyvere-Petyt. This printing-office was located in Bruges and spans several generations. It is interesting to see how these printers, living under the eyes of bishop Malou, did or did not execute his ideas about the depiction of the Immaculate Conception. The library of the city of Bruges, contains a collection of prints of this house[33]. The collection ranges from menus to devotional prints, from visiting-cards to diplomas. The wide dispersion of the Immaculate Conception image is shown by its presence on diplomas and certificates of membership of Marian congregations[34]. I discovered two main variants: Mary with her hands folded or crossed in front of her chest; and Mary with her hair covered by

---

32. The prints can be found in Appendix III.

33. The collection was in a rather deplorable condition: the prints were pasted in several large books. It was impossible to see the reverse side, except for some prints that had a text on the reverse side. The collection was not classified: menus, devotional prints, visiting cards, etc. were pasted in no arranged order.

34. Even schools that had names of saints other than Mary, had an image of the Immaculate Conception on their diplomas.

a veil and crown, or with her hair uncovered but crowned. Further details may differ. I will describe several representative examples, point out differences, and compare them with bishop Malou's description. First of all I will give an iconographical analysis, i.e. a description of what is to be seen on the prints. Next I will attempt a first iconological interpretation. Subsequently I will try to explain the pictures from the point of view of the women who saw them.

I. A certificate for the "Congrégation érigée à Soignies sous le titre de l'Immaculée Conception. Couvent des soeurs franciscaines."
This is a coloured print: in the top quarter we find the heading, i.e. the text "Congrégation érigée à Soignies sous le titre de l'Immaculée Conception. Couvent des soeurs franciscaines". This text is surrounded by branches and flowers. The banners of text "l'Immaculée Conception" and "Couvent des soeurs franciscaines" are carried by two angels. The other three quarters of the print can be divided in a top part and a lower part: in the four corners of this part we find four saints. Ste Anne (top left), Ste Agnès (top right), St Joseph (bottom left) and St Louis de Gonzage (bottom right). Between the two male saints we find a text in which the congregationalist promises to be a good child of Mary:

> Sainte Marie Mère de Dieu et Vierge, je .... vous choisis aujourd'hui pour ma Mère, ma Patronne et mon Avocate; je prends la ferme résolution de ne jamais Vous abandonner; de ne jamais rien dire ni faire contre Vous, et de ne permettre jamais que par mes inférieurs il soit fait quelque chose contre votre honneur. Je vous supplie donc de me recevoir pour votre perpétuelle servante; assistez-moi en toutes mes actions, et ne m'abbandonnez pas à l'heure de la mort. Ainsi-soit-il.
> Pour la plus grande gloire de Dieu et l'honneur de la Très-Sainte Vierge ...... a été reçue au nombre des enfants de Marie
>   Le Directeur,   La Préfette.

Between the two female saints we find a print of the Immaculate Conception. This figure is bigger than the saints. Whereas the saints are framed in squares, the Immaculate Conception is set in an oval. The Immaculate Conception has her hands folded in front of her chest, her head is inclined, her eyes are lowered. Her head is covered with a white veil piped with gold, which almost completely covers her hair. She is wearing a golden crown with red and green gems. The dress, almost completely covered by an artfully draped blue mantle, is old rose. She is standing on a globe, she is wearing shoes on both feet, the tops of which are visible, under her feet she is crushing a snake showing two sharp teeth, that is holding an apple in its mouth. Also to be seen are the two tips of the lunar sickle[35]. The Immaculate Conception is completely surrounded by a golden aureole, around her head is a red circle. Underneath the picture of the Immaculate Conception another text is written: "O Marie! Montrez-vous notre mère"

II. "Ecce Mater Tua".

This document is printed as a certificate for sisters who have fulfilled their noviciate and have been accepted for the vows of the third order. The margin of the certificate is completely decorated with flowers, leaves, and representations of St. Francis and St. Agnes. At the top of the document we find the Immaculate Conception. Two angels, above her head, carry the text "ecce mater tua". Two other angels, underneath her feet, show the text "regina sine labe concepta". In their other hand the two angels carry the text of the certificate itself. The Immaculate Conception is almost completely identical with the one described above. Certain details are different: the head of this Immaculate Conception is a little further inclined; beneath the globe we find blue flowers; the background colour of this certificate is green.

III. "Third Order of Penance"

This is a certificate of the order of St. Francis. In the top left corner we find the Immaculate Conception. The other corners show: St. Francis kneeling before the Crucified top right; St. Ludovice bottom right; St. Elisabeth bottom left. The Immaculate Conception is one and a half times the size of the other figures. Whereas the other Immaculate Conceptions stood erect, this Immaculate Conception bends the top part of her body backward. Her hair is uncovered and she is wearing a crown. Only one tip of her shoe can be seen, that on the left foot. Her clothes are bronze coloured. Under her foot we find a dragon with a fruit in its mouth. This dragon -- or is it a snake with paws? -- is also bronze.

IV. Ave Maria

This is a print that follows the instructions of bishop Malou rather literally. Mary is standing in an aureole. Her hands are held together in front of her chest. Her head is covered by a veil and (in deviation from Malou's prescriptions) she is wearing a crown . Her eyes are closed. She is wearing a dress and a mantle. She is standing in the moon sickle, and this sickle rests on the globe. The top of her right foot wearing a shoe is

35. About the origins of the lunar sickle. see Grzybkowski, 1988. He brings an interesting phenomenon to attention, namely the Virgin standing on the moon in which a female head is framed. His interpretation of this image is unsatisfactory and needs further research.

visible. It is treading on the serpent that is holding an apple in its mouth. Under the oval, two angels are carrying the text "Ave Maria". In the margin we read the text: "O Maria zonder vlek ontvangen bid voor ons die tot u onzen toevlugt nemen". This text runs from the left margin over the top margin to the right margin. At the bottom of the print we read: "100 dagen aflaet". Outside the margin of the print: I. Petyt, Brugge.

V. S M I C

This print differs greatly from the previous one. Again we see Mary in an oval, standing on the sickle of the moon. The difference is in the hairstyle. Mary's head is uncovered, and her hair falls down over her shoulders. Both feet are visible and they are both naked. Her hands are crossed in front of her chest. Her eyes are devoutly lowered. No paraphernalia are present. In the margin of the oval we once again read: "O Maria zonder vlek ontvangen bid voor ons die tot u onzen toevlucht nemen 100 dagen aflaat". The corners of the print have the letters: S M I C. Outside the print margin we find the signature: I. Petyt, Brugge.

VI. Congregatie van de onbevlekte ontvangenis van Maria

Mary is set in an oval. In the four corners of the print we find angels. The two angels in the upper corners are holding lilies, the two at the bottom have their hands folded. Mary is crowned but her hair is not covered. Her hands are folded in front of her chest. Her eyes are open but lowered. She is standing on a globe, with the top of her left foot with shoe visible. She stands on a dragon that is holding a fruit in its mouth. The text margin says: "Congregatie van de onbevlekte ontvangenis van Maria te Thielt ingesteld den 31 augustus 1834, moeder der bedrukten b.v.o.". Outside the printmargin: J. Petyt opvl. K. Vande Vyvere-Petyt, Brugge.

3.4.3. COMPARISON WITH MALOU

It seems that the house Vande Vyvere-Petit did not really take the demands of bishop Malou into consideration. It is only IV. Ave Maria that seems to have followed the instructions of Malou, and still some bending of the rules is to be noticed in that the Virgin is crowned. Malou's inventory of rules for depictions of the Immaculate Conception give the impression that he considered the Immaculate Conception on its own. However, the first three examples shown here -- and many others in the collection besides -- do not isolate the Immaculate Conception. They show it as part of something else, such as a certificate or a diploma. The Immaculate Conception here becomes more of an illustration than an image evoking contemplation. It is clear that the illustration still observes a ranking order: the Immaculate Conception occupies a central place, and it is larger than the other figures shown. There can be no doubt about the importance and pre-eminence of the Immaculate Conception.

It is remarkable that these different Immaculate Conceptions are all of the first type distinguished by Kolb (1984). The Mary of the Miraculous Medal seems not to have been as normative as could be expected, seeing that the apparition herself had ordered the minting of a medal. It seems as if the printers themselves decided how they would depict the Immaculate Virgin. There are some elements that are constant and which make the images look alike[36], but there is enough room left for variation. Seen from this perspective, the SMIC (V) image offers a different outlook on the Immaculate Conception. The naked feet and the uncovered head could suggest something more provocative than is usually contained in the images. On the other hand, its provocative potentialities should not be overestimated. The picture itself soon corrects any deviating ideas: first of all because of its form the picture clearly is an image of the Immaculate Conception; secondly there is Mary herself with her eyes devoutly lowered; thirdly the context of the devotional print means that whoever looks at it does so with a specific attitude of mind.

In order to bring together all the elements of this chapter in a conclusive interpretation we have to bring another aspect to the fore: the position of and ideas about women.

4. Interpreting the Nineteenth Century

Introduction

Interpreting the nineteenth century and its depiction of Mary is not an easy task, especially when one is focusing on the special relation between Mary and women. This focus encounters several difficulties. It is clear that the interest with which I turn to the nineteenth century is the understanding of the contemporary Marian presence. We have to face the question of how we can know something of the experience of non-language users -- those who are situated at the boundaries of discourse -- in this specific case women. What does the nineteenth century tell us about the religious experience of women? This question can hardly be

---

36. It is only after I had made the iconographical description that the differences became really meaningful for me. My first contact with the pictures left me with an idea of repetitiveness: I had the impression most depictions were more or less the same. This impression was mostly due to the fact that the pictures belong to one type of Immaculate Conception.

answered with the data that are available. The material about Mary is an obvious example of the male domination of cultural and religious media, more particularly that of mostly celibate men. We have little firsthand information either from or about women. What we would need is a library with diaries of ordinary women, or minutes of the conversations between women pilgrimaging to Mary, or notes of women's personal prayers to Mary. Again, this last example already presupposes that women would have felt the need to formulate personal prayers. Generally speaking, the twentieth-century Western European mind that has absorbed the message of individuality feels a slight touch of aversion when it thinks about standard formulations, pronounced by thousands and thousands. (When however at a popconcert thousands and thousands of people repeat the same sentences over and over again most of my generation does not consider this equally odd.) Where this repetitious element is concerned, we may think of the unpopularity of the rosary: the monotonous repetition of standardized sentences is not really popular. Even though counting beads and repeating prayers, reciting small commendations, etc. is part of many religions, it does not seem to be experienced as meaningful unless the recitation makes sense towards the person who says them. Even so-called senseless mumbling may be experienced as meaningful when it gives the mind the freedom to wonder.

I contend that what we have to be concerned about is the message that was proclaimed. We can try to disentangle the ideas that were transmitted, and of what those ideas could have been indicative in that particular community/society. This approach reacts against generalisations such as "Mary was the perfect mother because she kneels before her son" (S. de Beauvoir). Questions to be asked are: what kind of son, in what context, what kind of mother, what kind of kneeling: adoring, subservient, equalizing. Imagine the contrast with a person towering over a child, almost crushing it with its presence: in the case of the kneeling Mary, kneeling could mean showing reverence for the personality of the child, having respect for the child as child, the adult bridging the gap between herself and the child. I do not exclude that the conclusion could be that Mary was indeed the perfect mother because she knelt before her son, but after research I would know what in this specific context kneeling meant, what mother meant, and what son indicated. This sentence would not be a mere slogan, but a thoroughly researched statement.

When I look at the messages that are prevalent in a particular society, I focus on loose elements. With 'loose elements' I mean those pieces of the jigsaw that are open to multiple ways of interpretation. Such interpretation -- any interpretation -- are circumscribed by the nature of the society in which the message is received. The sentence "Jane does not want to go to school" can be interpreted, in Western[37] contemporary society, as an act of rebellion against the school system. We can even imagine that it might become a liberating slogan for all girls who do not want to go to school where teachers are allowed to have "intimate" contacts with the students. The simple observation "Jane does not want to go to school" obtains subversive power when read in this context. This interpretation is possible today because sexual harassment is a major issue. It needs a great deal of *Hineininterpretierung*, phantasy, and a-historical thinking to proclaim the sentence "Jane does not want to go school" to be a slogan against sexual harassment at school in nineteenth century society considering the fact that going to school was not a general practice for girls and sexual harassment unnamed.

Vice versa, it can be that a kneeling mother was indeed a powerful sign in a society different from twentieth century Western society. "In a different discourse, they (i.e. statements, E.M.) occupy a different position, respond to a different situation and are governed by a different structure and different laws of discourse" (M. Miles, 1985, 25).

My attempt is to provide a sharper and more balanced analysis than is given by the authors presented in the first chapter. By 'sharper' I mean with more open eyes to pro's and con's, i.e. with attention for both oppressive and enhancing elements. As M. Miles writes in the introduction to *Immaculate and Powerful*: "... religion can provide women with a critical perspective on and alternatives to the conditioning they receive as members of their societies (...) but it also inevitably forms part of women's cultural conditioning" (Atkinson, 1985, 2). Our question therefore should not only be: how oppressive were past images, but: why were they so successful? What was their attraction for women? Is it because the message those images conveyed was concomitant with the surrounding culture? In other words: was it attractive because it did not bring anything new, because it reinforced the existing themes? Or was it because it offered women something more? Did it provide them with an ideal that was worth following? Did it bring comfort?

I want to situate the discussion about the nineteenth century within the women's studies approach and debate. Although not a historian myself, I want to communicate with historians and add some personal research where I feel that historians fail to offer material to understand the contemporary interpretation of Mary. I will make use of studies I have at hand, and where necessary provide some research of my own. I focus

---

37. "Western" might still include too many countries to accommodate my example. I probably should say North America, Great Britain, the Netherlands and the Scandinavian countries.

on one particular area, i.e. Belgium, and with particular attention to popular expressions of devotion to Mary as we find them in written and printed sources. A general overview is first of all impossible and boring; furthermore it is far more interesting to focus on local policies and practices and see their effects on ideas about women and the use of women as carriers of ideas and religious values (see also Chapin Massey, 1985, 23-24).

To begin with I will situate the discussion about the nineteenth century as it is presented in the women's studies debate. It is remarkable that so many studies are focusing on the nineteenth century. Could the reason for this be that they are raising questions that are central to women's studies?

4.1. Women's Studies and the Nineteenth Century

The nineteenth century has a special attraction for people involved in women's studies. There are several reasons for this attraction: in the nineteenth century we encounter a historically new event. Women unite and fight for their rights. This is an international phenomenon: France, Great Britain, the United States of America, the Netherlands, Belgium - most Western countries are confronted with women who create an atmosphere of change. This movement will afterwards be labelled the first feminist wave[38]. Industrialisation changes the outlook of the world, and affects women's roles (Harrison, 1985, 42-53). Victorianism coloured the discourse, and motherhood became exulted as the sole ideal for women.

One particular facet of women's studies research of the nineteenth century, the question of the feminisation of culture, is one of the central issues in studying this period.

The first question to be asked, is whether nineteenth century culture was indeed feminised. A. Douglas (1977)[39] tried to provide an answer for nineteenth century America. Between 1820 and 1875,

"As the secular activities of American life were demonstrating their utter supremacy, religion became the message of America's official and conventional cultural life" (Douglas, 1977, 6).

38. For more information see: A.S. Kraditor, The Ideas of the Woman Suffrage Movement, 1890-1920, New York, Garden City Doubleday, 1971; S. Pankhurst, The Suffragette Movement. An Intimate Account of Persons and Ideals, London, Virago, 1977.

39. I referred to this book when describing the position of B. Corrado Pope (see p. 38-39). I now return to this question because it is important for further discussion. A sharpening of Douglas's position is found in Taves, 1987.

She notices an evolution in American Protestant religion in which by 1875 faith was no longer the subscription to a vast body of dogmas, but the affirmation of the importance of family morals, civic responsibility, and the social function of churchgoing (Douglas, 1977, 7). Calvinist theology almost disappeared. Douglas tries to provide an answer to this shift by looking at the changing function of the minister and at the place of women. The role of the clergy is declining (Douglas, 1977, 17-43) and "the independent woman with a mind and a life of her own slowly ceased to be considered of high value" (Douglas, 1977, 51).

> "Both liberal ministers and literary women had lost practical function within American society and were anxious to replace it with emotional indispensability; they turned of necessity from the exercise of power to the exertion of 'influence'. Both would in their own ways exchange dogma with prayer and knowledge, whether in the form of skills or of scholarship, for sensibility; they would substitute, in a sense, literature for life." (Douglas, 1977, 77)

For ministers, female influence became their major support. Their model was maternal power (Douglas, 1977, 97). Anti-intellectualism and a theology of feeling predominated. American culture is feminised:

> "It must be remembered how these people saw themselves, and with what reason: they were christians reinterpreting their faith as best they could in terms of the needs of their society. Their conscious motives were good - even praiseworthy; their effects were not altogether bad. Under the sanction of sentimentalism, lady and clergyman were able to cross the cruel lines laid down by sexual stereotyping in ways that were clearly historically important and undoubtedly personally fulfilling. She could become aggressive, even angry, in the name of various holy causes; he could become gentle, even nurturing, for the sake of moral overseeing. Whatever their ambiguities of motivation, both believed they had a genuine redemptive mission in their society: to propagate the potentially matriarchal virtues of nurture, generosity, and acceptance; to create the "culture of the feelings" that John Stuart Mill was to find during the same period in Wordsworth. It is hardly altogether their fault that their efforts intensified sentimental rather than matriarchal values" (Douglas, 1977, 10-11).

In Douglas's view nineteenth-century America was sentimentalised. This means that feminisation is narrowed to sentimentalism, and has little to do with the propagation and penetration of female values -- whatever these might be -- in society.

> "(...) America lost its male-dominated theological tradition without gaining a comprehensive feminism or an adequately modernized

religious sensibility. (...) The tragedy of nineteenth-century northeastern society is not the demise of Calvinist patriarchal structures, but rather the failure of a viable, sexually diversified culture to replace them. 'Feminization' inevitably guaranteed, not simply the loss of the finest values contained in Calvinism, but the continuation of male hegemony in different guises. The triumph of the 'feminizing', sentimental forces that would generate mass culture redefined and perhaps limited the possibilities for change in American society. Sentimentalism, with its tendency to obfuscate the visible dynamics of development, heralded the cultural sprawl that has increasingly characterised post-Victorian life" (Douglas, 1977, 13).

Taves elaborates and broadens Douglas's views by arguing that the shift in theology as shown by Douglas

"occurred across a range of denominations, both Catholic and Protestant; that while the shift was prefigured by developments in the early nineteenth century, it was primarily a mid-nineteenth-century development (1840-70) linked with the emergence of the Victorian family patterns most commonly associated with middle-class whites; and that the changes Douglas describes as "feminising" were not necessarily perceived in that way by mid-nineteenth-century Christians. The "feminisation" process, thus, might be better defined as the emergence of a sometimes-implicit association of femininity and religiosity" (Taves, 1987, 203).

Taves argues that this association was possible because male and female natures and social rules were seen as more and more polarised.

Douglas's question leads us to wonder whether we find the same situation in Catholic Europe. Both Pope and Michaud attempted to describe the place and position of woman in nineteenth century Europe. According to Michaud:

"Le XIXe siècle est le siècle de la Femme. Certes! Mais, dans l'abondante production sur les femmes, n'a-t-on pas trop oublié celle qui est peut-être à l'origine de toutes les autres, la femme *imaginaire*? Cette femme donnée en spectacle, cette femme statue, la Terreur de 1793 la célèbre comme "*la divinité du sanctuaire domestique*"; l'église catholique lui élève des autels et la proclame *immaculée*. Quelques années plus tôt, les missions saint-simoniennes ne s'étaient pas contentées de sillonner l'Europe; elles avaient poursuivi jusqu'en Orient la "*Femme Messie*". Qui aurait pensé que le modèle catholique fût à ce point prégnant dans la Révolution anticléricale et dans le mouvement socialiste? Où situer les poètes, dont on a voulu faire une caution à la médiocrité du siècle? Il est urgent de leur rendre justice. Goethe et Baudelaire sont aussi peu disposés l'un que l'autre à accepter les fadeurs de leurs contemporains: *l'éternel féminin* défie les classifications, et

Baudelaire lance ces mots fameux: "La femme est l'être qui projette la plus grande ombre ou la plus grande lumière dans nos rêves. (...) elle vit spirituellement dans les imaginations qu'elle hante et qu'elle féconde."" (Michaud, 1985, 9)

Michaud specifically looks at nineteenth-century artists. In the words of Baudelaire the imaginary woman is 'Muse et Madone'. Both Muse and Madonna are carnal as well as ideal. The Madonna is linked with the earth through her motherhood, her son secures her connection with heaven. The Muse is paramour and emblem for poetry (Michaud, 1985, 11). According to Michaud, a new relation becomes apparent between men and women in the nineteenth century and the Madonna: no longer

"une relation filiale de vénération ni d'adoration. Chez les artistes, le désir se mêle à la contemplation. Chez les prolétaires saint-simoniennes et celles qui, par la suite, poursuivent leur combat, la Vierge apparaît comme une figure de liberté. S'autorisant de la maternité spirituelle que l'Église reconnaît à Marie sur le peuple des croyants, les femmes socialistes réclament à leur tour une participation à la vie sociale" (Michaud, 1985, 10-11).

Michaud accentuates the crisis of religious life in eighteenth-century France and its continuation into the nineteenth century. The consequence of this crisis is a feminisation of religion. "Les hommes se détournent de plus en plus de la foi et des exercices du culte, alors que les femmes y restent attachées" (Michaud, 1985, 23). It is seen in the participation of women in the sodalities and the lack of men in them. But it is even more noticeable in the religious orders. The female religious orders stood firm after April 1790 when the constitutive Assembly forbade the taking of solemn vows and required the religious, both monks and nuns, to make officially known whether they would leave their monasteries and convents or continue living in them. The Act of August 1792 which decreed the suppression of religious congregations and the sale of their commodities, dispersed them into small groups, or left them on their own, but as soon as the situation showed signs of improving, the nuns started their zealous jobs again.

Michaud points to three consequences of the strong expansion of women congregations and its impact on future developments. First: the spreading of the idea that education and care of the sick naturally belonged to female religious life -- this idea was sustained by the civil authorities. Second: the first item was strongly connected with and influenced the second element, i.e. the conviction that christianisation takes place through women. Third: The institutions that are founded by preference appeal to Mary. These three elements could point to a feminisation of religious life in France. Michaud says in an affirmative voice: "La religion est féminine dans ses cadres et ses structures" (Michaud, 1985, 29). Structure and framework are feminine, but what about the apologetics? Chateaubriand's *Génie du Christianisme*, the book that preluded the Catholic restoration, gives the answer to this question according to Michaud. Chateaubriand agrees with Milton that religion is necessary for women, but even more "L'esprit du christianisme a une tendre sympathie avec le génie des mères" (*Le Génie du Christianisme*, 903, quoted in Michaud, 1985, 29). His defence of christianity heavily draws on the "feminine harmonies" of religion. Thus apologetics are also feminised.

Michaud clearly sees the discrepancy between this elevation of woman and feminine traits -- as especially pronounced in Mary -- and women in real life. The author stresses that the movement that celebrated Mary at the same time demoted woman:

> "Mais il est une question autrement plus insistante, et que l'Église tout au long de la période a refusé d'envisager: celle de la liberté féminine. Comment les femmes, en particulier, ont-elles réagi au modèle écrasant qui leur était tendu? Tant que la spiritualité mettait l'accent sur la *relation* singulière qui unit Marie à son fils, il restait au désir, à l'invention, à l'humanité une place pour s'accomplir. Mais comment faire pour survivre dans un système qui se fixe sur les *privilèges personnels* de la Vierge au risque de devenir l'exutoire malsain des refoulements cléricaux?" (Michaud, 1985, 78).

Michaud's conclusion is that religion was feminised in nineteenth century France, but this feminisation has to be understood on its own terms. It is not the contemporaneous wish for equality and mutuality. Feminisation in that society was a penetration of feminine values as defined by that society.

Pope also focuses on nineteenth century France but with special attention to the Marian events and their effects on French society. Pope summarises Douglas's book as describing feminisation in three stages: "a growing preponderance of women in congregations; the power that this preponderance gave women over religious life; and a 'softening' of theology and religious symbolism that followed as a consequence" (Pope, 1985, 193). I do not agree, however, with her interpretation of the second stage. What Douglas says is that ministers took on feminine traits, not that women took over the ministry. Douglas's argument is subtler than what Pope makes of it.

> "In contrast to Douglas's description of the American experience however, this trend did not lead to a female ideological ascendancy in the Catholic Church. The male hierarchy, as we have seen, not

only maintained but extended control of religious life by validating and popularizing certain affective religious practices and by tying them to the sacramental system" (Pope, 1985, 193).

I do not read this as being in contrast with Douglas's analysis. Pope can be accused of oversimplification: she confuses the terms "woman", "female", and "feminine"[40]. Did women have a preponderance in American nineteenth century religious life (Pope, 1985, 193) or did femininity? Douglas says ministers shifted from having power to exercising influence, and the independent woman disappeared. Where the situation in the Catholic Church was concerned one can similarly question whether this shift had much to do with women. Who shaped the femininity that is being described? I would not with the same rigidity as Pope in connection with Mary, affirm the thesis that men have shaped and defined female symbolism. I would like to modify this statement by saying that patriarchal society shaped female symbolism, i.e. a society of women and men where men are granted more access to public life than women and as a consequence are able to put their mark on ideology but in which women have the possibility to exercise *influence*, be it within the societal confines. It is difficult, however, to measure this influence as it does not express itself in institutional forms. The vagueness of the category *influence* makes it unsuitable for scientific analysis. Introducing this notion can nevertheless have a corrective effect on stringently proclaimed ideas about setting women against men, female against male.

Having started this overview of the interpretation of the nineteenth century by women's studies research with the question "was the nineteenth century feminised?", I should now attempt to give my answer. The authors mentioned here seem to agree that in the nineteenth century Western culture was feminised in one way or another. This feminisation however was a permeation of femininity as seen in the light of that particular society. What is important here is that this femininity and the values it represented did not only apply to women, but also started to be applicable to men -- be it certain categories of men, e.g. ministers -- and penetrated

---

40. Massey describes the terms in the following way: "the terms 'male' and 'female' designate relatively stable, if not absolutely clear, differences in biology. The terms 'masculine' and 'feminine', by contrast, designate historically contingent interpretations of the meanings of these biological sex differences. In interpreting the meaning of biological difference in relation to its particular social and economic arrangement, each society produces its own specific definitions of masculinity and femininity. Thus nothing metaphysical or natural can be claimed for the gender ideals of any society; gender is not given with a metaphysical soul or a biological body. The meaning of 'masculine' or 'feminine' depends on the particular pattern of personal growth determined by a particular historical family or parenting arrangement, which in turn is dependent on the particular social and economic conditions within different societies." (Massey, 1985, 10-11)

an important area of society, i.e. religion. The question thus cannot be answered with an unconditional yes or no. In the nineteenth century the Western world, i.e. the U.S.A. and Europe, was feminised, but this feminisation must be understood on its own terms, i.e. as a nineteenth century concept. It is easy to dismiss that particular kind of feminisation as oppressive towards women and to criticise the nineteenth century definition of the female from a twentieth century perspective. Nevertheless we have to remain aware that this definition is still influential.

At first sight the feminisation of religion in the nineteenth century could be interpreted as a firm base for a positive evolution in the twentieth century, positive that is from the point of view of the place of women in religion and society. History has shown us, however, that this process of feminisation met with increasing opposition. The feminisation that took place was on the one hand successful, but on the other also provoked protest. Why was it successful? And what elements evoked protest? The underlying and more important question is: what kind of woman did the nineteenth century have in mind? Why was that "woman" so eagerly embraced by many women, and forcefully rejected by others? Why does not she suit women a century later? It must be obvious that by asking these questions I regard the term 'woman' as indicating a carrier of cultural constructions. As Braidotti says 'woman' should be defined as "the stock of cumulated knowledge, the theories and representations of the female subject. This is no gratuitous appropriation, for 'I, woman' am affected directly and in my everyday life by what has been made of the subject woman (...)" (Braidotti, 1989, 101). I refer to the particular and specific image that a society has of what a "real" woman[41] is.

In the analysis of the figure of Mary we can find an answer to this question. Mary is an example, an expression of what kind of woman the nineteenth century had in mind: she reaches 'the highest plane of honour ever achieved by woman' (*Het nieuw Scherpenheuvels trompetjen*, 1835). An analysis of the political factors that influenced the rise and continuation of the popularity of Marian devotion will not give us a sufficient answer. I contend that a careful and meticulous reading of the widespread devotional literature should give us the missing clue, i.e. the language and images that were popular in describing women. Whereas some studies of political and ecclesiastical movements tend to arrange

41. Whenever one uses the term "woman" people will rise and ask: what about "what is a man"? I agree that this is a justifiable question. There are as many 'stories' about manhood, and masculinity, and "being a real man" as there about womanhood and femininity. I do not intend to deal with this question however, as it lies outside my range of aims. It will only be looked at as far as it can clarify what woman is.

data in neat and clear theories and hypotheses, reality proves to be more complicated. We do not have to do with one or more institutions that are able to impress their ideas upon the world, with the rest of the world simply accepting this. This is an oversimplified view of the exercise of power. We find, rather,

> "a network of relations, constantly in tension, in activity (...) This power is exercised rather than possessed; it is not the privilege, acquired or preserved, of the dominant class, but the overall effect of its strategic positions (...) These relations go right down to the depths of society; (...) they define innumerable points of confrontation, focuses of instability, each of which has its own risks of conflict, of struggles, and of an at least temporary inversion of the power relations" (Foucault, *Discipline and Punish*, quoted in Miles, 1985, 22-23).

Studying political moves, whether civil or ecclesiastical, we have to do with only one of these networks, and maybe one of the networks where direct confrontations are least fruitful. We also need to consider the influences of every day presences. In nineteenth century society we find, on the Roman Catholic side, the figure of Mary.

4.2. Women in the Nineteenth Century

"Le XIXe siècle est le siècle de la Femme. Certes!" (Michaud, 1985, 9). As I have pointed out before, it is almost impossible to extract the ideas women themselves had about Mary and womanhood. The written sources are dominated by male voices; the paintings, pictures, images are produced by men. Most of the ideas we receive are ideas that have gone through men's hands and minds. The sources that are directly related to women are often produced by men, or written by literate women who occupy an exceptional position. We can only sketch the climate that women lived in. We must try to re-create the atmosphere women in the nineteenth century breathed. We can reconstruct the message received by women. Possibly it will give a hint about how women thought, or felt they must think about themselves and their place in the world, about God and the participation of women in salvific events.

I will present some written sources produced by women themselves, some directed at women (see also the items already mentioned above), and sources, written by men, that deal with the woman question. I will also give a general view of the situation of women in Belgium in the nineteenth century, and the beginning of the twentieth century.

"Naître femme, au 19e siècle et pendant les trois premières décennies du 20e siècle, est plus dangereux que naître homme" (Lory, 1989,17). In Belgium, and in all of Europe, girls are more likely to die at an early age than boys (Poulain, 1989, 25). Statistics (Poulain, 1989, 26-30) show that during the period of 1841-1845 girls run a greater risk of dying from ages 1 to 20. The discrepancy is extremely high around their fifteenth birthday when 50% more girls die than boys. The higher death rate of girls in comparison with that of boys remains until 1930. There is however a decrease in the period of risk: in 1890 it extends from 4 to 19 years, in 1910 from 10 to 18 years, and in 1930 from 12 to 14 years. In Belgium the mortality rate of young people starts to improve from around 1870. From that moment on the discrepancy between the mortality rates of girls and boys starts to diminish. It is difficult to explain the causes behind these figures. Poulain and Taboutin remind us that biology does not provide an explanation: physically the female organism is more resistant than the male organism. They opt for a socio-economic and cultural explanation.

> "Il est clair qu'une défaveur sociale touchait les filles par rapport aux garçons dans ce contexte de la révolution industrielle, défaveur qui ne sera pas instantanément résolue par les lois de la fin du 19e siècle protégeant la condition féminine. On peut même penser que ces lois qui respectent la maternité de la femme risquent de dévaloriser la jeune femme sur le marché de l'emploi. Ainsi, tant que l'idée de l'enfant-objet qui rapporte se maintient, le garçon vaut plus que la fille et on imagine aisément que les parents privilégiaient les garçons par rapport aux filles, par exemple en matière de soins et d'alimentation" (Poulain, 1989, 31).

In this century of industrialism and change, women raise their voices, demanding to be treated as full citizens. In Belgium, feminism tackles some very general problems: the feminists strive for better schooling and training facilities, more professional opportunities for women and the adaptation of marital legislation. A strong impulse was received from the case of Marie Popelin. She had studied law[42] and wanted to take the oath but did not receive permission to do so because the profession of the law was open to men only. In 1892 the *Belgische liga voor rechten van de vrouw* (the Belgian League for Women's Rights) was founded. Among the founding members we find M. and L. Popelin, I. van Diest, H. and L. La Fontaine, and L. Frank. Their aim was to abolish marital power and to anchor family legislation in the basic principle of the equality of woman and man. They also strove for the participation of women in the supervision and the organisation of affairs of public interest.

The movement was far from being successful. It did not connect with most women's lives. This was probably due to the fact that the issues at

---

42. It was only from May 20, 1876 that women were allowed to study at university. It was not until 1890 that women could actually get access to a university.

stake were bourgeois questions. Most women were never in a position to go to university, and as a consequence were never confronted with the questions raised by Belgian feminists (de Weerdt, 1980. 69-77).

There is no question of one single feminist movement. At the end of the nineteenth century Belgium is divided into different political - ideological movements. These movements also influence daily life and those who function in it. The women's movement is not free from these ideological tides. Catholics, liberals, and socialists dominate Belgian society. Even within the same ideological families differences can be noted. Where the Catholics and the women's question are concerned, two groups can be distinguished. On the one hand there are the traditional Catholic women's clubs. They are traditionalist and take a conservative stand. On the other hand we find "Christian Feminism" from the movement founded at a rather late date (1905) by Louise van den Plas to counterpoise the liberal and socialist feminists. This movement offered an enlightened vision of women (Hermans and Struyf, 1984, 195; 203-204). Its objective was to sweep away prejudices against feminism and to offer women better education. The right was demanded for women to have personal properties, but the old code was not destroyed: even though woman and man were subject to the same ethical codes, the Pauline dictum remained untouched: man is the head of woman.

One of the publications directed especially at women is *De christene vrouw. Maandblad voor 'Mariakrans', Anti-socialistische vrouwenbond van Antwerpen*. That is to say: The christian woman. Monthly publication for the "Circle of Mary". The anti-socialist women's association of Antwerp. In the issue of June 1, 1902 an address on the women's question by Miss M.E. Belpaire, chairperson of the Association of Mary, is published. She tells women that they should all live up to Mary's example. She shows that women were present at all moments of historical interest. From creation onwards -- something was missing until woman was created -- she has been there. The first to receive the message of the completion of creation, i.e. the incarnation, was a woman: the holy Virgin Mary. And finally, under the cross we see the Mother of Sorrow. This scene leads Miss Belpaire to make the following remark: the role of men at the end of Jesus' life is not at all remarkable. The women were much more convincing: they are steadfast. This is the example women should follow today, especially in social institutions. Women should be present at decisive moments and stand by the side of the men. If women obtain more rights, they will also have to take on more duties. But, says Miss Belpaire, women are not afraid of this.

This encouraging woman's voice is an exception. The periodical usually contains pious stories, recipes, jokes, practical information, insurance, health, prayers, warnings against alcohol, etc. A fighting spirit is manifest in an article about the passion of the Lord:

> "Ah! truly, the role of woman played in this awful drama at Calvary, is magnificent and beyond all praise! The *weaker* sex showed here once more that it is more tenacious in faith than that sex that is called strong and prides itself on its strength; -- it was not only glorious but also heroic of these women to publicly show compassion and affection for the One who was scoffed at by a hostile and even armed crowd, who was despised and tortured! -- Honour, glory, and eternal exaltation for these heroic and noble women, who were compassionately gathered at the foot of Jesus' cross!" [43] (*De christene vrouw*, 1908, 31 author: P.B.).

This is clearly the voice of someone who tries to highlight the courageous attitude of women in the history of salvation.

In general we can say that the feminist wave that flowed through Europe in the nineteenth century was late in arriving in Belgium. It was mostly the privileged non-Catholic bourgeois women that were part of it. Even though the traditional Catholic societies provided a separate space for women, they seldom incited progressive thoughts. But every now and then a rebellious voice can be heard.

4.3. Ideas about Women

The nineteenth century can be characterised as a narrowing down of the identity of women. A process that started centuries ago now comes to a close: being a woman is being a mother. More and more motherhood has become the exclusive norm. This ideology is proclaimed from within the well-to-do middle classes and penetrates all layers of nineteenth century society. The family, with the child in a central position, is the cornerstone (Harrison, 1976, 81; French, 1985, 198). The standard is that of the man as the provider of the income and the woman as mother and educator (Wieringa, 1978, 106). Motherhood is a holy task (de Munter, 1982, 35; Badinter, 1980, 217-219). Women do not need to fulfil themselves in any other domain than in that of motherhood. "Women belong to the family,

---

43. "Ah! waarlijk, de rol door de vrouw in dit akelig drama van Calvarië gespeeld, is prachtig en boven alle lof! Het 'zwakke' geslacht heeft hier nog eens te meer getoond, dat het van kloeker godsdienstige constitutie is dan 'tgeen eigenlijk 't sterke genaamd wordt en ook volgeerne zich op zijne sterkte beroemt;- want niet alleen glorierijk, maar ook en vooral nog heldhaftig was het voor die vrouwen, alzoo in 't publiek medelijden en genegenheid te betoonen aan Dengene, die door een vijandige en bovendien nog gewapende menigt gehoond, veracht en gefolterd werd!- Eer, glorie en eeuwige verheerlijking dan ook aan dit heldhaftig en edel vrouwental, dat aan den voet van Jezus' kruis in medelijdende houding geschaard stond!"

not to politics. Nature predestined them for housework, not for public functions" (Bonald, quoted in de Beauvoir, 1949, 186). The man remains head of the family but no special attention is paid to his qualities as a father. The mother is educator and teacher. Nothing prevents her from making a success of this because she has a natural talent. Female nature orders her to be a good mother. Only two categories exist: good mothers and bad mothers. Bad mothers are those who do not take care of their children, who do not stay with their children, who do not deserve to use the title of mother because they are selfish, egoistic, and indifferent (Aron, 1980, 9-18; Badinter, 1980, 233-283; Harrison, 1976, 81). This ideal however could only be practised by a small group of women. Reality forced most women to struggle for life, a struggle that prevented them from staying at home, and concentrating unconditionally on their children[44].

The discussion in Belgium about the Bill concerning women's and children's labour (December 13, 1889) gives an impression of the prevailing ideas about women. This discussion had been held since 1840 (Nandrin, 1989, 12). The Catholic party wanted by all means to guard and preserve the morality of women. Léon De Bruyn therefore maintained on several occasions that

> "Jamais la femme ne devrait être obligée de quitter son foyer pour
> aller travailler au moment où son mari revient au logis, au moment
> où elle a à remplir des obligations familiales" (quoted in Nandrin,
> 1989, 15).

When it comes to maternal leave, it is not the mother that the Bill intends to protect but the child. It is remarkable that no regulation was made for the labour of adult women. This was due to the liberal economic principles that were adopted in Belgian politics: regulating the labour of adult women was contrary to the idea of non-interventionism.

The debates about the admission of women in government employment illustrates the kind of discussions that occupied the minds of nineteenth century Belgian politicians. The general regulations of the postal services (July 30 1845) explicitly denied women access to jobs. In 1862 this was extended to the administration of the Chemins de Fer, Postes, Télégraphes. On January 5, 1870 the exclusion came to an end.

---

44. It is impossible to sketch in a few pages the changes that industrialisation imposed in the nineteenth century and their effects on women's lives. I therefore refer to the articles of McDougall, McBride, and Corrado Pope in Bridenthal and Koonz, 1977 and their suggestions for further reading; the book by I. Weber-Kellerman (1983) focuses on German women's lives; a bibliography of the history of family and motherhood can be found in de Munter, 1982, 274-285.

The debates are dominated by two political families: the catholics and the liberals. The catholics want to keep women, especially married women, at home.

> "Le salaire de la femme appauvrit la famille: aucun salaire ne peut compenser les maux que crée son absence du foyer ... funeste désordre qui ne peut que compléter la ruine de la vie de famille" (Le moniteur des employées, Mai 27 1888, 2, quoted in Peemans, 1989, 83).

The liberals want women to gain access to administration jobs. There are limits however: it is "rendre un grand service aux hommes que de tenir ceux-ci à l'écart des emplois inférieurs" (L'Étoile belge, January 18 1893, quoted in Peemans, 1989, 83)[45].

Other sources inform us about the prevalent views regarding women. Criminological studies at the end of the nineteenth century show: "c'est toujours à travers son sexe et sa fonction de mère que la femme est jugée conforme ou non au rôle social qui lui est assigné de par sa nature" (Dupont-Bouchat, 1989, 97). Or as De Ryckere (1891) says:"Si le criminel représente dans nos sociétés policées la sauvagerie primitive, on a trouvé entre lui et la femme des similitudes frappantes" (quoted in Dupont-Bouchat, 1989, 97).

This image is counterbalanced by that in the media: Briot (1989) has analysed L'Illustration européenne (1870-1880) and on this basis outlines the prevailing image of the liberal Catholic bourgeois woman at the end of the nineteenth century. A little girl is supposed to be well-behaved and motionless, wearing pretty dresses unfit for play. Whenever she tries to perform an activity, catastrophe results, so it is wise to remain frozen. While growing up her main task is to become more and more incorporeal. Vitality and spontaneity must disappear. She may fill her days with musing about Love. If she is not dreaming about her beloved, her thoughts should be dedicated to her father, or brother, she must always think of a man. Her entire being must be absorbed by 'Love'. Three characters occupy the stage in the girl's life when she becomes nubile: the girl, her mother, and prospective candidates. Madame-mère is the person on which everything hinges. She will classify the suitors. "Quant à la jeune fille, l'usage du monde se charge de porter un correctif cuisant à sa vision sentimentale et romanesque de l'hymen" (Briot, 1989, 111). Contrary to all her musings, dowries appear to be the central issue in marriage. Even though marriage is not an easy task, it is the only means for women to

---

45. During the economic crisis of the 1930's, jobs at the central administrations were again reserved exclusively for men only.

fulfil their vocation: motherhood. "Épouse, mère, ménagère, c'est donc autour de ces trois rôles que devra s'articuler la destinée de cette jeune fille rêveuse, désoeuvrée, abîmée dans l'attente" (Briot, 1989, 112).

4.4. Conclusion

The nineteenth century Belgian woman cannot be described. Women themselves are separated into social classes. It is obvious that a middle class woman had less to do with the labour laws than women from the working-classes. It would be interesting to relate the mortality rates to class. The ideal of being a spouse and mother, always at home and ready to receive husband and children is obviously also class-bound. Catholic groups were intent on strengthening the prevalent ideology. They try to help women to confirm to this ideal role. Liberals seem to want to break this but they do not really succeed. Women have to cope with an image that on the one hand gives them the responsibility of educating of children, and on the other hand compares them with criminals, or less brutally puts them under the responsibility of men. Conflicting ideas and ideals, and a harsh reality define women's lives in nineteenth century Belgium.

5. Concluding remarks

> *"It is the misleading familiarity of 'history'*
> *which can break open the daily naturalism of*
> *what surrounds us"*
> D. Riley

I started the analysis of nineteenth century Marian devotion in Belgium by raising the question whether we should look at the nineteenth century as a century that has known a feminisation of its culture. My answer to that, in a general remark, was that we indeed have to consider this evolution in the nineteenth century, also in Europe, but that we have to be careful in valuing this evolution from an end-of-the-twentieth-century perspective. When I remark that it is ironical that the feminisation of culture went hand in hand with a decline of serious intellectual activity in Roman Catholicism, it becomes obvious that this remark is directed by the importance attached to intellectual activity in my own world today. Rather than give an evaluation of this evolution in the nineteenth century, it is important to understand its influence on our existence in the world today. Studying the nineteenth century is no nostalgic reflex, but a necessity.

The ideas about women in the Roman Catholic part of nineteenth century Belgium can be summarised as ambiguous. On the one hand we see that women were valued for their role as spouse and mother. Politicians try to protect women so that they can give themselves entirely to their 'holy' vocation. This idea is supported by religious discourse, in this specific case discourse about Mary. Even though the educational responsibility of women is emphasised, this does not lead to legal or spiritual adulthood of women. Whatever their position, they are always able to hand over final responsibility to a man, or seen from another perspective, they always have to obey to a higher authority: man. These ideas are not contradicted in religious texts, even the example of Mary shows that she always remains one step below the Father and the Son.

Mary is the most perfect example for women, especially when it comes to chaste behaviour. The emphasis on chastity for women in Marian devotional texts reveals the conflicting images about women: they are allowed to be responsible for children, but on the other hand women seem to be creatures who, if not forced to curb themselves, lead licentious lives. This idea explains why women should always be guarded by a man and why motherhood is the ultimate goal: man has the power and the authority to demand obedience, motherhood diverts attention from a lustful life. An outstanding example of the preoccupation with chastity is bishop Malou who does not allow Mary to be depicted with naked feet. He overlooks the message of innocence and humility that naked feet convey. The ideal woman is a woman who blamelessly devotes all her thoughts and attention to men. This attention and devotion is pervaded with chastity.

A remarkable element of this nineteenth-century country is the attempt at producing a coherent society that is truly Roman Catholic. Even art is involved in creating this society. 'True' religious art is supposed to be in conformity with the medieval ideal. The 'art' produced is at least recognisable as belonging to the Roman Catholic world. It is an element of the identity of Roman Catholics in Belgium. I do not go into the struggle for power that was connected with the attempt to give the neo-gothic style a dominant position. I only give consideration to the presence of this style as the outcome of the struggle.

Feminisation of this society has very little to do with the position and ideas about women. A certain pragmatism is evident: the ideal woman as modelled on Mary will never get into conflict with the liberal economic principles: an obedient woman who does not attempt to join the labour force, or who remains at least situated on its lower levels is politically and economically desirable. Feminisation only seems to take place as far as it reinforces the attempts to produce a coherent, Roman Catholic society.

It is very difficult to penetrate the reality of women's lives in nineteenth century Belgium and the meaning of Mary in those women's lives. I can only attempt to produce an interpretation that is not contradicted by the data that are available. Most ideals about women must be related to a bourgeois background. Working-class women did not have time to sit and devote all their thoughts to men. They neither had the urge to gain access to university as going to school was hardly within their reach. Survival was their first aim. Keeping in mind the mortality rates of girls, the struggle for survival was very real indeed. Keeping this kind of life in mind, it is possible to situate the devotion to Mary within this frame. We have seen that many of the attributes of Mary emphasised her compassionate and interceding characteristics. Mary is accessible for everything and everyone. Whatever one has on one's mind, it can be communicated to Mary. She offers solace: she has known sorrow, but has remained pure. She is omnipresent in a literal way: she is printed on all sorts of things. The rather loose way in which the commendations of the bishop were applied by the printer imply that not too much attention was given to the details in the depiction of the Immaculate Conception. First of all it was important just to have the Immaculate Conception printed: for this it sufficed to offer one type that could be recognised as the Immaculate Conception, how the details were filled in was less important. The presence of Mary in all aspects of life can provide a feeling of security: wherever you are, whatever you do, you can always rely on Mary.

This interpretation implies that Mary in the nineteenth century provided comfort to women. It made it possible for them to cope with life. The twentieth century emphasis on liberation and struggle seems to be at cross-purposes with this comforting position. Comfort often seems to breed resignation and possibly furthers stagnation. It is questionable however if any other message could have survived in that specific society, in which Roman catholics were in search of their identity. Every thing possible was done to streamline that identity.

In the next, and concluding chapter, we will have to take up this nineteenth century heritage and connect it with the analysis of contemporary appropriations of Mary.

Appendix I: events in the nineteenth century

1800-1823	Papacy of Pius VII	
1814	May	Pius VII back in Rome
August 7		Sollicitudo Omnium Ecclesiarum -restoration of the Jesuits
1823-1829	Papacy of Leo XII	
1825		Holy Year
1829-1830	Papacy of Pius VIII	
1830		Catherine Labouré's vision of the Miraculous Medal in the Rue du Bac
1831-1846	Papacy of Gregory XVI	
1832		Sterckx archbishop of Belgium
1838		First coronation of statue of Mary by Pope Gregory XVI in Rome, Santa Maria Maggiore
1842		Discovery of manuscript "Traité de la vraie dévotion à la Sainte Vierge" of Grignion de Montfort
1846		Mary Immaculate declared Patroness of United States
		Vision at La Salette
		Vision at Nouillan
1846-1878	Papacy of Pius IX	
1847		Restoration of Congregations of Mary and Associations of the Children of Mary by Pius IX
1849		"Ubi Primum" preparatory encyclical to Immaculate Conception
1851		Holy Year
		Official recognition of vision of La Salette by Pope Pius IX Coronation statue of Our Lady of the Future Mothers at Rome by Pope Pius IX
1854 Dec 8		Dogma of Immaculate Conception: Ineffabilis Deus (for an account of the drawing up of Ineffabilis Deus, see Söll, 1984, 209-213)
1858		Bernadette's visions at Lourdes
1864 Dec 8		Quanta Cura and Syllabus -denunciation of important ideas of modern life
1869-1870	Vatican Council	
July 18		Constitutio de Ecclesia -dogma of infallibility
1870 Sept 20	Fall of the Papal States	
1871		Visions at Pontmain

1872	Visions at Krüth-Neubois
1876	Visions at Pellevoisin; St.Palais; Marpingen
1877	Visions at Dittrichswald
1878-1903	Papacy of Leo XIII, Pope of the Rosary (twelve encyclicals about the rosary)
1879	Vision at Knock
1891 May 15	Rerum Novarum
1903-1914	Papacy of Pius X
1904	Coronation of Our Lady of Misericorde and the Immaculate Virgin in Rome
1907 July 3	Lamentabili -against modernism
Sept 8	Pascendi Dominici Gregis -against modernism

For an extended overview of devotion to Mary in Flanders, see Lehouck,1980.

Appendix II: Ineffabilis Deus

"... Ad honorem sanctae et individuae Trinitatis, ad decus et ornamentum Virginis Deiparae, ad exaltionem fidei catholicae et christianae religionis augmentum, auctoritate Domini nostri Iesu Christi, beatorum Apostolorum Petri et Pauli ac Nostra declaramus, pronuntiamus et definimus, doctrinam, quae tenet, beatissimam Virginem Mariam in primo instanti suae conceptionis fuisse singulari omnipotentis Dei gratia et privilegio, intuitu meritorum Christi Iesu Salvatoris humani generis, ab omni originalis culpae labe praeservatam immunem, esse a Deo revelatam atque idcirco ab omnibus fidelibus firmiter constanterque credendam.
Quapropter si qui secus ac a Nobis definitum est, quod Deus avertat, praesumpserint corde sentire, ii noverint ac porro sciant, se proprio iudicio condemnatos, naufragium circa fidem passos esse et ab unitate Ecclesiae defecisse, ac praeterea facto ipso suo semet oeni a iure statutis subiicere, si quod corde sentuint, verbo aut scripto vel alio quovis externo modo significare ausi fuerint."
(Denzinger 1641)

Appendix III: Prints

144

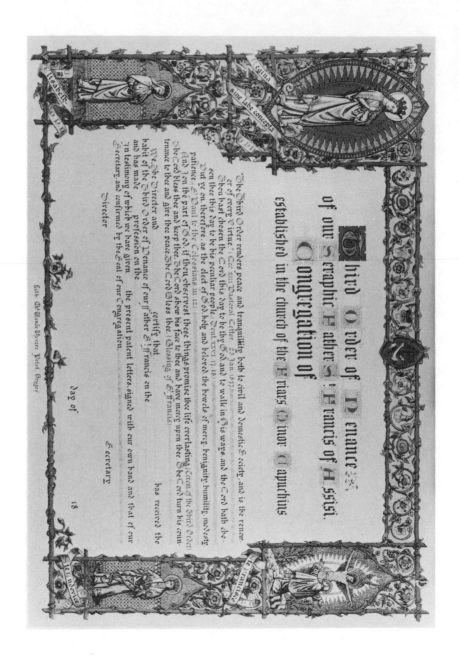

Third Order of Penance of our Seraphic Father St Francis of Assisi.

Congregation of

established in the church of the Friars Minor Capuchins

The Third Order renders peace and tranquillity both to civil and Domestic Society, and is the renewer of every Virtue.' (Leo XIII Pastoral Letter 25 Jan 1877)

Thou hast chosen the Lord this day to be thy God, and to walk in His ways, and the Lord hath chosen thee this day to be his peculiar people. (Deut. xxvi. 17, 18.)

Put ye on, therefore, as the elect of God, holy and beloved, the bowels of mercy, benignity, humility, modesty, patience.' (St Paul to the Colossians iii. 12.)

And if thou observest these things promise thee life everlasting. (Crown of the Third Order)

The Lord bless thee and keep thee. The Lord show his face to thee and have mercy upon thee. The Lord turn his countenance to thee and give thee peace. The Lord bless thee. (Blessing of St Francis.)

We, the Director and _____ certify that _____ has received the habit of the Third Order of Penance of our Father St Francis on the _____ profession on the _____ and has made

In testimony of which we have given the present patent letters, signed with our own hand and that of our Secretary, and confirmed by the Seal of our Congregation. _____

Director _____

Director _____ day of _____ 18

Secretary _____

Lith. The Gambezz Figueres Pdotz Brugge

Chapter 4

Desperately Seeking Mary

Introduction

We have arrived at the last chapter of this book. The building-bricks constructed in the previous chapters can be used as the basis of a constructive, provocative and evocative interpretation. After recapitulating the main points of the first three chapters, I will proceed to a further indication and delineation of the community that is engaged in interpreting Mary. Finally, I will attempt to present an interpretation of Mary that can empower women in a twentieth-century secularised society.

1. Seeking

In contrast with the theologians/philosophers of the first chapter, I do not want to offer a new interpretation of Mary. I radically want to situate the act of interpretation within the community of women who are confronted with Mary. I do not see a role for the theologian in providing yet another image of Mary. New images usually belong to the domain of poets, writers, painters, and seers. The interpretation is left in the hands of the community. "The theologian's task is neither to invent a new religion nor to leave his (sic) interpreters the task of determining the appropriateness of his (sic) categories to the Christian tradition" (Tracy, 1975, 72). The theologian can be left to unravel the process of interpretation and as such make a contribution. She can indicate where symbols are pointing and whether they are appropriately used.

Is it possible to re-interpret traditional symbols? Can we continue looking for salvation within the traditional religions? Or do we have to conclude that traditional religions -- in this particular case Christianity -- and its symbols are fundamentally corrupt? These were the questions that started this research and that were formulated at the end of the first chapter. The model of interpretation that we developed in chapter 2 shows us the possibilities that are still open for symbols like Mary. That model opened our eyes to the importance of tradition for the world that generates any story, any symbol. The Ricoeurian scheme emphasises the inevitable embeddedness of symbols in a pre-given world. This world not only determines meaning, it also is the condition for understanding a symbol, a story. Mary is a symbol that belongs to a specific story, to the story of Christianity. We cannot isolate Mary and try to fill her up with new meanings apart from the story that she arises from. The possibilities of the Mary symbol are streamlined and limited by the tradition in which she participates.

Mary belongs to the Christian story, she is an element in it and she derives meaning from her position in that story. I see Christianity as embodied in the community of people who, inspired by the story that is told around the life of Jesus, are committed to the project of a just world. When Mary is isolated from this story, we can no longer claim that she is Mary. Those authors who remove Mary from the Christian story to a completely different story cannot claim that this is still Mary. The proposals of Mary Daly, Carol Ochs, and others, imaginative as they are, must be dismissed as being not about Mary.

Halkes, Radford Ruether, Johnson, Schüssler Fiorenza, Gebara and Bingemer continue the dialogue with the Christian tradition. I have shown the flaws in their designs in the first chapter. I want to bring some elements to mind that have become clearer after the discussions in chapters 2 and 3. In chapter 2 we stressed the importance of the interpreting subject. Halkes, Radford Ruether and Johnson hardly specify this interpreting subject. They operate with a rather vague notion of 'woman'. It is as if 'woman' is defined as 'the person who needs to be liberated from sexism'. I want to redefine the project of 'liberation from sexism' into a project of 'bringing women into discourse'. This plan includes 'liberation from sexism' but moves beyond it as it has a constructive component. It furthermore implies the necessity to consider who 'women' are. The projects of Halkes, Radford Ruether and Johnson ought to be reconsidered in the light of a reflection on 'women'.

Seeing Mary as a symbol has widened the field of reference and has lifted her out of a context of ecclesiastical definition. The question asked at the end of the first chapter, 'is a dogmatic approach of Mary possible?', must be reviewed here. We first of all must clarify what 'dogmatic' is. It is not to be understood as the fixing of an ecclesiastical definition. I understand it as reflective and systematic thinking about the interpretation of the salvific events. A dogmatic approach of Mary is a reflection on the process of interpretation of Mary, fully acknowledging the historicity of any particular situation set in the context of a community. This community is committed to the liberation of women and men, finding its root model in the Bible and its ensuing modifications and interpretations. Mary has been generated by the Christian tradition. We cannot understand or interpret Mary without implicating that tradition. Mary as a religious symbol is rooted in the Mystery of Being as it is expressed within the Christian tradition.

We have seen that the story is not the only determining element in interpreting and understanding a symbol. We also have to take into account the interpreting subject. I emphasised the genderedness of the interpreting subject, and I showed how sexual difference is essential to any feminist claim. The interpreting subject, here defined as a community, cannot be disconnected from the interpretation. The community envisioned here, carries with it the liberating and the incapacitating definitions of womanhood. This community can only be a community of solidarity and resistance if the pain, suffering, and joy of women is integrally part of it. In this last chapter I will further explore the interpreting community as being a community that is committed to the Christian tradition. I will do this in dialogue with E. Schüssler Fiorenza and S.D. Welch. Next, I will make an attempt at an interpretation of Mary that can be meaningful today. Before turning to Schüssler Fiorenza and Welch, I will explain the title of this book, which is also the title of this chapter.

2.Desperately Seeking

The film *Desperately Seeking Susan* by Susan Seidelman, relates the story of a bored housewife Roberta, who gets involved in a tremendously exciting and life-changing adventure when, on an impulse, she tries to find out about a certain 'Susan'. It all begins when Roberta sees an advertisement in the newspaper: 'Desperately seeking Susan', accompanied with a place and date. Roberta is intrigued and at the appointed time goes to the meeting place. She finds out who Susan is, and overhears somebody saying that Susan loves 'trouble'. Roberta follows Susan and buys the jacket that Susan has traded in for a pair of boots. This is the beginning of a rollicking adventure. Amnesia and mistaken identity produce a series of ever more crazy situations. Roberta, in trying to solve the riddle of the advertisement, has to find the answer to several questions: who has written this ad, and for what reason, and who is Susan? In answering these questions Roberta becomes involved in the action: she cannot remain a mere observer, an outsider. Roberta participates in the story of Susan. She even becomes the main actor. *Desperately Seeking Susan* is not a film about Susan, it is a film about Roberta. In her search for Susan, she finally finds herself. During her amnesiac condition Roberta, thinking she is Susan, traces back Susan's steps, but nothing seems really familiar. When she regains her memory Roberta the housewife likewise appears to be unfamiliar. The whole adventure means that Roberta can never go back to her boring life as a wife of a succesful whirlpool salesman. The conversation at the end of the film between Roberta and her husband is hilarious and sad at the same time. Roberta's husband: "I want you to come home with me." Roberta: "Why?" And again, Roberta's husband: "I want you to come home with me". Roberta: "Why?" Even the second time, Roberta's husband is unable to give the simple and only appropriate answer: "Because I love you".

Instead he mutters something about "finding help" and "money is not the problem". He cannot understand that Roberta has fundamentally changed and is completely unable to revert to the 'old' Roberta. In her desperate search for Susan and herself she has been totally immersed in an activity that engages her entire person. It is impossible to eliminate everything that has happened with a simple shrug of the shoulders or with 'money is not a problem'. Roberta has become Roberta: she has become aware of herself as someone who is still called Roberta, still is Roberta, and at the same time is no more the Roberta of the beginning of the film.

Beside the obvious reference to Mary -- Madonna, the popstar who built her image on reversals of Roman Catholic elements, plays the part of Susan -- there are other reasons that led me to choose this film as an example. In this book I set out to find Mary. The questions asked were: who is she, who writes about her, and why? In this search for Mary a quest similar to Roberta's has taken place: I at first set out to find Mary but that soon turned out to be a dead-end. The variety of interpretations, however conflicting they often are, did not seem to offer any answer as to why one interpretation is preferable to another. It seemed to be a desperate search. As *Desperately Seeking Susan* showed us most of all Roberta's searching, so did this study especially highlight my hunt for an appropriate way of bringing Mary into the discourse. Rather than trying to find Mary, this book is about developing a model of interpretation. It consists of two components that are intricately linked to one another: a hermeneutical and an historical element. This model somehow looks like the journey that Roberta makes. Seeking Mary will be an expedition that involves the interpreting subject. In chapter two we dealt at length with this interpreting subject. It is an interpreting subject that does not appear from nowhere but which has a history. As Roberta can only be her true self after having retraced her own history, so we have to retrace the history of our own subjectivity as it has been defined in the past. In chapter 3 we identified the contribution of the nineteenth-century interpretation of Mary to the definition of female subjectivity. I will now return to the interpreting subject, especially to the aspect of 'we, women'. I will elaborate this 'collective' subject from a theological perspective.

3. Who is seeking?

Introduction

In chapter two, when presenting and exploring the debate, I referred to the discussion about female subjectivity. I finally followed Rosi Braidotti as, at this stage of the debate, she argued "in a brilliant reversal of the terms structuring debates on essentialism" (Brennan, 1989, 16) that the strategic politics of essentialism opened up possibilities of change. She offered a foundation for the claim that women should be interpretative subjects. Braidotti emphasised the crucial aspect of "we, women". This "we, women" is defined as "the movement of the liberation of the 'I' of each and every woman". Speaking as a theologian, I want to specify this community as being "the movement of the liberation of the 'I' of each and every woman, and the seeking of places of liberating revelation". I will take a look at the ideas of Elisabeth Schüssler Fiorenza and Sharon D. Welch to clarify this point. Schüssler Fiorenza introduced the idea of *ekklesia gynaikon* to identify the space where revelation is happening. Her insistence on the *ekklesia gynaikon* as a hermeneutic centre of interpretation is challenging. Sharon Welch spoke of communities of resistance and solidarity. In dialogue with these two authors, I will try to specify and delineate what "the movement of the liberation of the 'I' of each and every women, and the seeking of places of liberating revelation" means.

3.1. Ekklesia gynaikon

Elisabeth Schüssler Fiorenza introduces the idea of Woman-Church after a double-edged struggle with on the one hand the interpretation of biblical texts and on the other hand the attempt to bring women to the fore as historical agents. She subjects biblical texts to a litmus test consisting of the idea that the word of God must end all relations of dominance and exploitation. This test has arisen from the experiences of women. Therefore, she continues, the hermeneutic centre of interpretation for a feminist reading of the Bible is Woman-Church, i.e. the movement of self-identified women and women-identified-men in biblical religion (Schüssler Fiorenza, 1984, xiv). Woman-Church is the quest of women for self-affirmation, survival, power and self-determination, liberation from patriarchal alienation, marginalisation and oppression (Schüssler Fiorenza, 1985, 126). It is important that women take an option for their women-selves (Schüssler Fiorenza, 1984, xv). The place of validation of the interpretation of biblical texts is the emancipatory praxis of Woman-Church (Schüssler Fiorenza, 1984, 154, note 30). Elisabeth Sch üssler Fiorenza looks for places where divine revelation is taking place. She finds it in Woman-Church in the past and in the present.

> "The central commitment and accountability for feminist theologians is not the Church as a male institution but to women in the Churches, not the tradition as such but to a feminist transformation of Christian traditions, not to the Bible as a whole but to the liberating Word of God finding expression in the biblical writings" (Schüssler Fiorenza, 1984, 3).

Point of departure is the experience of the struggle for the liberation of women (Schüssler Fiorenza, 1984,13). Schüssler Fiorenza definitely does not want to use the term 'woman' or 'feminine' as a hermeneutical key. It could lead to a reproduction of Western totalizing gender dualism. This is a return to a logic of identity, an attempt at uniting particulars in an essence. In feminist biblical scholarship it leads to the creation of a 'canon within the canon', an organising principle. This finally ends with situating authority outside women. Authority becomes an external source and many texts would be rejected (Schüssler Fiorenza, 1989, 313-314). In order to escape the logic of identity Schüssler Fiorenza diverts the attention from a focus on women in the Bible to a feminist reconstruction of early Christianity, and from the formation of the canon and universalising principles to a discussion of the *process* of biblical interpretation and evaluation that encompasses the unfolding and the evaluation of oppressive as well as liberating functions of biblical texts in the lives and struggles of women (Schüssler Fiorenza, 1989, 314-315). Schüssler Fiorenza's project is situated at the crossroads of biblical historical literary criticism, liberation theology, and feminist theory (See also 1984, 85). All of this is encompassed in the matrix of a feminist commitment and the struggle for overcoming the patriarchal politics of otherness. Schüssler Fiorenza recognises the attempts of major authors to construct a feminist discourse about women.

> "Yet in this attempt to construct an oppositional discourse on woman or on gender differences feminist theory has kept in circulation the discourse of classical Western philosophy and theology on gender-dualism or gender-polarity that understands man as the subject of history, culture and religion and woman as the other" (Schüssler Fiorenza, 1989, 316).

Schüssler Fiorenza contends that unmasking the totalizing theorizing about the 'otherness of women' can enhance a thinking about woman in terms of a subject determined by a specific cultural and historical context and characterised by plurality amongst women. In her own words:

"(...) feminist identity is not based on the experience of biological sex or essential gender differences but on the common historical experience of women as unconsciously collaborating or struggling participants in patriarchal culture and history, (...)" (Schüssler Fiorenza, 1983, 31).

From within her own context Schüssler Fiorenza asks a question similar to the one asked by Rosi Braidotti:

"if just as race, nationality, or social status, so also gender is a socio-cultural-historical construct and not a feminine substance or universal female essence, then the question arises how women can transcend our being socially constructed as *woman* and at the same time become historical subjects as *women* struggling against patriarchal domination. If subjectivity is seen as totally determined by gender one ends up with feminine essentialism, if it is understood as genderless then one reverts to the generic human subject of liberalism for whom gender, class, or race are irrelevant" (Schüssler Fiorenza, 1989, 317, also 1984, 86).

Her remark about essentialism should be reviewed in the light of the illuminating explanation of the term's history given by Brennan (Brennan, 1989) and of the proposal by Braidotti. Schüssler Fiorenza thinks that she can move beyond the either-or position by reverting the attention to the Western 'politics of otherness', executing a continuous critical deconstruction of these politics, claiming and reconstructing women's own experiences, and sustaining a permanent reflection on their common differences.

Fiorenza seems to bring the group of women together under the common denominator of 'struggling against', 'struggling for'. This is a rather negative attitude. A suspicious questioner immediately asks: 'what if this common struggle is no longer necessary?' Schüssler Fiorenza herself encourages us to view "not only women's oppression but also women's power as the locus of revelation" (Schüssler Fiorenza, 1983, 35). This still remains a rather vague concept. In view of our reading of Braidotti it seems that Schüssler Fiorenza can only hold on to her claim if she draws on essentialism as a political factor. How can one claim one's own experience if there is no 'I' that can claim this experience? Should this reluctance to accept a radical recognition of the essential difference between women and men maybe be seen as a move that makes it possible to hold women and women-identified-men together in the ekklesia gynaikon? I contend that the ekklesia gynaikon can only embrace women and men when this radical difference is acknowledged. This radical difference could imply that liberating revelation is different for women and for men. This however does not necessarily lead to their occupying mutually exclusive spaces. This will become clearer from a reading of Welch. Before turning to Welch, we have to turn our attention to the question of 'authority'.

Schüssler Fiorenza's work is important as she has radically shifted the attention from the biblical texts to the *ekklesia gynaikon* as authoritative centre. The hermeneutic centre of interpretation is the movement of self-identified women and women-identified-men in biblical religion. The central issue for her is the *Wirkungsgeschichte* of the biblical texts in women's lives and how women can interpret them. My own focus is not limited to the biblical texts. I want to incorporate the traditions that those texts have inspired and that determine our reading of the texts today. Mary is one of the symbols that has been generated by that Christian tradition, which includes biblical texts. It is obvious from my reading of Ricoeur that I believe that it is meaningless to speak of authority apart from the hermeneutic enterprise. This involves both text and interpreting subject. The 'hermeneutic centre of interpretation' is the interpreting subject within the hermeneutic activity, which means that interpreting subject and text, in their interplay, are the authoritative centre. Authority does neither lie in the text nor in the interpreting community, but in the interchange between them.

3.2. Communities of resistance and solidarity

More reflection about communities can be found in the work of the theologian Sharon D. Welch. She attempts to write a feminist theology of liberation. Point of departure for her book is an analysis of contemporary Christianity. Western Christianity, so her analysis runs, is immersed in a situation of crisis and she accepts the challenge to find a way of dealing with this crisis. Welch sees liberation theology as a fruitful partner in the discussion. It is not her aim to construct a system in which language about God will be correlated with ontological systems or to develop a coherent system of reference to the Divine, i.e. the traditional task of fundamental theology (Welch, 1985, 6). Her own interest lies in developing a theology that does not situate the question of truth in the correspondence of language about God to something eternal but in the creation of a community of peace, justice, and equality. The truth-question becomes a question of praxis. Welch does not study the content of faith and the symbols of Christianity, but the praxis: "The discernment of the social and political function of symbols and images is a new task for theologians" (Welch, 1985, 16). It is naïve to suppose that the oppressive history of Christianity would be due to a wrong interpretation of its symbols (Welch, 1985, 54). In her continuous dialogue with liberation theology Welch also communicates with the ideas of Michel Foucault.

Welch experiences her own position as double-edged. She takes the position of the oppressor as well as that of oppressed. On the one hand she belongs to white bourgeois U.S., on the other hand she is a woman. The tension between these two positions is a concern of ongoing reflection in her book. She moves between nihilistic relativism and a commitment to the struggle against oppression. This involves a conscious choice for and affirmation of the possibility of liberation, the resistance against oppression and an attempt to understand freedom and its conditions. The nihilistic pole expresses the awareness of discrepancies between ideals and praxis, the impossibility to make pronouncements about certain knowledge and final liberation (Welch, 1985, 14).

Welch's position as a feminist theologian is characterised by this oscillation between commitment and scepticism. A feminist theology must be rooted in the liberating praxis of sisterhood. This is an explicit identification with a specific group. It is the horizon that determines Welch's entire project.

> "I maintain this perspective but do so with a note of skepticism. I agree that it is important to identify one's perspective and to choose to enter the 'battle for truth' on the side of the oppressed, yet I do so for reasons different from those given by some liberation theologians. Rather than grounding this choice in some atemporal or noncontingent structure -- tradition, revelation, the person and work of Jesus -- I understand this choice to be a moral one, a choice not free from the concomitant element of risk" (Welch, 1985, 26)[1].

The 'epistemological privilege of the oppressed' does not automatically imply that the insights that come forward from that area are true. The validity of this perspective is its praxis: social and political emancipation (Welch, 1985, 27).

All theological discourse is temporal and cannot be identified with true Christianity. Welch condemns the idea that something ought to be true because it is 'original', e.g. because it has always been in the Bible or because it has known a very long tradition.

> "The identification of continuity with truth evades the complex history of discourse. It also evades the question of truth and attempts to return to a traditional notion of truth as propositional" (Welch, 1985, 52).

---

1. In her book, *A Feminist Ethic of Risk* (Welch, 1990), Welch struggles against the paralysing despair which she encounters in white bourgeois U.S. society. The texts of black Afro-American women inspire, even force her to develop an ethic of risk. I will return to these ideas.

The identification of truth with continuity is not tenable: it makes possible all kinds of Christianity, from the most oppressive to the most liberating variety.

I value Welch's approach because of her balancing between commitment and skepticism. Furthermore, I agree with her idea about connecting symbols with social practices instead of correlating them with "coherent systems of references to the divine". It must be clear that I do not share her idea that the misinterpretation of symbols cannot be seen as a cause of an oppressive Christianity when it comes to Mary. Welch contends that the oppressiveness could lie in the symbols themselves. She can only hold on to this idea if she conceptualizes symbols as isolated elements. In turning to Ricoeur I have extensively argued that symbols must be seen as functioning within a text, and as being interpreted by a subject. It is thus impossible to understand symbols as corrupt in themselves. My model of interpretation tries to control the process of interpretation, and as such tries to work towards liberating perspectives on Mary. The side of the interpreting subject, defined as "we, women" etcetera, directs interpretations towards liberating interpretations for women.

In Welch's approach we also encounter the same problem as we mentioned with Schüssler Fiorenza: the commitment for a specific group is voiced in terms of 'struggle against'. There is no positive identification. I call to mind Braidotti's remark that there is a stronger bond among women than an ethics of solidarity or a mere sharing of common interests. I contend, however, that this ethics of solidarity is the ground where women and men come together. In emphasizing the essential commonality of women, i.e. the fact that they are women, one could get lost in a so-called separatist movement. This has never been my aim. The 'feminist cogito' (Braidotti) is necessary if women want to claim their own interpretations. The community of resistance and solidarity should be seen as a community of women and men, who learn to live with and struggle for the acceptance of differences; and who acknowledge that liberating revelation could be entirely different for each of the sexes.

*

* *

Interpretation will emerge within the interpreting community. From the dialogue with Schüssler Fiorenza and Welch, as conducted in the previous chapters, the interpretative community considered here can be described as follows: it is a community of women united in the liberation of the 'I' of each and every woman, seeking liberation in the process of dealing with the text one encounters, not discarding tradition but working through it, and as such unexpectedly finding itself enwrapped in revelatory moments. It is this community that is the active participant in the imaginative process. It is a community which is open to a community of resistance and solidarity in which women and men take part, realising that differences do not have to divide but are the mode for revelation to happen. The community referred to here participates in Christianity's quest for justice and wholeness. Christianity is to be understood as the ekklesia inspired and formed by the biblical texts. The Bible is not a timeless archetype but a structuring prototype, a formative root model, an experiential authority that "can 'render God' although it is written in the 'language of men'" (Schüssler Fiorenza, 1984, xvi-xvii).

The hermeneutic approach explains the differences between women, between women and men, in interpretations of Mary: the pre-understanding of the text in which Mary appears is different. I have given an example of determining factors in that pre-understanding in analysing Mary in nineteenth century Roman Catholic Flanders. This tradition already streamlines the possible interpretations. Differences among women will have to be specified, and these differences need not lead to ruptures. Understanding the backgrounds can bring forth understanding.

As I explained earlier, S. Welch's oscillation between scepticism and commitment is a position I recognise very well. It is a feeling of being torn between hope and despair. Welch has tried to reconcile the paralysing scepticism in developing an ethic of risk. She makes use of novels written by Afro-American women. In those novels she finds the characteristics of an ethic of risk: "a redefinition of responsible action, grounding in community, and strategic risk-taking" (Welch, 1990, 20). Her conclusion is that

> "Middle-class people can be empowered by a recognition of the power of the divine in their love and courage. They bear witness to the transcendent, healing power of love; they bear witness to the beauty and wonder of life. They are a dangerous memory" (Welch, 1990, 180).

Welch tries to present us with an ethic that enables people to fight against despair, that empowers them for continuous commitment. My question is whether traditional religious symbols can still give rise to thought given our twentieth century situation. Up till now I have shown *how* this can take place. Now is the moment to investigate if Mary can indeed be a vital symbol that gives rise to thought. Whereas Welch has found inspiration in the novels of African-American women, I turn to a Dutch, feminist film to explore this question. In a secularised society, reference to the religious dimension of life is not evident, and the traditional means of reference seem to be drained of meaning. A reading, or rereading of the biblical text for example seems to become a mere repetition of empty talk. As I said at the beginning of this chapter, we need poets, novelists, seers, and I will now add film directors, to open windows for inspiring rereadings. The film *Gebroken Spiegels* (Broken Mirrors) offers us a renewing view. It is a film about violence against women. I have chosen this film because it deals with a question that leaves me with a fundamental sense of despair: the pervasive and persistent violence against women in our society. The permanent fight against this violence needs to be nurtured by empowering symbols. A paralysing despair becomes operative after each hearing of yet another story of violence. Are there any signs that point to empowering symbols in a secularised society?

4. Broken Mirrors: provocative\evocative interpretation

I have chosen the film *Gebroken Spiegels* by Marleen Gorris (1984) as the confronting story. I will first tell the story of the film. Next I will attempt an interpretation.

Gebroken Spiegels tells two stories. We follow the story of Diane, mother of one child and married to a junkie, who starts working in 'Happy House', a sex club. We see her together with other prostitutes in 'Happy House'. The film shows us how they get to know one another, how relations develop among them. We also get acquainted with the 'guests' of 'Happy House', the cruelties, the frustrations, the boredom. It seems to be a hopeless situation that culminates in the stabbing of one of the prostitutes by a 'guest' gone beserk. Parallel to this story we see the kidnapping of Bea, a housewife. She is locked up in a cellar and is exposed to the cruel and freakish whims of a man until she finally dies. The man takes photographs of his victim in the successive stages of the imprisonment. He pastes these photographs underneath the pictures of his previous victims. The two stories come together at the end of the film.

At the end of the film, after Irma, one of the prostitutes in 'Happy House', has been stabbed, a 'customer' offers help and takes her to the hospital, accompanied by two other prostitutes Diane and Dora. When they come back to 'Happy House', the atmosphere is stifling. The women are in a despondent mood. They thank the man for helping them. The man, however, does not leave. At that moment Haydn's *Stabat Mater* is played. We see a close-up of the man's hands. He pulls off his gloves and grabs for something in the inside pocket of his coat. -- One instant, having the previous events in mind, the viewer expects him to pull a gun. -- He takes out his wallet. He wants to get what men come for in a brothel. He insists. Diane takes a gun and points it at him. He still does not understand that the women are serious, that he must leave. Diane shoots at him. The bullet misses him by an inch. He finally receives the message and leaves. The shot of the man taking out his wallet is taken from a similar position as the one of the murderer of the parallel story taking his camera. This shot joins the two stories and the viewer now knows that this man is the murderer. Diane's action becomes an act of judgment, even though she does not know that this man is a murderer. Diane shoots the mirror in 'Happy House' to smithereens and leaves the house with Dora.

The film has been interpreted as being a film about violence against women. Anneke Smelik (Smelik, 1989) has analysed *Gebroken Spiegels* and interprets this violence as inherent to a patriarchal world. The women in the brothel, the imprisoned housewife, they are all victims of violence. Their subjectivity is stolen from them. The world is represented as a brothel. The two stories that are told revolve around the same fundamental conflict between two value systems: one in which women are objects and one in which women are subjects. The violence done to the women emphasises their being objects. The subjectivity of the women is represented in their telling of the story: the women represent the history told, they tell the story (Smelik, 1989, 240). We see the brothel through the eyes of the women. We look at the women and we look from inside the women[2]. The men are shown in a completely different way: they remain anonymous. We never share their gazes, but look at them from the outside. Their looking reveals a sadistic and perverted, even lethal voyeurism. The different position of women and men is emphasised by the cinematic language. It creates empathy and identification with the women. As soon as a man enters on the scene perspectives change. The spectator somehow experiences the objectification of the women. The women's answer to their systematic denigration in *Gebroken Spiegels* is at first characterised by cynicism, silence, or rebelliousness, the inability to escape from the position of the objectified woman. It is only after having aimed a gun at the murderer/whorer that they are able to smash the mirror, the mirror that captures an objectified and objectifying image of the women.

I agree with Smelik's analysis, but I want to go a step further. The film brings us more than violence and stolen subjectivity. I contend that this film can be interpreted as a deeply religious film that alludes to a liberating revelation. There are two clues: the *Stabat Mater* at the end of the film, and the presence of an invisible man singing a traditional hymn about Mary at the beginning of the film. These two elements, and I

---

2. Smelik explains how this effect is obtained through cinematic means, i.e. through the focalisation of the women.

contend they are crucial elements in the film, can be seen as pointers that raise the film to another level. The positioning of these two scenes does not seem to be accidental. It is as if the film is enclosed by references to Mary.

Reading the film with the symbol of Mary -- however slightly the reference to her at first sight may seem to be -- as a central hinge adds a new dimension to it. I will show how the film can be read as a locus of revelatory liberation for women. My interpretation of the film is an example of and exercise in clarifying the interpretative process. It will become clear how my interpretation is guided, and propelled by the confrontation of the text, in this case *Gebroken Spiegels*, and the subject. In the third chapter, I described the meaning and place of Mary in nineteenth-century Flanders, a heritage I had to specify as, at an unconscious level, it belongs to the definition of who I am, a woman belonging to and connected with the movement of women striving for the liberation of the 'I' of women. Encountering the symbol of Mary in a text opens up a world of 'pre-understanding'. I do not read Mary with a blank mind, she refers to a multitude of images and stories. In writing the third chapter I clarified the pre-given world that is inherent in the text, in my text. What Ricoeur has called Mimesis I, and which is a moment in the interpretative process, was extensively unraveled in this third chapter. It is the world I take along in the interpretative process, in the confrontation with the text. My world is also determined by my commitment to the feminist movement. When I see the film *Gebroken Spiegels* and I take in two references to Mary, these references do not fall on untilled soil. It explains why these references can go unnoticed by others. I will show that when these two references to Mary are taken as anchors for interpreting this film, we discover a film that can be seen as pointing at a liberating revelation for women.

At the beginning of the film, we follow Dora, one of the prostitutes. On the ground where she lives, we see a hovel. Dora talks to the man, André, living in the hut. She tells him what worries her. We never see André. He is a voice, mysterious, a thorn in the side of the neighbours. Dora cares for him, and receives comfort from their conversations. One day, when Dora leaves for her 'job', André sings: "Immaculate and pure art Thou, o holy Mary"[3]. It does not seem to be an accusation or a reprimand. It adds to the mystery of André: why does he sing this? Why do we get the impression that this song should not be interpreted as a moralising comment from André? One day, when Dora returns home, she discovers that the cabin has disappeared. One of the neighbours has

---

3. "Onbevlekt en rein zijt gij, O heilige Maria"

complained to the authorities and the hovel and André have been removed. No more conciliatory talks, no more comforting words. The film continues.

At the end of the film, when the two stories come together, one of the main parts is played by the music. Off-screen, we softly hear Haydn's *Stabat Mater*. We hear it, increasing in volume, till the end of the film. The dialogue and other sounds in the film are subdued. The music breathes a comforting, luring, and beneficent atmosphere. The music leads us, despite distress, violence, and humiliation, to the insight that this moment of misery is not the end. The music is powerful, even if one does not know which music it is. The end of the film, however, becomes more revealing when it is connected to the text of the *Stabat Mater*. The *Stabat Mater* shows us Mary mourning at the cross of her son. The text asks *fac me tecum plangere*, let us weep and mourn with Mary. Make us share the pain. The text and the music do not end on a sad note. The text asks for the soul to be received in paradise when the body dies. The music underscores this request for an open end. The use of this music in the film reads as an appeal to the spectator -- and all cinematic means used in this film fortify this appeal -- to share in the feelings of the women. Paradise is not some otherworldly space but is the active step of the women: they leave 'Happy House'.

The man in the cabin singing with his broken voice, the cultivated, enrapturing music of Haydn are thought-provoking elements. The man André, invisible but present, irresistibly makes us think of a comforting Father-God. He is not a God who punishes, or criticises. In the man himself we already see a reversal of certain images: a person living in a shabby cabin showing excentric behaviour, but comforting. If we indeed follow the allusion to the Father-God we arrive at an image of God where we do not expect it (it is tempting to compare the cabin with the stable of Betlehem), an image that breaks with any idea of power and judgment, an image that emphasises compassion and dialogue. When André sings "Immaculate and Pure art Thou" he is mocking any judgment that could be passed on Dora. Whatever she does, she is Immaculate and Pure. This is a second reversal: whereas Mary's purity has often been used as being in contrast with the behaviour of most women, here it is offered as a positive identity. The prostitute Dora is more Immaculate (without sin) and Pure than the world of violence in which she lives.

The disappearance of André leaves Dora alone. Where can she find consolation? The film moves in an ever tighter spiral of violence done to women. It seems to lead to despair and impotence. Still at the end we see Diane and Dora leave 'Happy House'. We arrive at a third and fundamental reversal: from resignation and trying to deal with the situation as it is, to an active involvement that pushes them outside the spiral of violence. The music indicates that it is more than the proverbial last straw that brings about this action. It is the real sharing of suffering and mourning, and the conviction that this cannot be the end.

The conversations with André offered solace. This time the new-found strength brings more than just the means to cope with this life. The shared sorrow and grief enable Dora and Diane to leave the world of violence behind. They take a step towards another life.

5. Seeking Mary without despair

I must further clarify the meaning of this film for a feminist interpretation of Mary. The starting-point for this entire research of Mary, was the search for meaningful symbols that enable us to express questions about life and death in a twentieth-century Western and secularised society. The fundamental question is whether traditional symbols can enable us to formulate our longings and doubts. I tried to answer this question by focussing on Mary. The model of interpretation I have developed here has shown how traditional symbols can be appropriated today, how they offer an opening for imaginative use.

I return to the reversals I have signalled in the film. First of all I want to take another look at the reversal of the meaning of Immaculate and Pure. We have seen that the nineteenth-century society that we studied in chapter 3 had a strong inclination towards interpreting Mary as set apart from humanity, and especially from women, because she was Immaculate. The ideal woman was a woman who blamelessly devoted all her thoughts and attention to men, a chaste attention and devotion. An ideal that could hardly be realised by nineteenth-century women. The Immaculate Conception and chastity became almost synonymous. Original sin is interpreted in terms of sexual conduct. These nineteenth-century elements are on hand in *Gebroken Spiegels*. The prostitutes are expected to devote their entire self to their customers. They must be obedient and fulfil the wishes of those men. The prostitutes do not live up to the traditional standards as they are unable to give 'chaste' attention. An outsider's perspective would cast blame on these women. The film, however, shows how being Immaculate and Pure is connected with living in a violent society. In this film, the behaviour of 'the customers' is pointed at as sinful. The violence against women is named as sinful. Immaculate and Pure is the woman who does not lose her integrity in this violent world. The use of the Mary symbol in this film gives rise to thought. The Immaculate Conception, which refers to the conditions necessary for Jesus' birth, could be interpreted as a conception without violence. God's realm can only become real when violence against women is banned.

The other reversal at which I want to take a closer look is the reference to the *Stabat Mater*. I indicated the comforting tone of the music. We have seen that in the nineteenth century Mary was omnipresent and accessible. She was someone that everybody could turn to, someone who comforted the afflicted. We have also seen that this did not make for change but rather affirmed resignation. In using the *Stabat Mater*, Gorris leads us beyond the stage of enduring resignation. She shows how shared grief can empower us to break the spiral of violence against women. The *Stabat Mater* is a meditation on John 19:26-27. Jesus is dying, Mary and the beloved disciple are standing by the cross. Jesus' life of righting relations and empowering people with stories about God's Realm, is ended by an act of violence. A new period is about to start: an era without Jesus. The disciples will have to become active. Together with the beloved disciple, Mary becomes the symbol of the community that must live with the unacceptable fact of Jesus' violent death. The relations between people will change in this period after Jesus' death. Mary is no longer adressed as 'mother' by Jesus. He says: *gynai*, woman. He tells the disciple: "Behold, your mother", and to Mary he says: "Woman, behold, your son". And the disciple takes Mary into his house.

The thirteenth-century poet who wrote the *Stabat Mater* meditated on that moment under the cross. The poet identifies this scene as a moment of intense grief and mourning. The poem asks us to participate in this moment of mourning. It tells us that we should mourn, but not alone. We must take the others into our house and mourn together. Contrary to the nineteenth-century type of paralysing consolation, we are shown here that shared grief is not the end, and that it does not necessarily lead to the acceptance of the present conditions. It is the beginning of an era of new relationships between people. The poet of the *Stabat Mater* asks for us to be taken into paradise, *Gebroken Spiegels* shows us the women stepping out of the world of violence: we see them as Immaculate and Pure.

Commitment to the liberation of the 'I' of each and every woman can be wearying. It demands a continuous fighting spirit. This continuous struggle can lead to a situation of complete burn-out if the fighting spirit is not nourished. I think such nourishment can be drawn, as the film and the poem have shown, from the admittance of shared grief and mourning. Mourning is connected with vulnerability. It is the acceptance of the limits of the human race and the abandonment to the Mystery of Being. Mourning is connected with the capacity to let things go, but it also contains the dream of another life. The dreams rising from the shared mourning put us on the way to another world. Mary standing at the foot of the cross, together with the beloved disciple, has become a symbol of the community that must learn to live without Jesus' presence. It is a community that is allowed to express its grief, but knows that this grief is not the end.

Gorris's use of references to Mary gave rise to a reflection about the power of shared mourning and the Immaculate and Pure position of women in a violent society. In using traditional elements, namely the reference to Mary, *Gebroken Spiegels* reveals a liberating solidarity for women, nurturing and sustaining strength, drawing power from Who Cannot Be Named. I suspect the film reveals something completely different to men. It is up to them to discover what it is. The community of resistance and solidarity of women and men may get a chance if men will seriously start to think about violence against women. It must be clear that every one who says, like Roberta's husband in *Desperately Seeking Susan*, "I want you to come home with me", looks as foolish as Roberta's husband did.

Bibliography (1829-1913) (chronological)

L. DE BRUSSI
1829   Nieuwe maand van Maria, aen haere eer toegewijd, of gevolg van lezingen nopens de mysteriën van de Allerheyligste Maegd en de bezonderste waerheden der zaligheyd voor alle dagen van Mey, na het fransch. St. Nicolaas, A.C. Ruhart- van Beesen.

N.N.
1829   Het geestelijk roozelaerken der allerheyligste maegd en moeder Gods Maria. Of verscheyde manieren om den heyligen Roozenkrans Godvruchtiglyk te bidden. Turnhout, Brepols.

P. GENTIL
1838   La solitude des vierges, ou, La vie et les vertus de la très Sainte Vierge. Tirées de l'évangile et des saints pères, mises en méditatioons pour une retraite de huit jours. Modèle de perfection proposé à toutes les Vierges consacrées à Dieu, soit par les voeux de Religion, soit par l'état d'une vie plus retirée dans le monde. Lyon, Teyert et cie.

N.N.
1835   Godsdienstig handboekje voor alle Roomsch katholyken bevattende toepasselijke gebeden ten dienste van hen die eene novene van de H. Maagd Maria willen houden om, in allen nood, haren bijstand af te smeeken, en bijzonderlijk ingerigt bij het dragen van de onlangs geslagen medailje ter eere van hare Onbevlekte Ontvangenis en algemeen bekend onder den naam van Mirakuleuze Medailje. Turnhout, Glénisson en van Genechten.

J.B. VERHOEVEN
1835   Het nieuw scherpenheuvels trompetjen uyt blazende verscheyde geestelyke liedekens, tot meerdere eer Gods, en den allerheyligste Maegd en Moeder Gods Maria. Byeengezameld door J.B. Verhoeven. Turnhout, Glénison en van Genechten.

C. VICTOR D'ANGLAIS
1836   L'homme du monde aux pieds de Marie. Rouen, G. Remillet - G. Le Grand Fleury.

N.N.
1836   Manier om godvruchtiglyk en met profijt der zielen het heylig Roozenkransken van Maria, ingesteld door den H. Dominicus. Turnhout, Glénisson en van Genechten.

N.N.
1839   Navolging der Allerheyligste Maegd Maria volgens het voorbeeld van de navolging van Christus. Uyt het Fransch vertaeld. Tweede uytgave, merkelijk verbeterd. Gent, J. Rousseau.

M.G. SCHELLENS
1839   Sermoonen op de bijzonderste feestdagen van het Jaer. Mechelen, P.J. Hanicq.

A.V.D.H.
1843   Navolging der Allerheyligste Maegd Maria, op de wijze van de Navolging van Christus. Kortrijk, Beynaert-Feys.

170

N.N.
1845   De ware bron des geluks, of het heil der christenen in het navolgen van Maria, bevattende 31 overwegingen, voor iederen dag der maend naer verkiezing, op de Deugden van de H. Maegd. Uit het fransch door een kloosterling van Latrappe. Gent, wwe. Vander Schelden.

H.J.G. VAN NOUHUYS
1851   Hymnen en gebeden ter eere der Allerheyligste Maagd. C.L.van Langenhuysen.

L. MEYERE, FAVRE, ZWYZEN, e.a.
1855   De standaerd der ware devotie tot de allerheiligste Maegd. Nieuwe Maend van Mei. Brussel, Loven.

L. LEYNEN
1854   De lof van Maria door Dionisius den Karthuizer, uit het latijn vertaeld door L. Leynen. Hasselt, P.F. Milis. dl1.
1855   dl.2.

Eenen dienaer van Maria.
1855   Verzameling van sermoonen voor elken dag der maend mei over de voorregten van de allerheiligste maegd Maria en namelijk over hare onbevlekte ontvangenis, ter gebruike der heeren geestelijken. Brussel, Goemaere.

R.P. SPEELMAN
1856   La Vierge Immaculée, Patronne de la Belgique -ou- témoingages de foi et de dévotion à l'Immaculée Conception, recueillis dans les annales belges, depuis les temps les plus reculés jusqu'à nos jours. Tournai, Casterman et fils.

J.B. MALOU
1856   Iconographie de l'immaculée conception de la Très Sainte Vierge Marie ou de la meilleure manière de représenter ce mystère. Bruxelles, Goemaere.

A.D.R.
1856   Les vierges miraculeuses de la Belgique, Histoire des sanctuaires ou elles sont vénérées, légendes, pèlerinages, confréries, bibliographie. Bruxelles, Deprez-Paart.

T.R.P. VENTURA DE RAULICA
1860   Les délices de la piété traité sur le culte de la très-sainte vierge. Paris, J.-P. Camus.

N.N.
1862   Maria. Leerares der liefde tot Jezus, in 't Italiaensch uitgegeven door E.P. Barnabieter. Gent, Ad. Rousseau en zusters.

N.N.
1864   De schoonste maand mijner moeder of keus van 31 lezingen voor de maand van Maria. Gent, Vander Schelden.

Eenen priester van het bisdom Brugge
1865   Sermoenen op de deugden van Maria voor de meimaend en congregatien. Rousselaere, L.L. Stock en zusters.

E. MENNE
1866   Sermoonen op de voornaamste feestdagen der allerheiligste Maagd Maria, vrij omgewerkt door S.R. De Becker. Mechelen, Van Moer.

F. ARIAS
1867   De deugden van de Moeder Gods. Gent, Rousseau en zusters.

N.N.
1868   Manuel à l'usage de la congrégation des enfants de Maria placée sous le patronage de cette sainte et immaculée vierge et de sainte Agnès, vierge et martyre. Gand, Vander Schelden.

DE SÉGUR
1868   De H. Maagd. Godvruchtige lezingen voor de maand van Maria. 's Hertogenbosch, W. van Gulick.

A. BAYLE
1870   Marie au coeur de la jeune fille, ouvrage traduit de l'italien. Paris, Librairie Ambroise Bray, Bray et Retaux successeurs.

J. HILLEGEER
1874   Verschijning van Onze-Lieve-Vrouw te Lourdes. Geneesmiddel voor alle zieken. Gent, J. en H. Vander Schelden.

N.N.
1875   Manuel historique, théorique et pratique à l'usage des serviteurs de l'Immaculée Conception sous titre de N.-D. de Lourdes. Bruxelles, Paris.

C. GAY
1877   Conférences aux mères chrétiennes. Poitiers, Paris, Librairie de Henri Oudin.

N.N.
1884   Encyclopédie de la Prédication Contemporaine. Mois de Marie. Marseille.

A. PIRENNE
1885   Sermons sur la Ste. Vierge. Liège.

ANRIEMMA
1890   Marie parout, Marie toujours. Tournai.

A. VAN DENDERWINDEKEN
1890   Maria, Moeder van Smerten of volledig handboek der godsvrucht tot O.L.V. van zeven weeën. Gent, Vander Schelden.

N.N.
1890   Maria's heiligdommen in Nederland en België. Den Bosch, De Kathol. Ill.

S. SCHOUTENS
1890   Maria's Vlaanderen of beschrijving van de wonderbeelden en merkweerdige bedevaartplaatsen van O.L.V. in Oost- en West-Vlaanderen. Antwerpen.

O. COPPIN
1891   Aux pieds de Marie. Louvain.

GUILLERMIN
1893   Choix de Discours et Allocutions des plus célèbres orateurs contemporains sur la T.S.V. Bloud.

C.H.T. JAMAR
1893   Ziedaar uwe Moeder. Gent.

G. KERBOSCH
1893   Maria, toonbeeld aller deugden. Een volledig Gebed- en overwegingsboek inzonderheid voor katholieke Jongedochters. Roermond, H. van der Marck.

N.N.
1893   Maand van Onze Lieve Vrouw van het H.Hert, gevolgd door oefeningen onder de H. Mis, biecht- en communieoefeningen, enz. Averbode, Compiet.

N.N.
1893   Petites méditations pour tous les jours du mois à l'usage des Enfants de Marie. Tournai.

N.N.
1893   Navolging der Allerheiligste Maagd maria. Gent, Vanderschelden.
N.N.
1894   Le Manuel des enfants de Marie ou livre de prières. Malines, H. Dessain.
C.G.M. DE BUSSCHERE
1895   Maria's Rozenkrans. Oostende.
N.N.
1898   Handboek voor de minnars der H.H.Harten van Jesus en Maria.
        Turnhout, Brepols en Dierickx.
P. BRUCKER
1900   Les Congrégations mariales comme moyen d'action religieuses et morale.
        Reims.
C.H.T. JAMAR
1900   Het gulden boekje van Maria's lijden. Gent.
N.N.
1900   Nouveau formulaire de Prières dédié aux enfants de Marie. Anvers,
        Spitaels.
G. VAN GUIJCK
1900   De Zeester. Brugge, van de Vyvere-Petyt.
N.N.
1901   Litanies de Notre Dame. Namur, Godenne.
A. WEYERS
1901   Moeder Maria. Gebeden- en meditatieboek. Turnhout, Brepols en
        Dierickx Zoon.
L.A. CATHERIN
1902   La femme à l'école du Rosaire. Manuel des mères chrétiennes. Lille.
E. FAGUETTE
1902   Glorie aan Maria vol Barmhartigheid. Anvers, De Vlijt.
C. VAN SULL
1903   Nouveau mois de Marie, ill. Bruxelles.
J. VAN VOLKXEM
1903   Le culte de Marie proposé aux jeunes gens. Liège.
F. BOURNAND
1904   La Sainte Vierge dans les Arts. Paris, Tolra et Simonet.
S. DAEMS
1904   Kanselstoffen. zesde boekdeel, Maria- en Heiligenverering. Averbode,
        Abdij van Averbode.
EDELIN
1904   Instructions aux enfants de Marie. Paris.
J.L.H.
1904   La dévotion à la T.S.V.M. en examples. Tongres, Vranken-
        Dommershausen.
A, VERMEERSCH
1904   Sermon en l'honneur de l'Immaculée Conception. Louvain.
N.N.
1904   Volledig meiboekje. Averbode, Abdij van Averbode.
N.N.
1905   De Bedruktste der Moeders of de VII weeën van Maria. Averbode.
GODTS
1905   Prière à la T.S. Vierge. Tournai, Casterman.
MICHEL
1905   Instructions sur les principaux faits de la vie de la Ste Vierge. Namur.

N.N.
1906   Le plus précieux de tous les trésor pour la jeune fille. Conseils et
        exemples spécialement offerts aux enfants de Marie. Lille, Gramint.
Mariakrans Antwerpen (ed.)
1907   Cathechetische verhandeling over christenen vrouwenbeweging te
        Antwerpen. Antwerpen, Dirix-Van Riet.
H.M.H. BARTELS
1908   Maria ons voorbeeld. Brussel.
J. CLÉMENT
1908   Iconographie Mariale. La représentatioon de la Madone à travers les ages.
        Montluçon.
N.N.
1908   Getijden der Onbevlekte Ontvangenis. Turnhout, Brepols en Dierickx.
P.V. DELAPORTE
1909   Poésies Eucharistiques et Mariales. Bruxelles, Albert de Wit.
F. FRANSSEN
1909   Toespraken 1 en 2 serie, 3 en 4, op feestdagen van Jezus en Maria.
        Nijmegen, Malmberg.
N.N.
1909   Gebeden voor de vergaderingen der Congregatie van O.L.V.. Brugge, A.
        De Rycke-Vernimme.
OSSEDAT
1909   Dogme et peinture. Lille.
ANSFRIDUS
1910   Kleine meimaand der kinderen van Maria. Brugge, Verbeke-Loys.
V. CAPPE
1912   La femme belge. Éducation et action sociales. Rapports et documents avec
        une lettre-préface de S.E. le Cardinale Mercier. Bibliothèque de la Revue
        Sociale Catholique. Louvain.

Periodicals

De christene vrouw. Maandblad voor "Mariakrans" Antisocialistische Vrouwenbond van
Antwerpen 1(juni 1902)1 - 8(jan. 1909)1.
Maria's kransken. Maandblad voor de katholieken in België ter bevordering van de
rozenkrans. jan 1895 - dec 1902.

Bibliography

ADLER M.
  1982   Meanings of Matriarchy, in C, SPRETNAK(ed.), The Politics of Women's
            Spirituality. Essays on the Rise of Spiritual Power within the Feminist
            Movement. New York, Anchor Press, 127-137.
ALCOFF L.
  1988   Cultural Feminism versus Post-Structuralism: The Identity Crisis in
            Feminist Theory, in Signs. Journal of Women in Culture and Society, 13,3,
            405-436.
ARON J.P.
  1980   Misérable et glorieuse, la femme au XIX siècle. Paris, Fayard.
ATKINSON C.W., C.H. BUCHANAN, M.R. MILES, (ed.)
  1985   Immaculate and Powerful. The Female in Sacred Image and ocial Reality.
            The Harvard Women's Studies in Religion Series. Boston, Beacon Press.
AUBERT R.
  1952   Histoire de l'église depuis les origines jusqu'à nos jours. vol. 21 Le
            pontificat de Pie IX (1846-1878). Paris, Bloud & Gay.
  1955   L'Episcopat belge et la proclamation du dogme de l'Immaculée
            Conception en 1854, in J. COPPENS, Études sur l'Immaculée Conception.
            Sources et sens de la doctrine. Gembloux, Brugge, 63-99.
BADINTER E.
  1980   L'amour en plus. Histoire de l'amour maternel (XVIIe-XXe siècle). Paris,
            Flammarion.
BAL M.
  1988   Verkrachting verbeeld. Seksueel geweld in cultuur gebracht. Utrecht,
            H&S.
  1990   Over haar lijk. Waarheid, wetenschap en cultuurverschil. De Leidse Annie
            Romein-Verschoorlezing. Amsterdam, Uitgeverij An Dekker.
BAMBERGER J.
  1974   The Myth of Matriarchy. Why Men Rule in Primitive Society, in M.Z.
            ROSALDO, A. LAMPHERE (ed.), Woman, Culture, and Society.
            Stanford, Standford University Press, 263-280.
BEAUVOIR S. de
  1949   Le deuxième sexe. 1. Les faits et les mythes. 2. L'expérience vécue. Paris,
            Gallimard.
BEINERT W.
  1988   Maria in der Feministischen Theologie. Regensburg, Verlag Butzon &
            Bercker Kevelaer, Kleine Schriften des Internationalen Mariologischen
            Arbeitskreises Kevelaer. (also in Catholica 42(1988)1, 1-27).
BEINERT W., H. PETRI, (ed)
  1984   Handbuch der Marienkunde. Regensburg, Verlag Friedrich Pustet.
            BERTELS K.
  1978   Vrouw, man, kind. Lijnen van vroeger naar nu. Baarn, Ambo.
BERTIER de SAUVIGNY G. de
  1965   De kerk in het tijdperk van de restauratie (1801-1848). Geschiedenis van
            de kerk dl.VIII. Hilversum, Antwerpen, Uitgev. P. Brand.

176

BINFORD S.R.
1982   Myths and Matriarchies. in C. SPRETNAK, The Politics of Women's Spirituality. Essays on the Rise of Spiritual Power Within the Feminist Movement. New York, Anchor Press/Doubleday, 541-549.

BOFF L.
1989   The Maternal Face of God. The Feminine and Its Religious Expressions. London, Collins (orig. 1979).

BODDINGTON P.R.
1988   The Issue of Women's Philosophy. in GRIFFITHS M., M. WHITFORD (ed.), Feminist Perspectives in Philosophy. London, Macmillan Press, 205-223.

BOUDENS R.
1984   Inleiding, in M.CLOET, Het bisdom Brugge (1559-1984). Bisschoppen, priesters, gelovigen. Brugge, Westvlaams verbond voor kringen van heemkunde, 339-345.

BOUDEWIJNSE H.B.
1990   The Ritual Study of Victor Turner. An Anthropological Approach and Its Psychological Impact. in H.-G. HEIMBROCK, H.B. BOUDEWIJNSE, Current Studies on Rituals. Perspectives for the Psychology of Religion. Amsterdam, Rodopi, 1-17

BRAIDOTTI R.
1987   Envy: or With My Brains and Your Looks, in JARDINE A. (ed.), Men in Feminism. New York, London, Methuen. 1987, 233-241.
1989   The Politics of Ontological Difference, in T. BRENNAN (ed.), Between Feminism and Psychoanalysis. New York, London, Routledge, 89-105.

BRANDENBURG A.
1965   Maria in der evangelischen Theologie der Gegenwart. Paderborn, Verlag Bonifacius-Druckerei.
1975   Zeitgemässe Marienlehre. Das Lehrschreiben Papst Paul VI. Maria und Kirche - Krise des Reformatorischen, in Catholica, -Vierteljahresschrift für ökumenische Theologie 29, 195-210.

BRENNAN T.,(ed.)
1989   Between Feminism and Psychoanalysis. London, New York, Routledge.

BRIDENTHAL R., C. KOONZ, ed.
1977   Becoming Visible. Women in European History. Boston, Houghton Mifflin Company.

BRIOT B.
1989   "Gai, gai, marions-les" Les jeunes filles dans "L'Illustration européenne" 1870-1880. in COURTOIS L. (ed.), Femmes des années 80. Un siècle de condition féminine en Belgique (1889-1989). Louvain-la- Neuve, Bruxelles, Academia, Crédit Communal de Belgique, 109-113.

BROUNS M.
1989   De lotgevallen van een concept, in Tijdschrift voor Vrouwenstudies, 10, 3, 466-468.

BYNUM C. Walker, S. HARRELL, P. RICHMAN, ed.
1986   Gender and Religion: On the Complexity of Symbols. Boston, Beacon Press.

CANNON K.G., B.W. HARRISON, a.o.
1985   God's Fierce Whimsy. Christian Feminism and Theological Education. New York, The Pilgrim Press.

CARR A.
1982   Is a Christian Feminist Theology Possible? in Theological Studies, 43,2, 279-297.
1988   Transforming Grace. Christian Tradition and Women's Eperience. San Francisco, Harper & Row.
CARROLL M.P.
1986   The Cult of the Virgin Mary. Psychological Origins. Princeton, Princeton University Press.
CAUWE R.
1964   Mgr. Malou, in Collationes Brugenses et Gandavenses, 10, 433-462.
1984   Jan-Baptist Malou (1848-1864), in M. CLOET, e. a., Het bisdom Brugge (1559-1984). Bisschoppen, priesters, gelovigen. Brugge, Westvlaams verbond van kringen voor heemkunde, 357-364.
CAWS M.A.
1986   Ladies Shot and Painted: Female Embodiment in Surrealist Art, in S. Rubin SULEIMAN , The Female Body in Western Culture. Contemporary Perspectives, Cambridge MA, Harvard University Press, 262-287.
CHRIST C.P.
1979   Why Women Need the Goddess: Phenomenological, Psychological, and Political Reflections, in C.P. CHRIST, J. PLASKOW, Womanspirit Rising. A Feminist Reader in Religion. San Francisco, Harper & Row, 273-287.
CLARK S.H.
1990   Paul Ricoeur. London, New York, Routledge.
CLEEVEN J. van
1988   Neogotiek en neogotismen. De neogotiek als component van de 19e-eeuwse stijl in België, in J. de MAYER, De Sint Lucasscholen en de neo-gothiek. Leuven, Universitaire Pers Leuven, 17-55.
CLOET M.(ed.)
1984   Het bisdom Brugge (1559-1984). Bisschoppen, priesters, gelovigen. Brugge, Westvlaams verbond voor heemkunde.
CODE L.
1988   Experience, Knowledge, and Responsibility. in GRIFFITHS M., M. WHITFORD (ed.), Feminist Perspectives in Philosophy. London, Macmillan Press, 187-204.
COOEY P.M., S.A. FARMER, M.E. ROSS, ed.
1987   Embodied Love. Sensuality and Relationship as Feminist Values. San Francisco, Harper & Row.
1987a   The World Become Flesh: Woman's Body, Language, and Value, in COOEY P.M. (ed.), Embodied Love. Sensuality and Relationship as Feminist Values. San Francisco, Harper & Row, 17-33.
COURTH F.
1986   Maria im aktuellen ökumenischen Gespräch, in Trierer Theologische Zeitschrift, 95, 38-53.
1989   Kontroverspunkte im ökumenischen Gespräch über die Mutter Jesu und Ansätze zu Ihrer Überwindung. in H. PETRI, Divergenzen in der Mariologie. Zur oekumenischen Diskussion um die Mutter Jesu. Regensburg, Verlag Friedrich Pustet, 1989, 9-433.
COURTOIS L., F. ROSART, J. PIROTTE (ed.)
1989   Femmes des années 80. Un siècle de condition féminine en Belgique (1889-1989). Louvain-la-Neuve, Bruxelles, Academia, Crédit Communal de Belgique.

178

DALY M.
1974   Beyond God the Father. Toward a Philosophy of Women's Liberation.
        Boston, Beacon Press.
1975   The Church and the Second Sex. With a New Feminist Postchristian
        Introduction by the Author. New York, Harper & Row.
1978   Gyn/Ecology. The Methaethics of Radical Feminism. Boston, Beacon
        Press.
1984   Pure Lust. Elemental Feminist Philosophy. Boston, Beacon Press.
1987   Websters' First New Intergalactic Wickedary of the English Language (in
        Cahoots with Jane Caputi). London, The Women's Press.
DANNEELS G., E. HENAU, W. ROSSEL, F. VANDERHEYDEN
1988   Maria en de nieuwe evangelisatie. Averbode, Apeldoorn, Altoria.
DELIUS W.
1963   Geschichte der Marienverehrung. München, E. Reinhardt.
DEMAREST H.
1982   Brugse devotieprenten van O.L.Vrouw ten tijde van Guido Gezelle.
        Brugge, Heemkundige kring Maurits Van Coppenolle Sint-Andries
        Brugge.
DEMOLDER J.
1984   De sociale bijstand in België tussen Kerk en Staat; and Motieven van de
        negentiende eeuwse religiositeit, in P. VANDERMEERSCH, (ed),
        Psychiatrie, godsdienst en gezag. De ontstaansgeschiedenis van de
        psychiatrie in België als paradigma. Leuven, Amersfoort, Acco, 107-124;
        125-136.
DENZINGER H., A. SCHÖNMETZER
1965   Symbolorum. Definitionum et declarationum de rebus fidei et morum.
        Barcelona, Freiburg, Herder.
DOUGLAS A.
1977   The Feminization of American Culture. New York, A.A. Knopf.
DRESEN G.
1986   Einde van de Inquisitie, geboorte van een Ander. Verhalen van de liefde
        in een voorstel tot ethiek. in Ter Elfder Ure, 29,2, 178-212.
DÜFEL H.
1962   Luthers Stellung zur Marienverehrung. (Kirche und Konfession, Bd. 13)
        Göttingen, Vandenhoeck & Ruprecht.
DUPONT- BOUCHAT M.-S., F. ALEXANDRE, S. LAURENT
1989   En marge du travail: Femmes criminelles - Femmes en prison. in
        COURTOIS L. (ed.), Femmes des années 80. Un siècle de condition
        féminine en Belgique (1889-1989). Louvain-la- Neuve, Bruxelles,
        Academia, Crédit Communal de Belgique, 97-105.
DUPRONT A.
1987   Du sacré. Croisades et pélerinages. Images et langages. Moyenne,
        Éditions Gallimard, Bibliothèque des Histoires.
EVDOKIMOV
1978   La femme et le salut du monde. Paris, Desclée de Brouwer.
ELIZONDO V.
1983   Maria en de armen: een model van evangeliserend oecumenisme, in
        Concilium, 8, 76-82.
ESTRADE J.B.
1899   Les apparitions de Lourdes. Tours, Maison Mame.
FARMER S.A.
1987   Introduction, in COOEY P.M. (ed.), Embodied Love. Sensuality and
        Relationship as Feminist Values. San Francisco, Harper & Row, 1-13.

FEINER J., L. VISCHER (ED.)
1973　Neues Glaubensbuch. Der gemeinsame christliche Glaube. Freiburg,
　　　Verlag Herder.
FIORENZA E. Schüssler
1975　Feminist Theology as a Critical Theology of Liberation, in Theological
　　　Studies, 36, 4, 605-626.
1979　Feminist Spirituality, Christian Identity, and Catholic Vision, in C.P. Christ
　　　and J. PLASKOW, Womanspirit Rising. A Feminist Reader in Religion.
　　　New York, Harper & Row, 1979, 136-148. (orig. in National Institute for
　　　Campus Ministries Journal, Fall 1978)
1983　In Memory of Her. A Feminist Theological Reconstruction of Christian
　　　Origins. London, SCM Press Ltd.
1984　Bread Not Stone. The Challenge of Feminist Biblical Interpretation.
　　　Boston, Beacon Press.
1985　The Will to Choose or to Reject: Continuing Our Critical Work, in L.M.
　　　RUSSELL, Feminist Interpretation of the Bible. Philadelphia,
　　　Westminster Press, 125-136.
1989　The Politics of Otherness. in M.C. ELLIS, O. MADURO (ed.), The
　　　Future of Liberation Theology: Essays in Honor of Gustavo Gutierrez.
　　　Maryknoll, N.Y., Orbis Books, 311-325.
FRENCH M.
1985　Beyond Power. On Women, Men, and Morals. London, Jonathan Cape.
FREUD S.
1953-66　The Standard Edition of the Complete Psychological Works of Sigmund
　　　Freud. Ed. by J. Strachey. London, Hogarth Press.
GEBARA I., M. BINGEMER
1989　Mary. Mother of God, Mother of the Poor. New York, Orbis Books.
GOLD P. Schine
1985　The Lady and the Virgin. Image, Attitude, and Experience in Twelfth-
　　　Century France. Chicago, University of Chicago Press.
GOLDENBERG N.
1976　A Feminist Critique of Jung, in Signs. Journal of Women in Culture and
　　　Society, 2, 2, 443-449.
1979　Changing of the Gods. Feminism and the End of Traditional Religion.
　　　Boston, Beacon Press.
1985　Archetypal Theory and the Separation of Mind and Body: Reason Enough
　　　to Turn to Freud?, in Journal of Feminist Studies in Religion, 1, 1, 55-72.
1986　Anger in the Body: Feminism, Religion, and Kleinian Psychoanalytic
　　　Theory, in Journal of Feminist Studies in Religion, 2, 39-49.
GOMBRICH E.H.
1982　The Image and the Eye. Further Studies in the Psychology of Pictorial
　　　Representation. Oxford, Phaidon Press.
GRIFFITHS M., M. WHITFORD (ed.)
1988　Feminist Perspectives in Philosophy. London, Macmillan Press.
GRZYBKOWSKI A.
1988　Maria über der Frau im Monde, in Das Munster. Zeitschrift für christliche
　　　Kunst und Kunstwissenschaft, 4, 41, 302-309.
HAEGEN R. van der
1989　In het spoor van seksuele differentie. Nijmegen, SUN.

180

HALKES C.J.M.
1962   Maria, de gelovige mens, in Ter Elfder Ure, 9, 37-44.
1975   Beeld van Maria: van inperking naar bevrijding, in Getuigenis, 20, 203-207.
1977   Een 'andere' Maria, in Rondom het woord, 19, 79-95. (zelfde artikel in C.
        BUDDING, C. HALKES, Als vrouwen aan het woord komen. Kampen,
        1978, 79-95)
1980   Met Myriam is het begonnen. Opstandige vrouwen op zoek naar hun
        geloof. Kampen, Uitg. Kok.
1980   De ambiguiteit van de Mariaverering in relatie tot de onderdrukking en
        bevrijding van vrouwen, in Wending, 35, 122-127.
1983   Mary and Women, in Concilium, 160, 66-73.
1984   Zoekend naar wat verloren ging. Enkele aanzetten voor een feministische
        theologie. Baarn, Ten Have.
HARRISON B. Wildung
1985   The Effect of Industrialization on the Role of Women in Society, in C.S.
        ROBB (ed.), Making the Connections. Essays in Feminist Social Ethics.
        Boston, Beacon Press, 42-53. (orig. in Concilium, 3(1976), 91-103)
HAWKESWORTH M.E.
1989   Knowers, Knowing, Known: Feminist Theory and Claims of Truth, in
        Signs. Journal of Women in Culture and Society, 14, 3, 535-557.
HERMANS A., A.M. STRUYF
1984   Opvattingen over opvoeding in de vrouwenbeweging in België, eind 19de -
        begin 20ste eeuw, in Pedagogisch Tijdschrift, 9, 4, 195-205.
HEUVEL J. van den
1984   Volksdevotie en vroomheid (1834-1952), in M. CLOET, Het bisdom
        Brugge (1559-1984). Bisschoppen, priesters en gelovigen. Brugge,
        Westvlaams verbond van kringen voor heemkunde, 459-472.
HIGONNET M.
1986   Speaking Silences: Women's Suicide, in S. Rubin SULEIMAN , The
        Female Body in Western Culture. Contemporary Perspectives, Cambridge
        MA, Harvard University Press, 68-83.
IRIGARAY L.
1987   Egales à qui? in Critique, 43(May)480, 420-437.
JARDINE A.A.
1985   Gynesis. Configurations of Womanhood and Modernity. Ithaca/London,
        Cornell University Press.
JEDIN H. (hrsg.)
1962-1979 Handbuch der Kirchengeschichte. Freiburg, Herder.
JOHNSON E.A.
1984   Mary and Contemporary Christology: Rahner and Schillebeeckx, in Église
        et Théologie, 15, 155-182.
1985a   The Symbolic Character of Theological Statements about Mary. in Journal
        of Ecumenical Studies, 22,2, 312-335.
1985b   The Marian Tradition and the Reality of Women. in Horizons, 12, 1, 116-
        135.
JOY M.
1990   Equality or Divinity. A False Dichotomy? in Journal of Feminist Studies in
        Religion, 6,1, 9-24.
KAEMMERLING H.E.
1979   Ikonographie und Ikonologie. Theorien, Entwicklung, Probleme. Köln,
        DuMont.

KASSEL M.
1983   Mary and the Human Psyche Considered in the Light of Depth
        Psychology, in Concilium, 160, 74-82.
KATOPPO M.
1979   Bewogen en vrij. Theologie van een Aziatische vrouw. Kampen, Uitgev.
        Kok. (orig. Compassionate and Free)
KEMP W.
1985   Der Betrachter ist im Bild. Kunstwissenschaft und Rezeptionsästhetik.
        Köln, Dumont Taschenbücher.
KENIS L.
1989   De theologische faculteit te Leuven in de negentiende eeuw. 1834-
        1889.(Unpublished ThD., K.U.Leuven), Leuven.
KERTELGE K.
1986   Maria, die Mutter Jesu, in der Heiligen Schrift. Ein Beitrag zum
        ökumenischen und innerkatholischen Gespräch, in Catholica -
        Vierteljahrschrift für ökumenische Theologie, 40, 253-269.
KOLB K.
1984   Typologie der Gnadenbilder, in W. BEINERT, P. HEINRICH, Handbuch
        der Marienkunde. Regensburg, Verlag Friedrich Pustet, 849-882.
KRELIG G.
1959   Maria, in Nederlands Katholieke Stemmen, LV, 137-144.
KRISTEVA J.
1983   Stabat Mater. in Histoire d'amour. Paris, Denoël, 295-327 (orig.
        Héréthique de l'amour, in Tel Quel, 74(1977); transl by A. Goldhammer
        in S. Suleiman 1986, 99-118).
LACKMANN T.
1985   Maria als Modell der nachfolge Christi im evangelisch-katholisch
        Gespräch, in Erneuerung in Kirche und Gesellschaft, 25, 31-37.
LAMBERTS E.
1972   Kerk en liberalisme in het bisdom Gent (1821-1857). Bijdrage tot de studie
        van het liberaal-katholicisme en het ultramontanisme. Leuven,
        Universiteitsbibliotheek, Universitaire Uitgaven. Werken op het gebied van
        de geschiedenis en de filologie, 5e reeks, deel 8.
LANGEMEYER B.
1967   Konziliare Mariologie und biblische Typologie. Zum ökumenischen
        Gespräch über Maria nach dem Konzil, in Catholica, -Vierteljahresschrift
        für ökumenische Theologie 21, 295-316.
LANGER S.K.
1980   Philosophy in a New Key: a Study in the Symbolism of Reason, Rite, and
        Art. Cambridge, Harvard University Press. (Orig. 1942)
1964   Philosophical Sketches. A Study of the Human Mind in Relation to
        Feeling, Explored throough Art, Language, and Symbol. New York,
        Mentor Books. (Orig. 1962)
LAURENTIN R.
1963   La question Mariale. Paris, Éditions du Seuil.
1965   La Vierge au Concile; présentation, texte et traduction du chapitre VIII
        de la Constitution dogmatique Lumen Gentium. Paris, Lethielleux.
1968   Court traité sur la vierge Maria. Paris, P.Lethielleux.
1976-1978 Catherine Labouré. Documents. 2 vols. Paris, Lethielleux
1977   Clés pour une approche symbolique de Marie, in Études Mariales.
        Bulletins de la Société Française d'Études Mariales: Images et sanctuaires
        de Marie. Études pluridisciplinaires de symbolique religieuse, 42-57.
1980   Vie de Catherine Labouré. 2 vols. Paris, DDB.

182

LAURENTIN R, A. DURAND
1970   Pontmain: histoire authentique, documents. Paris, Lethellieux.
LAURETIS T. de
1984   Alice Doesn't. Feminism, Semiotics, Cinema. Bloomington, Indiana
        University Press.
1986(ed.) Feminist Studies. Critical Studies. Bloomington, Indiana University Press.
LEHOUCK N.
1980   Volksdevotie en bedevaartpraktijk in Vlaanderen. Analytisch en
        vergelijkend onderzoek van de Mariaverering 1830-1925. Gent
        (onuitgegeven licentiaatsverhandeling).
Lexikon der Marienkunde. Regensburg, Pustet.
1957-68
LOGISTER W.
1990   Tendensen in de mariologie sinds 1950, in Kosmos + Oecumene, 03, 62-
        69.
LONERGAN B.J.F.
1957   Insight. A Study of Human Understanding. London, Danton, Longman &
        Todd.
LORY J.
1989   Naître femme et le devenir. in COURTOIS L. (ed.), Femmes des années
        80. Un siècle de condition féminine en Belgique (1889-1989). Louvain-la-
        Neuve, Bruxelles, Academia, Crédit Communal de Belgique,, 17-18.
LUKKEN G.M.
1986   Semiotische analyse van een bidprentje, in Jaarboek voor Liturgie-
        onderzoek, deel 2, 12-21.
MARTINA G.
1986   Pio IX (1851-1866). Roma, Editrice Pontifica Universita Gregoriana.
MASCALL E.L.
1957   Words and Images. A Study in Theological Discourse. London, Longmans,
        Green & Co.
MASSEY M. Chapin
1985   Feminine Soul: The Fate of an Ideal. Boston, Beacon Press.
1987   Religion, Gender, and Ideology. A Historical Exploration, in Journal of
        Religion, 67, 2, 151-163.
MAYER J. de (red)
1988   De Sint Lucasscholen en de neo-gothiek. Leuven, Universitaire Pers
        Leuven.
McBRIDE T.
1977   The Long Road Home; Women's Work and Industrialization, in R.
        BRIDENTHAL, Becoming Visible. Women in European History. Boston,
        Houghton Mifflin Company, 280-295.
McDOUGALL M.L.
1977   Working-Class Women During the Industrial Revolution, 1780-1914, in R.
        BRIDENTHAL, Becoming Visible. Women in European History. Boston,
        Houghton Mifflin Company, 255-279.
McFAGUE S.
1982   Metaphorical Theology. Models of God in Religious Language.
        Philadelphia, Fortress Press.
McLAUGHLIN E.
1979   The Christian Past: Does It Hold a Future for Women? in C.P. CHRIST,
        J. PLASKOW, Womanspirit Rising. A Feminist Reader in Religion. San
        Francisco, Harper & Row, 93-106.

MEYER-WILMES H.
1990   Rebellion auf der Grenze. Ortsbestimmung feministischer Theologie. Freiburg, Herder.
MICHAUD S.
1982   Muse et madone. Visages de la femme, de la révolution française aux apparitions de Lourdes. Paris, Éd. du Seuil.
MICHIE H.
1987   The Flesh Made Word. Female Figures and Women's Bodies. New York/Oxford, Oxford University Press.
MICHIELSENS M.
1990   Luce Irigaray en seksuele (in)differentie, in M. SCHEYS (red.), Rapporten en perspectieven omtrent vrouwenstudies 2. Brussel, V.U.B.-Press, 13-30.
MIEGGE G.
1962   Die Jungfrau Maria. Studie zur Geschichte der Marienlehre. Göttingen, Vandenhoeck & Ruprecht.
MILES M.R.
1985   Image as Insight. Visual Understanding in Western Christianity and Secular Culture. Boston, Beacon Press.
1985   Introduction, in C.W.ATKINSON, Immaculate and Powerful. The Female in Sacred Image and Social Reality. Boston, Beacon Press, 1-14.
1986   The Virgin's One Bare Breast: Female Nudity and Religious Meaning in Tuscan Early Renaissance Culture, in S. Rubin SULEIMAN, The Female Body in Western Culture. Contemporary Perspectives, Cambridge MA, Harvard University Press, 193-208.
1988   Practicing Christianity. Critical Perpectives for an Embodied Spirituality. New York, Cross Road.
MILLER N.
1986   Changing the Subject: Authorship, Writing, and the Reader, in T. de LAURETIS (ed.), Feminist Studies. Critical Studies. Bloomington, Indiana University Press, 102-120.
MORTON N.
1985   The Journey is Home. Boston, Beacon Press.
MULACK C.
1985   Maria. Die geheime Göttin im Christentum. Stuttgart, Kreuz Verlag.
MUNTER A. de
1982   Moeders en opvoeding. Een bibliografische oriëntatie. Leuven, Acco.
MUSSNER F.
1964   Der Glaube Mariens im Lichte des Römersbriefes, in Catholica - Vierteljahresschrift für ökumenische Theologie 18, 258-268.
1967   Lk 1,48f.; 27f. und die Anfänge der Marienverehrung in der Urkirche, in Catholica -Vierteljahresschrift für ökumenische Theologie 21, 287-294.
NANDRIN J.-P.
1989   A la recherche d'un acte fondateur mythique. La loi du 13 décembre 1889 sur le travail des femmes et des enfants. in COURTOIS L. (ed.), Femmes des années 80. Un siècle de condition féminine en Belgique (1889-1989). Louvain-la- Neuve, Bruxelles, Academia, Crédit Communal de Belgique,, 11-16.
NÉDONCELLE M.
1936   Les leçons spirituelles du XIXe siècle. Paris, Bloud & Gay.
NELSON J.L.
1977   Virgin Territory: Recent Historical Work on Marian Belief and Cult, in Journal of Religion and Religions, 7, autumn, 206-225.

184

NEUMANN E.
  1955   The Great Mother. An Analysis of the Archetype. London, Routledge &
          Kegan Paul Ltd.
NICOLAS M.-J.
  1977   Le sens des images dans une théologie de l'incarnation, in Études
          Mariales. Bulletin de la Société Française d'Études Mariales: Images et
          sanctuaires de Marie. Étude pluridisciplinaire de symbolique religieuse, 24-
          32.
OBERMAN H.A.
  1964   The Virgin Mary in Evangelical Perspective, in Journal of Ecumenical
          Studies, 1, 2, 271-298.
OCHS C.
  1977   Behind the Sex of God. Toward a New Consciousness. Transcending
          Matriarchy and Patriarchy. Boston, Beacon Press.
OTT H.
  1984   Steht Maria zwischen den Konfessionen? (Fragen eines evangelischen
          Theologen an die katholische Marienlehre), in R. STAUFFER, In
          necessariis unitas. Mélanges offert à Jean-Louis Leuba. Paris, 304-319.
OUTSHOORN J.
  1989   Een irriterend onderwerp. Verschuivende conceptualiseringen van het
          sekseverschil. Nijmegen, SUN.
PAGELS E.
  1979   What Became of God the Mother? in C.P. CHRIST, J. PLASKOW,
          Womanspirit Rising. A Feminist Reader in Religion. San Francisco,
          Harper & Row, 107-119.
PANOFSKY E.
  1987   Meaning in the Visual Arts. Papers in and on Art History.
          Harmondsworth, Penguin Books. (orig. 1955)
PEEMANS F.
  1989   L'employée de l'État. Espace de travail et espace sociologique (fin 19e s.-
          années 1950). in COURTOIS L. (ed.), Femmes des années 80. Un siècle
          de condition féminine en Belgique (1889-1989). Louvain-la- Neuve,
          Bruxelles, Academia, Crédit Communal de Belgique,, 81-85.
PETRI H.
  1984   Maria und die Oekumene, in W. BEINERT, Handbuch der Marienkunde.
          Regensburg, Verlag Friedrich Pustet, 315-359.
  1989   Divergenzen in der Mariologie. Zur oekumenischen Diskussion um die
          Mutter Jesu. Regensburg, Verlag Friedrich Pustet.
PHILIPS G.
  1954   Maria en de Kerk, in Nederlandse Katholieke Stemmen, L, 241-251.
POOLE F.J. Porter
  1986   Metaphors and Maps: Towards Comparison in the Anthropology of
          Religion, in Journal of the American Academy of Religion, LIV/3, 411-
          457.
POPE B. Corrado
  1977   Angels in the Devil's Workshop. Leisured and Charitable Women in
          Nineteenth-Century England and France, in R. BRIDENTHAL, Becoming
          Visible. Women in European History. Boston, Houghton Mifflin
          Company, 296-324.
  1985   Immaculate and Powerful. The Marian Revival in the Nineteenth Century,
          in C.W. ATKINSON, C.H. BUCHANAN, M.R. MILES (ed.), Immaculate
          and Powerful. The Female in Sacred Image and Social Reality. The

Harvard Women's Studies in Religion Series, Boston, Beacon Press, 173-200.

POST P.G.J.
1986   Bidprentjes als liturgische bron. Benadering vanuit iconografie, semiotiek en mentaliteitsgeschiedenis, in Jaarboek voor Liturgie-onderzoek, deel 2, 1-11.

1987   Bedevaart, liturgie en artes. Methodische noties vanuit een onderzoeksprogramma bij S. Sinding-Larsen's 'Iconography and Ritual', in Jaarboek voor liturgie-onderzoek, deel 3, 111-139.

1988   Iconisering of ontbeelding? Enkele notities over de ontwikkeling van de beeldzijde van bidprentjes met de ikoon als invalshoek, in Jaarboek voor Liturgie-onderzoek, deel 4, 235-277.

POST P.G.J. (red.)
1990   Verbeelding van vroomheid. De devotieprent als cultuurwetenschappelijke bron. Themanummer van het Volkskundig Bulletin, 16, 3.

POULAIN M., D. TABUTIN
1989   La surmortalité des petites filles, in COURTOIS L. (ed.), Femmes des années 80. Un siècle de condition féminine en Belgique (1889-1989). Louvain-la- Neuve, Bruxelles, Academia, Crédit Communal de Belgique, 25-31.

PRESTON J.J. (ed.)
1982   Mother Worship. Theme and Variations. Chapel Hill, The University of North Carolina Press.

PRUYSER P.
1983   The Play of Imagination. New York, The International Universities Press.

RAEDTS P.
1990   De christelijke middeleeuwen als mythe, in Tijdschrift voor Theologie. 30.2. 146-158.

RAHNER K., H. VORGRIMLER
1965   Klein theologisch woordenboek. Hilversum, Antwerpen, Uitgeverij Paul Brand.

RICH A.
1976   Of Woman Born. Motherhood as Experience and Institution. New York, W.W. Norton & Co.

RICOEUR P.
1960   Finitude et culpabilité. I. L'homme faillible. II. La symbolique du mal. Paris, Éditions Montaigne.

1962   The Hermeneutics of Symbols and Philosophical Reflection. in International Philosophical Quarterly, II, 2, 191-218 (transl. of Herméneutique des symboles et réflexion philosophique, in Archivio di Filosofia (il problema della demitizzazione) Atti del Convegno. Roma, 1961, 31(1961) 1-2, 51-73).

1965   De l'interprétation. Essai sur Freud. Paris, Éditions du Seuil.

1969   Le conflit des interprétations. Essais d'herméneutique. Paris, Éditions du Seuil.

1972   The Symbol Gives Rise to Thought. in Walter H. CAPPS, Ways of Understanding Religion. New York, The Macmillan Company, 309-317.

1974   Philosophy and Religious Language. in Journal of Religion, 54, 71-86.

1976   Interpretation Theory. Discourse and the Surplus of Meaning.

1983   Temps et Récit. Paris, Editions du Seuil.

1986   Du texte à l'action. Essais d'herméneutique II. Paris, Editions du Seuil.

RIDDER C.de
1960   Maria Medeverlosseres? De discussie in de huidige Rooms-katholieke
        theologie over de medewerking van de Moeder Gods in het
        verlossingswerk. Utrecht, J. Hoeyenborch.
RILEY D.
1988   'Am I that Name?' Feminism and the Category of Women in History.
        Houndmills, Macmillan Press.
RITSCHL D.
1986   Konzepte. Ökumene, Medizin, Ethik. Gesammelte Aufsätze. München,
        Chr. Kaiser Verlag.
ROGIER L.J.
1964   De kerk in het tijdperk van verlichting en revolutie. Antwerpen,
        Hilversum, P. Brand.
RORTY R.
1980   Philosophy and the Mirror of Nature. Oxford, Basil Blackwell.
RUETHER R. Radford
1972   Liberation Theology. Human Hope Confronts Christian History and
        American Power. New York, Paulist Press.
1975   New Woman New Earth. Sexist Ideologies and Human Liberation. San
        Francisco, Harper & Row.
1977   Mary - The Feminine Face of the Church. Philadelphia, Westminster
        Press.
1981   To Change the World. Christology and Cultural Criticism. London, SCM
        Press.
1983   Sexism and Godtalk. Toward a Feminist Theology. London, SCM Press.
1985a   Womanguides. Readings Toward a Feminist Theology. Boston, Beacon
        Press.
1985b   Feminist Interpretation. A Method of Correlation. in L. RUSSELL,
        Feminist Interpretation of the Bible. Philadelphia, Westminster Press, 111-
        124.
1989   Disputed Questions. On Being a Christian. Maryknoll, Orbis Books.
RUETHER R.Radford, E.C. BIANCHI
1976   From Machismo to Mutuality. Woman - Man Liberation. New York,
        Paulist Press.
RUSSELL L.M. (ed.)
1985   Feminist Interpretation of the Bible. Philadelphia, Westminster Press.
RUSSELL L.M., K. PUI-LAN, A.M. ISASI-DIAZ, K.G. CANNON
1988   Inheriting Our Mothers' Gardens. Feminist Theology in Third World
        Perspective. Philadelphia, The Westminster Press.
SANDSTROM A.R.
1982   The Tonantsi Cult of the Eastern Nahua, in J.J. PRESTON (ed.), Mother
        Worship. Theme and Variations. Chapel Hill, The University of North
        Carolina Press, 25-50.
SCHEELE P.-W.
1975   Maria in der Gemeinschaft und Geschichte Israels, in Catholica -
        Vierteljahresschrift für ökumenische Theologie 29, 92-113.
SCHIMMELPFENNIG R.
1952   Die Geschichte der Marienverehrung im deutschem Protestantismus.
        Paderborn, F. Schöningh.
SCHMIDT P.
1975   Maria und das Magnificat. Maria im Heilshandeln gottes im Alten und
        Neuen Gottesvolkes, in Catholica -Vierteljahresschrift für ökumenische
        Theologie 29, 230-246.

SCHOONBAERT L.M.A. (ed.)
1986   Religieuze thematiek in de Belgische kunst 1875-1985. Brussel,
        A.S.L.K.SCHOONBAERT L.M.A.
1986   Religieuze thematiek in de Belgische kunst van 1875 tot heden, in
        Religieuze thematiek in de Belgische kunst 1875-1985. Brussel, A.S.L.K.,
        13-35.
SCHOONENBERG P.
1962   Het geloof van ons doopsel. Gesprekken over de apostolische
        geloofsbelijdenis. Vierde deel: De macht der zonde. Inleiding op de
        verlossingsleer. 's-Hertogenbosch, L.C.G. Malmberg.
SCHÜTTE H.
1985   Ziel: Kirchengemeinschaft. Zur ökumenischen Orientierung. Paderborn.
SCOTT J.W.
1986   Gender: A Useful Category of Analysis, in American Historical Review,
        1053-1075.
SELLER A.
1988   Realism versus Relativism: Towards a Politically Adequate Epistemology.
        in GRIFFITHS M., M. WHITFORD (ed.), Feminist Perspectives in
        Philosophy. London, Macmillan Press, 169-186.
SEMMELROTH O.
1960   Maria of Christus? Christus als doel der Mariaverering, overwegingen.
        Tielt, Lannoo.
SHIACH M.
1989   'Their "symbolic" exists, it holds power - we, the sowers of disorder, know
        it only too well' in BRENNAN T. (ed.), Between Feminism and
        Psychoanalysis. London, New York, Routledge, 153-167.
SIMON A.
1949   L'église catholique et les débuts de la Belgique indépendante. Wetteren,
        Éditions Scaldis.
1950   Le cardinal Sterckx et son temps (1792-1867). Wetteren, Éditions Scaldis.
SIMONS M.A.
1984   Motherhood, Feminism, and Identity, in Women's Studies International
        Forum, 7,5, 349-359.
SOETING A.
1980   Protestanten en de Mariologie. in Tenminste-Jaarboeken, Kampen, Kok,
        51-65.
SÖLL G.
1971   Dogma und Dogmenentwicklung. (Handbuch der Dogmengeschichte,
        Band 1 Faszikel 5). Freiburg, Herder.
1984   Maria in der Geschichte von Theologie und Frömmigkeit, in W.
        BEINERT, Handbuch der Marienkunde. Regensburg, Verlag Friedrich
        Pustet, 93-231.
SÖLLE D.
1978   Sympathie. Theologisch-politische Traktate. Stuttgart, Kreuz Verlag.
SOSKICE J.M.
1985   Metaphor and Religious Language. Oxford, Clarendon Press.
SPELMAN E.V.
1982   Woman as Body: Ancient and Contemporary Views, in Feminist Studies,
        8,1, 109-131.
SPRETNAK C. (ed.)
1982   The Politics of Women's Spirituality. Essays on the Rise of Spiritual Power
        within the Feminist Movement. New York, Anchor Press, Doubleday.

188

SULEIMAN S.Rubin, ed.
1986a   The Female Body in Western Culture. Contemporary Perspectives.
         Cambridge MA, Harvard University Press.
1986b   (Re)Writing the Body: The Politics and Poetics of Female Eroticism, in S.
         Rubin SULEIMAN, The Female Body in Western Culture. Contemporary
         Perspectives, Cambridge MA, Harvard University Press, 7-29.
STALPAERT H.
1976   Brugse devotieprenten van O.L.Vrouw. Brugge, Heemkundige kring
         Maurits Van Coppenolle Sint-Andries Brugge.
TAPPOLET W.
1962   Das Marienlob der Reformatoren. Martin luther, Johannes Calvin,
         Huldrych Zwingli, Heinrich Bullinger. Tübingen, Katzmann.
TAVES A.
1987   Mothers and Children and the Legacy of Mid-nineteenth-Century
         American Christianity, in The Journal of Religion, 67,2, 203-219.
THIJS A.K.L.
1986   Devotie, winst en politiek: achtergronden van de produktie van
         neogotische devotieprenten in Vlaanderen tijdens de tweede helft van de
         negentiende eeuw. in J. ANDRIESSEN, A. KEERSMAEKERS, P.
         LENDERS, Cultuurgeschiedenis in de nederlanden van de renaissance
         naar de romantiek. (Liber Amicorum). Leuven, Amersfoort, Acco, 279-
         295.
THURIAN M.
1962   Marie, Mère du Seigneur, figure de l'Église. Taizé, Presses de Taizé.
TILLICH P.
1955   Religious Symbols and Our Knowledge of God. in The Christian Scholar,
         38,3, 189-197.
TRACY D.
1975   Blessed Rage for Order. The New Pluralism in Theology. New York,
         Seabury Press.
TURNER V., E. TURNER
1982   Postindustrial Marian Pilgrimage, in J.J. PRESTON, Mother Worship.
         Theme and Variations. Chapel Hill, The University of North Carolina
         Press, 145-173.
VAN DEN BERGH K.
1975   Bidprentjes in de Zuidelijke Nederlanden. Brussel, Aurelia Books.
VANDERMEERSCH P.
1978   Het gekke verlangen. Psychotherapie en ethiek. Antwerpen, De
         Nederlandse Boekhandel.
1984(ed.) Psychiatrie, godsdienst en gezag. De ontstaansgeschiedenis van de
         psychiatrie in België als paradigma. Leuven, Amersfoort, Acco.
VANSINA F.D.
1985   Paul Ricoeur. Bibliographie systématique de ses écrits et des publications
         consacrées à sa pensée (1935-1984). - A Primary and Secondary Systematic
         Bibliography (1935-1984). Leuven, Bibliothèque Philosophique de Louvain,
         Ed. Peeters.
VICKERS N.J.
1986   "This Heraldry in Lucrece' Face", in S. Rubin SULEIMAN , The Female
         Body in Western Culture. Contemporary Perspectives, Cambridge MA,
         Harvard University Press, 209-222.
VINTGES K.
1989   De ambiguiteiten van Simone de Beauvoir, in Tijdschrift voor
         Vrouwenstudies, 10,1, 117-129.

VOSS G.
1981   Maria zwischen den Konfessionen, in Una Sancta, 36, 76-88.
WALKER A.
1989   God Is Inside You and Inside Everybody Else, in J. PLASKOW, C.P.
        CHRIST, Weaving the Visions. New Patterns in Feminist Spirituality. San
        Francisco, Harper & Row, 101-104.
WARNER M.
1976   Alone of All Her Sex. The Myth and the Cult of the Virgin Mary.
        London, Pan Books.
1985   Monuments and Maidens. The Allegory of the Female Form. London,
        Weidenfeld & Nicolson Ltd.
WARNOCK
1976   Imagination. London, Faber.
WEBER-KELLERMAN I.
1983   Frauenleben im 19. Jahrhundert. Empire und Romantik, Biedermeier,
        Gründerzeit. München, Verlag C.H.Beck.
WEERDT D. de
1980   En de vrouwen? Vrouw, vrouwenbeweging en feminisme in België 1830-
        1960. Gent, Masereelfonds.
WELCH S.D.
1985   Communities of Resistance and Solidarity. A Feminist Theology of
        Liberation. New York, Orbis Books.
1990   A Feminist Ethic of Risk. Minneapolis, Fortress Press.
WIERINGA F., S. LEYDESDORFF, J. OUTSHOORN
1978   Huis uit, huis in, in K. BERTELS, Vrouw, man, kind. Lijnen van vroeger
        naar nu. Baarn, Ambo, 89-110.
WHITE H.
1987   The Content of the Form. Narrative Discourse and Historical
        Representation. Baltimore, London, The John Hopkins University Press.
WHITFORD M.
1988   Luce Irigaray's Critique of Rationality. in GRIFFITHS M., M.
        WHITFORD (ed.), Feminist Perspectives in Philosophy. London,
        Macmillan Press, 109-130.
IJSSELING S.
1990   Mimesis. Over schijn en zijn. Baarn, Ambo.

THURIAN M.
1962   Marie, Mère du Seigneur, figure de l'Église. Taizé, Presses de Taizé.
TILLICH P.
1955   Religious Symbols and Our Knowledge of God. in The Christian Scholar,
        38,3, 189-197.
TRACY D.
1975   Blessed Rage for Order. The New Pluralism in Theology. New York,
        Seabury Press.
TURNER V., E. TURNER
1982   Postindustrial Marian Pilgrimage, in J.J. PRESTON, Mother Worship.
        Theme and Variations. Chapel Hill, The University of North Carolina
        Press, 145-173.
VAN DEN BERGH K.
1975   Bidprentjes in de Zuidelijke Nederlanden. Brussel, Aurelia Books.

190

VANDERMEERSCH P.
1978   Het gekke verlangen. Psychotherapie en ethiek. Antwerpen, De
        Nederlandse Boekhandel.
1984(ed) Psychiatrie, godsdienst en gezag. De ontstaansgeschiedenis van de
        psychiatrie in België als paradigma. Leuven, Amersfoort, Acco.
VANSINA F.D.
1985   Paul Ricoeur. Bibliographie systématique de ses écrits et des publications
        consacrées à sa pensée (1935-1984). - A Primary and Secondary Systematic
        Bibliography (1935-1984). Leuven, Bibliothèque Philosophique de Louvain,
        Ed. Peeters.
VICKERS N.J.
1986   "This Heraldry in Lucrece' Face", in S. Rubin SULEIMAN , The Female
        Body in Western Culture. Contemporary Perspectives, Cambridge MA,
        Harvard University Press, 209-222.
VINTGES K.
1989   De ambiguiteiten van Simone de Beauvoir, in Tijdschrift voor
        Vrouwenstudies, 10,1, 117-129.
VOSS G.
1981   Maria zwischen den Konfessionen, in Una Sancta, 36, 76-88.
WALKER A.
1989   God Is Inside You and Inside Everybody Else, in J. PLASKOW, C.P.
        CHRIST, Weaving the Visions. New Patterns in Feminist Spirituality. San
        Francisco, Harper & Row, 101-104.
WARNER M.
1976   Alone of All Her Sex. The Myth and the Cult of the Virgin Mary.
        London, Pan Books.
1985   Monuments and Maidens. The Allegory of the Female Form. London,
        Weidenfeld & Nicolson Ltd.
WARNOCK
1976   Imagination. London, Faber.
WEBER-KELLERMAN I.
1983   Frauenleben im 19. Jahrhundert. Empire und Romantik, Biedermeier,
        Gründerzeit. München, Verlag C.H.Beck.
WEERDT D. de
1980   En de vrouwen? Vrouw, vrouwenbeweging en feminisme in België 1830-
        1960. Gent, Masereelfonds.
WELCH S.D.
1985   Communities of Resistance and Solidarity. A Feminist Theology of
        Liberation. New York, Orbis Books.
1990   A Feminist Ethic of Risk. Minneapolis, Fortress Press.
WIERINGA F., S. LEYDESDORFF, J. OUTSHOORN
1978   Huis uit, huis in, in K. BERTELS, Vrouw, man, kind. Lijnen van vroeger
        naar nu. Baarn, Ambo, 89-110.
WHITE H.
1987   The Content of the Form. Narrative Discourse and Historical
        Representation. Baltimore, London, The John Hopkins University Press.
WHITFORD M.
1988   Luce Irigaray's Critique of Rationality. in GRIFFITHS M., M.
        WHITFORD (ed.), Feminist Perspectives in Philosophy. London,
        Macmillan Press, 109-130.
IJSSELING S.
1990   Mimesis. Over schijn en zijn. Baarn, Ambo.

Nederlandse samenvatting

Is het mogelijk om vanuit feministisch perspectief over Maria te spreken? Kan een traditioneel en beladen beeld een nieuwe inhoud krijgen? Hoe vindt het proces van interpretatie van een dergelijk beeld plaats? In de feministisch-theologische discussie bestaan grote onduidelijkheden met betrekking tot het omgaan met traditioneel overgeleverde beelden. Zijn de traditionele beelden nog levensvatbaar? Bezitten ze een bevrijdend perspectief voor vrouwen? Of zijn ze volledig onbruikbaar geworden door eeuwenlang patriarchaal misbruik? De figuur van Maria is hier een voorbeeld van: de reacties binnen vrouwenstudies theologie verlopen van een volledige afwijzing van Maria tot pogingen tot herinterpretatie. In deze dissertatie wordt de vraag naar het interpretatieproces gesteld.

In het eerste hoofdstuk, *Feminist Interpretations of Mary*, wordt een overzicht gegeven van diverse feministische interpretaties van de figuur van Maria. Na een situering van de recente mariologische discussies en achtergronden komen achtereenvolgens aan bod: C. Halkes, R. Radford Ruether, E. Schüssler Fiorenza, E Johnson, I Gebara en M. Bingemer, M. Daly, C. Ochs en C. Mulack, M. Kassel, M. Warner, P. Schine Gold en B. Corrado Pope. De auteurs worden gesitueerd binnen haar eigen context. Naast de presentatie en situering van de auteurs worden kritische vragen geformuleerd t.o.v. haar specifieke interpretatie van Maria. Het hoofdstuk wordt afgerond met een verdieping van twee vragen die bij alle auteurs opduiken: enerzijds de vraag naar 'wat' wordt geïnterpreteerd (wordt Maria gepercipieerd als een symbool, een dogmatisch gegeven, een element dat nu eenmaal tot het volksgeloof behoort, een psychische structuur, een instrument van machtsuitoefening) en 'wie' interpreteert (stelt men zich op het standpunt van de 'neutrale' wetenschapper of wordt bijvoorbeeld een verbondenheid met de vrouwenbeweging verdisconteerd). Anderzijds wordt de kwestie van de 'historische achteloosheid' van de meeste auteurs geconstateerd. 'Maria' is een gegeven dat aan steeds wisselende interpretaties onderhevig is geweest. Historische precisering en situering is noodzakelijk.

In hoofdstuk twee, *A Feminist Model of Interpretation*, wordt ingegaan op de vragen: 'wat' wordt geïnterpreteerd en 'wie' interpreteert. Wat betreft de eerste vraag, 'wat' wordt geïnterpreteerd, wordt geopteerd voor een exploratie van Maria als symbool. Hiertoe wordt een theoretisch kader uitgewerkt waarbinnen het begrip symbool wordt afgebakend. Er wordt gekozen voor een hermeneutische aanpak zoals gesuggereerd in het werk van P. Ricoeur. Wat betreft de tweede vraag, 'wie' interpreteert wordt geargumenteerd dat het zinvol is om van een vrouwelijk interpreterend subject uit te gaan.

Het hoofdstuk is als volgt opgebouwd: In een eerste paragraaf wordt aan de hand van enkele studies een korte aanduiding gegeven van de verwerking van de problematiek symbolen, vrouwen als symbolen, vrouwelijke symbolen binnen vrouwenstudiesonderzoek. De studie van Warner (*Monuments and Maidens*) en de bundels *Immaculate and Powerful* en *Gender and Religion* tonen aan dat een uitgewerkt theoretisch kader ofwel ontbreekt ofwel onvoldoende is uitgewerkt. In de tweede paragraaf wordt toegewerkt naar het idee van *symbolic imagination*. Na een eerste, intuïtieve exploratie van de samenhang tussen taal, beelden en symbolen wordt een meer systematische uiteenzetting over symbooltheorieën gegeven. Het is niet de bedoeling om een uitgebreide presentatie en evaluatie van alle mogelijke symbooltheorieën te geven, maar om de hermeneutische theorie van P. Ricoeur te situeren. Ricoeur definieert symbolen als participerend in een verhaal. De betekenis van het symbool is afhankelijk van de plaats die het in het verhaal inneemt. Een symbool zonder verhaal of context bestaat niet. Zo valt ook Maria als symbool niet te begrijpen zonder erkenning van de context, van het verhaal waarin ze functioneert. Belangrijk bij de activiteit van het symboliseren is de plaats van de *imagination*. Dit is een actief proces dat een spel van vernieuwing en sedimentatie activeert.

De plaats van het symboliserende subject is in het Ricoeuriaanse schema cruciaal. Dit is bij Ricoeur een sekse- en/of genderloos subject. Feministische theorievorming wijst op het problematische karakter van het zogenaamde neutrale subject. De huidige stand van zaken binnen vrouwenstudies benadrukt dat het 'vrouwelijk subject' niet te conceptualiseren is. De nadruk komt te liggen op een gemeenschap van vrouwen die als collectiviteit haar zelfdefinitie in handen nemen. Deze idee wordt ontwikkeld met behulp van R. Braidotti's concept van de politiek van ontologische differentie.

In het derde hoofdstuk, *Mary: A Nineteenth Century Heritage*, wordt nader aandacht besteed aan de 'historische achteloosheid'. Tevens wordt de contextgebondenheid -- belangrijke categorie in het paradigma van Ricoeur -- van interpretaties van het symbool Maria gepreciseerd. Hiertoe wordt de negentiende eeuwse erfenis van actuele herinterpretaties van Maria ontrafeld. De negentiende eeuwse Maria wordt gereconstrueerd en het belang dat binnen vrouwenstudies wordt gehecht aan de negentiende eeuw als mogelijke gefeminiseerde eeuw wordt geanalyseerd. Dit hoofdstuk dient een dubbel doel: het blootleggen van de verbondenheid van de twintigste eeuw met de negentiende (de erfenis van de beeldvorming rondom Maria) alsook het scherp stellen van de verschillen (het interpreteren en omgaan met Maria vanuit een feministisch bewustzijn, geworteld in een feministische gemeenschap).

Drie redenen bepalen de aandacht voor de negentiende eeuwse Maria: eerst en vooral biedt de studie van de negentiende eeuw ons de problematiek van het Mariavereringsmechanisme in close-up. Ten tweede blijkt dat de lappendeken die Maria is in de negentiende eeuw tot een soort voltooiing komt. Ten derde vormt de negentiende eeuwse Mariabeeldvorming, en in een bredere kontekst de gehele negentiende eeuw de achtergrond voor het huidige feministische onderzoek.

Het hoofdstuk is als volgt opgebouwd: eerst wordt een algemeen inzicht geboden in het Europese katholieke negentiende eeuwse klimaat, met bijzondere aandacht voor de plaats van Maria. Vervolgens wordt een beperking ingevoerd en concentreert de studie zich op de Belgische mariale devotie. Deze beperking stelt ons in staat het mechanisme van de Mariaverering in detail en van nabij te bestuderen. De iconografie van Maria krijgt een centrale plaats. Tenslotte wordt de relatie tussen deze specifieke Maria en vrouwen in de negentiende eeuw gelegd.

Het vierde hoofdstuk, *Desperately Seeking Mary*, bevat naast een recapitulatie van de kernpunten van de eerste drie hoofdstukken een verdere indicatie en afbakening van de interpreterende gemeenschap die zich voor Maria geplaatst ziet. Aan het einde van het hoofdstuk wordt een poging tot interpretatie van Maria voor twintigste eeuwse vrouwen in een geseculariseerde maatschappij gepresenteerd. De interpreterende gemeenschap wordt omschreven als een gemeenschap van vrouwen die streeft naar de bevrijding van het 'ik' van alle vrouwen en die zoekt naar bevrijding in het proces van interpretatie van wat voor haar ligt. Traditie wordt niet opzij gezet maar gezien als een erfenis waar men zich doorheen moet werken. Deze activiteit kan soms leiden tot momenten van onverwachte openbaring. Het is tevens een gemeenschap gevormd door vrouwen en mannen die openstaat voor vormen van verzet en solidariteit. Verschillen (bv. vrouw of man) hoeven geen scheidslijn te zijn. Deze gemeenschap laat zich inspireren door de bijbelse teksten.

De interpretatie van de film *Gebroken spiegels* is een aanzet tot en voorbeeld van creatief symboliseren. In het proces van interpretatie wordt duidelijk hoe de subtiele refererenties naar Maria in deze film ons op het spoor zetten van een bevrijdend beeld: Maria die te denken geeft over de kracht van gedeeld rouwen en van de Onbevlekte en Reine positie van vrouwen in een wereld vol geweld.